BASKETBALL

Steps to Success

Hal Wissel, DPE
Director of Player Personnel
New Jersey Nets, National Basketball Association

President, Basketball World, Inc.
Springfield, Massachusetts

Human Kinetics

Library of Congress Cataloging-in-Publication Data

Wissel, Hal, 1939-
    Basketball : steps to success / Hal Wissel.
        p.   cm.
    Includes bibliographical references.
    ISBN 0-87322-691-7
    1. Basketball--Training.   2. Basketball--Coaching.   I. Title.
    GV885.35.W55   1994
    796.323'07--dc20   94-4549
                                                                              CIP

ISBN: 0-87322-691-7

Acquisitions Editor: Brian Holding; **Developmental Editor:** Judy Patterson Wright, PhD; **Assistant Editors:** Ed Giles, Dawn Roselund, and John Wentworth; **Copyeditor:** Anne Mischakoff Heiles; **Proofreader:** Pam Johnson; **Production Director:** Ernie Noa; **Typesetter:** Kathy Boudreau-Fuoss; **Text Design:** Keith Blomberg; **Layout Artists:** Kathy Boudreau-Fuoss and Denise Lowry; **Illustrator:** Keith Blomberg; **Court Diagrams:** Craig Ronto; **Cover Designer:** Jack Davis; **Cover Photo:** Wilmer Zehr; **Printer:** United Graphics

Instructional Designer for the Steps to Success Activity Series: Joan N. Vickers, EdD, University of Calgary, Calgary, Alberta, Canada

Human Kinetics books are available at special discounts for bulk purchase. Special editions or book excerpts can also be created to specification. For details, contact the Special Sales Manager at Human Kinetics.

Printed in the United States of America

10   9   8   7   6   5

Human Kinetics
P.O. Box 5076, Champaign, IL 61825-5076
1-800-747-4457
Web site: http://www.humankinetics.com/

United States: Human Kinetics, P.O. Box 5076, Champaign, IL 61825-5076
1-800-747-4457
e-mail: humank@hkusa.com

Canada: Human Kinetics, Box 24040, Windsor, ON N8Y 4Y9
1-800-465-7301 (in Canada only)
e-mail: humank@hkcanada.com

Europe: Human Kinetics, P.O. Box IW14, Leeds LS16 6TR, United Kingdom
(44) 1132 781708
e-mail: humank@hkeurope.com

Australia: Human Kinetics, 57A Price Avenue, Lower Mitcham, South Australia 5062
(08) 277 1555
e-mail: humank@hkaustralia.com

New Zealand: Human Kinetics, P.O. Box 105-231, Auckland 1
(09) 523 3462
e-mail: humank@hknewz.com

Contents

Preface

The motivation for writing this book comes from over 30 years of coaching basketball players from youth to NBA level. There are many books available on basketball team play. Some of these concentrate on team drills. My previous book, *Becoming a Basketball Player: Individual Drills*, contains drills that you can practice alone. This book focuses on the development of fundamental skills and their integration into team play through individual, small group, and team lead-up drills.

This book is a resource for teachers and coaches. It is also a guide for parents who want to encourage their youngsters. But primarily this book has been written for *you*, the player. Players who love the game continually seek ways to improve. They ask, What is the most important attribute for becoming a better player? I strongly believe that desire and self-confidence are the key factors to success. That you have purchased this book and are taking the time to read it demonstrates your desire. Disciplined practice of the principles contained in the book will improve your skills and build your confidence.

Basketball is unique because it is not only the ultimate team game but also an individual game. Improving yourself as a player helps your team. Basketball, more than any other sport, requires integration of individual talent into unselfish team play. First, it requires the sound execution of fundamental skills, which, once learned, can be connected into the game. Drills are used to instill confidence, to transfer skills to game situations, and to contribute toward long-term enjoyment of playing basketball.

Despite the size, conditioning, and talent of today's basketball players, who succeeds and who fails in the sport is still determined by who possesses fundamental skills. Larry Bird, Magic Johnson, and Michael Jordan are examples of players who had obvious physical talent for the game but who reached their high level of performance because they practiced hard and often to become proficient in every basketball fundamental and then used those skills to maximize the performance of their teammates. Larry Bird is a great example of a player who practiced often. After dominating other players on a playground in Gary, Indiana, in the summer before his high school junior year, Larry was asked by one of his friends if he had been playing much ball. Bird's answer was simple: "Every day, all day."[1] New York Knicks coach Pat Riley talks about Magic Johnson as a role model, saying, "The most fundamental player I've ever been around in my life was Magic Johnson. People don't understand that. They saw all the flash. He made those plays too, but he was very solid, fundamental."[2] Michael Jordan derived sheer joy in playing and was so obsessed with winning that he constantly pushed himself to work harder than anyone in practice. Jordan cared about fulfilling his potential, and he is a model for those who strive to bring out the best in themselves.

The fundamental skills of basketball include footwork, shooting, passing and catching, dribbling, rebounding, using moves with the ball, moving without the ball, and defending. You and your coach should determine priorities. However, many young players become frustrated when they cannot shoot or handle the ball. Confidence-building offensive skills should be emphasized early because these skills take more time to master than skills that do not involve the ball.

Improvement for the more advanced player comes from game competition and individual practice. Seek out the strongest competition. Strong competition helps you improve and also reveals your weaknesses. Work to overcome these weaknesses. It is easy to practice something you already do well, and that is what average players do. The way to get better is to make your weaknesses your strengths. If you have trouble shooting, learn to shoot the correct way, and then *practice*. Correct practice fosters improvement. If you have trouble dribbling with your weak hand, for instance, practice dribbling with that hand. If you need to improve your defensive quickness or jumping ability, practice defensive footwork and jumping drills. You will not

---

[1]Bird, L. & Ryan, B. (1989). Larry Bird—Drive: The story of my life. New York: Doubleday.
[2]Kerber, F. (December 14, 1993, p. 84). Knick Notes. New York Post.

only improve your skills but, more importantly, you'll build your confidence.

Failure in athletics is often caused by a confidence problem rather than a physical limitation. I have coached for many years and feel strongly that success depends above all on getting players to believe in themselves. We all realize that your confidence is greatest after you have achieved success. However, before success is ever achieved you can best develop your confidence through practice. It is common to think of self-confidence in relation to natural physical talent. It is a mistake, however, to consider physical talent alone. There will always be times when you compete against opponents who are more physically talented than you are. Many players tend to lack confidence in such situations. To have the confidence to defeat more physically talented athletes, you must believe that you have worked harder and are better prepared, particularly in fundamental skills.

As in any project of this magnitude, many people have contributed to its successful completion. I would like to thank Human Kinetics for the opportunity to share my basketball experiences with others. Particular thanks go to Dr. Judy Patterson Wright, my developmental editor, whose patience, suggestions, and good humor helped me persevere through the writing. Thanks to Keith Blomberg, Art Director for Human Kinetics, who did the illustrations. Thanks to the subjects for the photos used for the illustrations, Lafayette College student-athletes Keith Brazzo, Charles Dodge, Elliot Fontaine, Ross Gay, Stephanie Hayes, Jon Norton, Nuno Santo, Christine Sieling, and Leslie Yuen.

This book is based not only on my experiences as a coach but also on my study of the publications on playing and coaching basketball, attendance at numerous coaching clinics, and discussing basketball with many coaches and players. I would like to express my sincere appreciation to Paul Ryan, my high school coach; Dr. Edward S. Steitz, my college mentor and advisor and the coach who gave me my first opportunity to coach on the college level; the inspiring coaches I have worked under, especially Hubie Brown, Mike Dunleavy, Frank Hamblen, Del Harris, Frank Layden, and Lee Rose, who gave me opportunities to work in the National Basketball Association; my loyal and dedicated assistant coaches Wes Aldrich, Ralph Arietta, P.J. Carlesimo, Tim Cohane, Seth Hicks, Kevin McGinniss, Scott Pospichal, Joe Servon, Sam Tolkoff, and Drew Tucker; Hank Slider, a master teacher who contributed greatly to my knowledge and understanding of shooting; and Stan Kellner, coach, author, and clinician, who stimulated my interest and research in sports psychology. Special thanks to the many dedicated players I have had the privilege of teaching and coaching and who continue to be a source of inspiration.

Last, thanks to my wife, Trudy, and our children, Steve, Scott, David, Paul, and Sharon for listening to ideas, reading copy, questioning methods, serving as subjects for the photos for the illustrations and, especially, for their love, understanding, and inspiration.

Hal Wissel

Dedicated to Dr. Edward S. Steitz

The Steps to Success Staircase

Get ready to climb a staircase—one that will lead you to become an accomplished basketball player. You cannot leap to the top; you get there by climbing one step at a time.

Each of the 10 steps you will take is a smooth transition from the one before. The first few steps of the staircase provide a solid foundation of fundamental skills and concepts. As you practice each of the fundamental skills, your progress will allow you to connect skills. Practicing common combinations of basketball skills will give you the experience you need to make quick, intelligent decisions on the basketball court. You will learn to make the right moves in various game situations—whether you're shooting, passing, dribbling, making an offensive move, rebounding, or playing defense. A commitment to practice leads to improved basketball skills, which in turn leads to enhanced confidence. Confidence in skills leads to success in games and renews commitment to practicing. This is a familiar cycle to all those who have achieved success.

At its best, basketball is a team game. As you near the top of the staircase, you will become more confident in your ability to play and communicate with teammates, complementing each other's talents—moving without the ball, executing two and three person plays, fast breaking, and playing team offense and defense.

Familiarize yourself with this section as well as "The Game of Basketball" and "Preparing Your Body for Success" sections in order to understand how to set up your practice sessions around the steps.

Follow the same sequence each step (chapter) of the way:

1. Read the explanations of what is covered in the step, why the step is important, and how to execute or perform the step's focus, which may be a basic skill, concept, or tactic, or combination of the three.

2. Follow the numbered illustrations showing exactly how to position your body to execute each basic skill successfully. There are three general parts to each skill: preparation phase (starting position), execution phase (performing the skill that is the focus of the step), and follow-through phase (reaching a finish position or following through to starting position).

3. Look over the common errors that may occur and the recommendations for how to correct them.

4. The drills will help you improve your skills through repetition and purposeful practice. Read the directions and the Success Goals for each drill. Practice accordingly and record your scores. Compare your score with the Success Goals for the drill. You need to meet the Success Goals of each drill before moving on to the next one because the drills are arranged in an easy-to-difficult progression. This sequence is designed specifically to help you achieve continual success.

5. As soon as you can reach all the Success Goals for one step, you are ready for a qualified observer—such as your teacher, coach, or skilled player—to evaluate your basic skill technique against the Keys to Success Checklist. This is a qualitative or subjective evaluation of your basic technique or form, because using correct form can enhance your performance.

6. Repeat these procedures for each of the 10 Steps to Success. Then rate yourself according to the directions in the "Rating Your Total Progress" section.

Good luck on your step-by-step journey to developing your basketball skills, building confidence, experiencing success, and having fun!

Key to diagrams

→ = Path of player

– – → = Pass

〜〜〜→ = Dribble

——| = Screen

0 = Offensive player
X = Defensive player
C = Coach

Offensive players by position
1 = Point guard
2 = Shooting guard
3 = Small forward
4 = Power forward
5 = Center

① = Point guard with ball

② = Shooting guard with ball

③ = Small forward with ball

④ = Power forward with ball

⑤ = Center with ball

Defensive players by assignment

X_1 = Player assigned to 1

X_2 = Player assigned to 2

X_3 = Player assigned to 3

X_4 = Player assigned to 4

X_5 = Player assigned to 5

The Game of Basketball

Basketball was invented in December 1891 by Dr. James Naismith, a faculty member at the International YMCA Training School in Springfield, Massachusetts (known now as Springfield College). Naismith invented basketball in response to an assignment by Dr. Luther Gulick, the director of the physical education department, who assigned Naismith the task of devising a competitive game like football or lacrosse that could be played indoors during the cold winter months. Basketball immediately became popular and quickly spread nationally and internationally due to the travels of the YMCA Training School graduates.

Competition among colleges spread after the turn of the twentieth century. The National Invitation Tournament (the first national collegiate tournament) was initiated in 1938, and the National Collegiate Athletic Association tournament was started in 1939. Professional leagues were formed as early as 1906. The National Basketball Association (NBA), the major professional basketball league, was formed in 1946. Basketball first became a part of the Olympics in 1936.

BASKETBALL TODAY

Today, basketball is the fastest growing sport in the world. Some of the reasons for the game's growth include the following:

1. Basketball is a tremendously popular spectator sport, particularly on television. The televising of NBA games worldwide and of men's and women's college games nationally has influenced many people to participate in the sport.

2. The nature of the game keeps people involved. Although basketball was invented as an indoor sport, it is now played indoors and outdoors in all seasons. Almost 40% of play is outside in an unorganized environment.

3. Basketball is for everyone. Although basketball is an extremely youthful sport with participation heaviest among teenage males, it is played by both sexes of all ages and sizes and also by the physically challenged, including those in wheelchairs. Although there are advantages to being tall, there are also many opportunities for the skillful smaller player. Participation among older players and female players is growing. More girls play interscholastic high school basketball than any other sport, and women's support groups are building networks that will continue the expansion of female participation.

4. Basketball is growing rapidly outside the United States and international competition is creating even greater excitement and participation in the sport. The addition of NBA players into Olympic competition in 1992 has had a tremendous impact on the popularity of basketball, a game that was already being played throughout the world. Currently, there are basketball federations in almost 200 countries.

5. Basketball competition is unique because, unlike other sports, it can be easily modified. Although most organized basketball competition consists of teams of five players, unorganized basketball competition can be played from fullcourt 5-on-5 down to smaller groups of halfcourt 3-on-3, 2-on-2, and 1-on-1. There has been a particularly rapid growth in organized 3-on-3 basketball tournaments. The NBA is now leading the way by sponsoring NBA Hoop It Up tournaments in over 60 countries. There has also been growth in individual competition in the form of free throw and other shooting contests sponsored by schools, clubs, and other organizations.

6. Basketball can be played alone. All you need is a ball, a basket, a confined space (such as a driveway or playground), and your imagination to provide a competitive game-like experience that other sports simply cannot match.

PLAYING THE GAME

The game of basketball is played by two teams of five players on a court. The objective of each team is to score by putting a ball into its own basket and to prevent the other team from doing so. The ball can be advanced only by passing with the hands or by dribbling (batting, pushing, or tapping) the ball on the floor once or several times without touching it with both hands simultaneously.

Fundamental skills include footwork, shooting, passing and catching, dribbling, rebounding, using moves with the ball, moving without the ball, and defending.

Although players are allowed to play in any position, the most common positions of the five players on a team are point guard or #1 (best ball handler), shooting guard or #2 (best outside shooter), small forward or #3 (versatile inside and outside player), power forward or #4 (strong rebounding forward), and center or #5 (inside scorer, rebounder, and shot blocker).

RULES

Currently there are several sets of basketball rules in the world. International rules for competition between nations are established by the Federation Internationale de Basketball (FIBA). In the United States, professional players play under the rules of the National Basketball Association (NBA). College men and women play under separate sets of rules as established by the National Collegiate Athletic Association (NCAA). High schools play by rules established by the National Federation of State High School Associations. In recent years there has been a movement toward uniformity in rules. Differences remain, mostly in degree of length, distance, and time, rather than in substance and content. To foster children's enjoyment and development, modified rules calling for smaller basketballs, lower baskets, and scaled-down courts have been devised.

Player Equipment

Basketball shoes are necessary for traction on the court. Athletic shorts, tank tops or loose fitting T-shirts, and white socks are recommended. You may wear soft pads to protect your knees and elbows and eyeglass protectors or goggles to protect your eyes. Jewelry is illegal.

Basketball, Basket, and Backboards

Basketballs are spherical and an approved orange color. The circumference of the men's ball is a maximum of 30 inches and a minimum of 29-1/2 inches, and the circumference of the women's ball is a maximum of 29 inches and a minimum of 28-1/2 inches. The backboard is a rectangle, with a flat surface, measuring 6 feet horizontally and either 3-1/2 feet or 4 feet vertically. A rectangular box measuring 24 inches horizontally and 18 inches vertically is centered on the backboard behind the ring (rim) with the top edge of its baseline level with the ring. Each basket is 18 inches in inside diameter and is attached to the backboard with its upper edge 10 feet above the floor and its nearest inside edge 6 inches from the backboard.

Court Dimensions and Markings

The playing court is a rectangular surface free from obstructions with dimensions of 50 feet by 94 feet (usually 84 feet for high schools). Markings designating specific areas of the court are illustrated in Figure 1.

Court areas are referred to by specific names. The boundary lines at each side and each end of the court are called the *sideline* and *endline* or *baseline*, respectively. A team's *frontcourt* refers to the half of the court between its end line and the nearer edge of the *division* or *midcourt line* including the basket, and the *backcourt* includes the other half of the court where your opponent's basket is located. Your team must advance the ball over the midcourt line within 10 seconds, and once the ball is in the frontcourt it is a violation if it is returned backcourt. There are three circles on the court—a *free throw circle* at each end and a *center circle*. The *free throw line*, 15 feet from the backboard, dissects each free throw circle. Lines from the ends of the free throw line to the baseline are called *lane lines* and along with the free throw line and baseline mark an area called the *free throw lane* or *key*. Offensive players cannot stay in the lane for more than 3 consecutive seconds unless a shot is taken. The college and high school 3-point line is marked at 19 feet, 9 inches (NBA line is 23 feet, 9 inches) from the center of the basket. Additional markings on each side of the lane lines are called the *block* and *hash marks*.

Scoring

A goal from the field beyond the 3-point line counts 3 points, any other field goal counts 2 points, and a free throw counts 1 point.

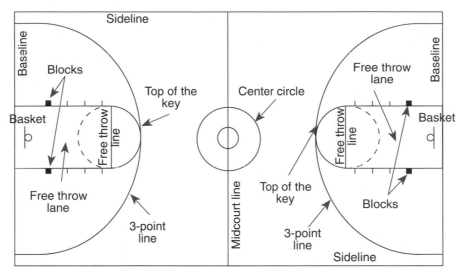

Figure 1 Basketball court markings.

Length of Game

Professional games consist of 4 quarters of 12 minutes each. College games consist of 2 halves of 20 minutes each. High school games consist of 4 quarters of 8 minutes each. Overtime periods are used for tie games. The length of the youth games are adjusted according to the ages of the players. The game clock is stopped between quarters or halves, during time-outs, when the ball goes out of bounds, and when free throws are attempted. Shot clocks vary in length for professional, international, college men, college women, and high school competition.

Fouls

Fouls are called by officials for the purpose of not allowing a team to gain an advantage through rough play. Fouls carry penalties. When you commit five fouls, you are disqualified from the game. When you foul an opponent in the act of shooting, the opponent is awarded 2 free throws. When you foul an opponent other than when shooting, the opponent is awarded the ball out of bounds. When your team commits more than a specified amount of fouls in a quarter or a half, the opposing team is allowed to shoot bonus free throws for nonshooting fouls. Some of the types of fouls are listed here:

• *Holding, pushing, charging, tripping, or impeding an opponent's progress*—extending a body or body part into other than a normal position, or using any rough tactics

• *Using your hands on an opponent*—using your hands in any way that inhibits the freedom of movement of the opponent or acts as an aid in stopping or starting

• *Extending your arms to hinder your opponent*—extending your arms fully or partially, other than vertically, so that freedom of movement of an opponent is hindered when contact with your arms occurs

• *Illegal screen*—when setting a screen you are still moving when the defender makes contact

Violations

Ball-handling and time violations cause your team to lose possession of the ball to the defense. Some of the more common violations are listed here:

• Ball-handing violations

   Out of bounds—causing the ball to go out of bounds

   Over-and-back—causing the ball to return to the backcourt after it has crossed into the frontcourt without the defense touching it

   Traveling—taking more than one step before the start of a dribble, or taking two or more steps before releasing a pass or shot

   Double dribble—resuming dribbling after having stopped dribbling or dribbling with both hands simultaneously

   Charging—running into or pushing a stationary defender

- Time violations

  5 seconds to inbound—failure for the ball to   be caught within 5 seconds after a made   basket or after the official hands the ball   to the inbounder

  10 seconds in backcourt—taking 10 or more seconds to get the ball across the midcourt line

  3 seconds in lane—being in the offensive free throw lane for 3 or more seconds without a member of your team shooting

ORGANIZATIONS

Various governing bodies currently provide rules for basketball competition in the United States. The majority of girls' and boys' high school play is governed by the National Federation of State High School Associations (NFSHSA). For rules information and interpretation contact:

NFSHSA
11724 Plaza Circle
Box 20626
Kansas City, MO 64195

Collegiate competition for both men and women is controlled by the National Collegiate Athletic Association (NCAA), the National Association for Intercollegiate Athletics (NAIA), or the National Junior College Athletic Association (NJCAA). These organizations oversee seasonal play and administer national championships. Questions concerning player eligibility, national championship format, recruiting rules, and so forth should be directed to the appropriate governing body:

NCAA
6201 College Boulevard
Overland Park, KS 66211-2422

NAIA
6120 South Yale Avenue
Suite 1450
Tulsa, OK 74136

NJCAA
P.O. Box 7305
Colorado Springs, CO 80933

The organization responsible for participation of United States men's and women's teams in international competition is USA Basketball. The international body with jurisdiction over the sport of basketball is the Federation Internationale de Basketball (FIBA). For information concerning international competition and rules, contact:

USA Basketball
1750 East Boulder Street
Colorado Springs, CO 80909-5777

FIBA
P.O. Box 70 06 07
Kistlerhofstrasse 168
W-800 Munchen 70
Federal Republic of Germany

Preparing Your Body for Success

Warm-up activities such as trotting, changing pace and direction, short sprints, and executing defensive slides for about 5 minutes followed by a stretching routine are important to physically and mentally prepare you for strenuous basketball activity. Preparing your body for basketball practice or a game involves three phases: a 5-minute warm-up to increase your heart rate, stretching, and basketball warm-up drills.

WARM-UP

The first phase of preparing your body for strenuous basketball activity is to warm up with 5 minutes of offensive and defensive footwork. This will increase your blood circulation and gradually begin to prepare your body for the demands you are going to put on it.

When warming up with offensive and defensive footwork, you will move from baseline to baseline using a third of the width of the floor (lane line to lane line or lane line to sideline). A detailed description of footwork can be found in Step 1.

Offensive Footwork

Select from the following footwork options:

1. *Trot.* Use easy running from baseline to baseline and return. Do at least 2 round-trips.

2. *Sprint.* Run to halfcourt, change pace to a trot, and continue to the opposite baseline. Return in the same manner.

3. *Change of Pace.* Run from baseline to baseline with at least three quick changes of pace from sprint to trot to sprint. Return in the same manner.

4. *Change of Direction.* Run from baseline to baseline making changes of direction. Start in an offensive stance with your left foot touching the intersection of the baseline and lane line on your left. Run diagonally at a 45-degree angle to the lane line on your right. Make a sharp 90-degree change of direction from right to left, and run diagonally to the imaginary lane line extended on your left. Make a sharp 90-degree change of direction from left to right. Continue changing direction at each imaginary lane line extended as

you proceed to the opposite baseline. Return in the same manner.

5. *One-Two Stops.* Run to the opposite baseline making four one-two stops as you go. Alternate the foot you land on first on each one-two stop. Land on your left foot first on one stop, then on your right foot first on the next stop. Return in the same manner.

Defensive Footwork

Start with your back to the far basket in a staggered defensive stance with one foot up, touching the baseline, and your other foot spread directly back.

1. *Zigzag.* Use defensive retreat steps to move diagonally back until your back foot touches the nearest sideline or lane line. Quickly drop step with your lead foot and use retreat steps to move diagonally back until your back foot touches the nearest imaginary lane line extended or sideline. Continue changing direction at each imaginary lane line extended or sideline as you proceed to the opposite baseline. Return in the same manner.

2. *Defensive Attack and Retreat.* Use defensive attack and retreat steps until your back foot touches the halfcourt line. Quickly drop step moving your other foot back and move backward to the baseline using attack and retreat steps until your back foot touches the baseline. Vary your attack and retreat steps as you move down the floor. Return in the same manner.

3. *Reverse-Run-and-Turn.* Move backward using defensive attack and retreat steps. Imagine that a dribbler beats your lead foot and you must recover by using a reverse-run-and-turn. Reverse to the side of your lead foot, keeping your vision on the imaginary dribbler, and run at least three steps before establishing a defensive position with your original lead foot up. From baseline to the halfcourt line, make two reverse-run-and-turns starting with your left foot forward. From halfcourt line to the opposite baseline, make two reverse-run-and-turns starting with your right foot forward. Return in the same manner.

STRETCHING

Stretching increases your readiness to perform and helps prevent injuries. Hold each stretch position for 8 to 10 seconds, then relax. Avoid bouncing. Concentrate on your body and relax as you stretch. You may prefer to close your eyes as you stretch to more easily focus on the muscles you are stretching. Take care to prevent injury by moving slowly when changing from one stretching position to another. Go to the point to where you feel a moderate amount of tension and then relax mentally as you hold the stretch.

Stretching can also increase flexibility. To develop flexibility, move further into each stretch rather than ending the stretch at 8 to 10 seconds. Move further into the stretch until again you feel mild tension and then hold the position for 20 to 30 seconds.

The following stretching exercises are designed to develop flexibility throughout your body with emphasis on stretching the muscles used for playing basketball. For best results, these exercises should be done in sequence from upper body to lower body.

Head and Neck

Neck Stretch: Stand in a balanced stance with head erect. Lean your head to the right, ear to shoulder, relax, and slowly count to 10. Lean your head to the left, ear to shoulder, relax, and slowly count to 10. Repeat both sides 3 times.

Shoulders

1. Chest and Shoulder Stretch: Grasp your hands together behind your back and slowly lift them upward. If you are not able to grasp your hands, simply reach back as far as possible. For an additional stretch, bend at the waist and raise your arms higher. Repeat 3 times.

2. Upper Back, Shoulder, and Arm Stretch: With your right hand, grasp your left elbow and pull it slowly across your chest toward your right shoulder. You will feel the stretch along the outside of your left shoulder and arm. Repeat with your other shoulder and arm. Vary this stretch by pulling across and down over your chest and upper stomach. Repeat each 3 times.

3. Shoulder and Triceps Stretch: Bring both arms overhead and hold your left elbow with your right hand. Allow your left arm to bend at the elbow and let your left hand rest against the back of your right shoulder. Pull with your right hand to slowly move the left elbow behind your head until you feel a stretch. Repeat with the other arm. Repeat each 3 times.

Arms

Arm Circles: With your arms stretched at shoulder height, circle your arms in small, tight circles forward 10 times, then backward 10 times. Next, slowly do 10 forward arm circles using small, then gradually larger circles. Reverse direction and make 10 gradually larger circles backward. Repeat total sequence 3 times.

Trunk

1. Side Bends: With your feet shoulder-width apart, join hands overhead and bend your trunk to the left, keeping your shoul-

ders and hips square to the front. Relax, then attempt to increase your stretch. Repeat to the opposite side. Repeat both sides 3 times.

2. Trunk Rotation: Starting in a balanced stance extend both arms horizontally to the left. Rotate your trunk, hips, and arms, first to the right, then to the left. This counts as one repetition. Repeat 3 times. Next do 3 repetitions rotating your arms and trunk in opposition to your hips.

Legs

1. Standing Hamstring Stretch: With your feet shoulder-width apart, slowly bend forward at the waist and attempt to touch your fingers to the ground while keeping your knees slightly bent. Relax your upper body, especially your arms and neck. You should feel the stretch in your hamstrings behind your knees. Hold your stretch and *do not bounce*. Slowly rotate up to a standing position. Repeat 3 times. A slightly different stretch occurs when you cross one foot in front of the other.

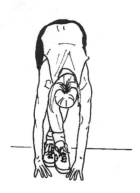

2. Groin, Hip, and Inner Leg Stretch: From a standing position, spread your feet about 3 feet apart. Bend one knee to the side, shifting your weight to that side and keeping the foot of the bent leg flat on the floor. Extend your other leg with the inner part of the ankle of the extended leg touching the floor. Feel the stretch in your groin, hip, and inner leg. Perform the same stretch with your other leg. Repeat 3 times.

3. Quadriceps Stretch: Using a wall or stationary object for balance, grasp your right foot with your left hand and pull so that your heel moves back toward your buttocks. You should feel the stretch along the front of your right thigh. Repeat with your left leg and right hand. You can add an additional stretch by

leaning forward at the waist. Repeat each 3 times.

4. Calf and Achilles Tendon Stretch: Stand about 3 feet away from a wall or stationary object. With your feet together and your knees locked, lean forward. Apply a stretch on your calves and achilles tendons by slowly leaning toward the wall. Be sure to keep your heels flat on the floor and your back straight. You can feel an additional stretch by slightly bending one knee at a time. Repeat 3 times.

5. Sitting Groin Stretch: Sit with your knees spread in front of you and the soles of your feet touching. Grab your ankles and place your elbows on the inner parts of your knees. Use your elbows to gently push down on the inside of your knees. You should feel the stretch in the groin area. Repeat 3 times.

6. Sitting Hamstrings Stretch: Sit with your right leg straight and the sole of your left foot slightly touching the inside of your right knee. Slowly bend at your waist, reaching for your right foot. Keep the toes of your right foot up while relaxing your ankles and toes. You should feel the stretch in the back of your right thigh. Perform the same stretch with your left leg. Repeat 3 times.

Back and Hips

1. Back and Hips Stretch: Sit with your right leg straight. Bend your left leg, crossing your left foot over and resting it to the outside of your knee with the sole flat on the floor. Then push against the outside of your upper left thigh with your right elbow, just above the knee. Use your right elbow to keep this leg stationary as you perform the stretch. Next, place your left hand behind your buttocks, slowly turn your head to look

over your left shoulder and rotate your upper body toward your left hand and arm. You should feel the stretch in your lower back, hips, and buttocks. Perform the stretch with your other leg. Repeat each 3 times.

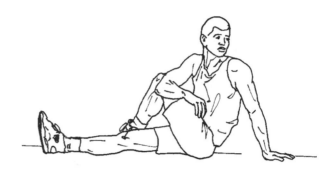

2. Lying Back Stretch: Lie on your back. Slowly bring your knees up toward your chin, while grabbing the backs of your upper legs with your hands. Do *not* grab below the front of your knees, as this puts pressure on your knees. Lift your hips slightly off the floor. You should feel the stretch in your lower back. Repeat 3 times.

Ankles

Ankle Stretch: Stand with your feet flat on the floor. Slowly roll your weight onto your heels, raising your toes off the floor; then roll down onto your toes, raising your heels off the floor. Next, slowly roll your weight onto the inside of your feet, raising the outside of your feet off the floor; then roll down onto the outside of your feet, raising the inside of your feet off the floor. Hold each position for

8 seconds. Repeat each position 3 times. You can also stretch your ankles by walking on your heels, toes, inside of your feet, and outside of your feet. Walk for several steps in each position before changing.

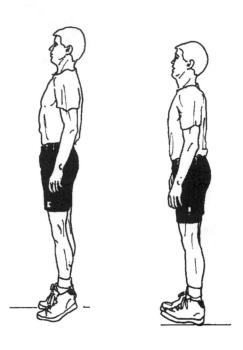

BASKETBALL WARM-UP DRILLS

The ball-handling warm-up described in Step 3 and the dribble warm-up and two-ball dribble drills described in Step 4 are excellent warm-ups for your entire body, and they also enhance ball-handling and dribbling skills and increase confidence. Step 2 describes several shooting warm-up drills. The hook shot warm-up and alternate hand hook shooting drill are excellent drills for loosening your shoulders while helping you develop your strong- and weak-hand hook shot. The shooting warm-up helps you warm up for shooting, while enhancing shooting mechanics, rhythm, and confidence. One-foot vertical jump training described in Step 1 and tossback passing described in Step 3 are also excellent basketball warm-up drills that improve skill and confidence.

COOL-DOWN PERIOD

At the end of basketball practice, take about 5 minutes to cool down. This is an excellent time to stretch, because your muscles are warm. Choose at least one stretching exercise for each body part.

Step 1   Offensive and Defensive Footwork: Improve Balance and Quickness

Although basketball is a team game, individual execution of fundamental skills is essential before you can play well as a team. Shooting, passing, dribbling, rebounding, defending, moving with the ball, and moving without the ball are the fundamental skills to master. If you are a beginning player, practice to learn these fundamentals. If you are an experienced player, work to strengthen any fundamental skills that are weak and perfect those that are strong.

The prerequisites for soundly executing each of the fundamental skills are *balance* and *quickness*. It is common to associate basketball success with height or size, but balance and quickness are the most important physical attributes you can have as a player. There is little you can do to increase your height, but balance and quickness for executing basketball skills can be improved through practice.

Balance means that you have your body parts under control and in a state of readiness to make quick movements. Quickness is an asset only if you can still execute properly. To rush or hurry is different from being quick. If you rush—using unusual haste or performing too rapidly—you're apt to make mistakes. Rushing reflects a lack of emotional as well as physical balance or control.

Quickness refers to your speed of movement in performing a skill (not just running speed). Quickness is specific to the fundamental being performed, like quick movement of your feet on defense, quickly going for a rebound, or a quick release of your shot.

WHY BALANCE, QUICKNESS, AND FOOTWORK ARE IMPORTANT

How quickly you can execute each fundamental skill with balance, or control, will be a major factor in your progress. Each fundamental skill must first be learned correctly and then practiced to the point that execution becomes automatic. Once you've reached this level, then you can emphasize quickness. Balance, or being under control, is the critical factor to increasing quickness in a skill.

Quickness and balance are closely related to footwork, which is basic to all fundamental basketball skills. Being ready to start, stop, and move in any direction with quickness and balance requires good footwork. Developing your footwork lays the foundation; effective footwork lets you keep your body under control so you can move with timing, deception, and quickness.

Good footwork is important to both offense and defense. As an offensive player you have the advantage over your defender in knowing what move you will make and when. Offensive footwork is used to fake your defender off balance, move off screens, cut to the basket, prevent charging into a defender, and to elude a block out when going for an offensive rebound.

Developing good footwork is especially important when playing defense. You can try to anticipate moves, but you'll never be certain what your opponent will do. Much of your defensive success will depend on your ability to react instantly in any direction to the moves of your opponent—which requires executing defensive footwork with balance and quickness. With hard work you can even improve your defensive footwork to the level that you can force your opponent to react to you. Good footwork can enable you to disrupt the offensive poise of your opponent, force low percentage shots, and force turnovers.

You may question just how much you can increase your natural quickness. Quickness is in large measure determined by genetics. But, by thoroughly understanding the basic mechanics of footwork, you can definitely improve your quickness, if you work at it.

I've heard some coaches say that Michael Jordan was born with great natural ability and that young players cannot hope to develop Jordan's quickness and jumping ability. This type of thinking fails to consider that although Jordan was naturally gifted, he also worked very hard to improve every facet of his game. Other naturally gifted NBA players capable of equally amazing feats simply lack Jordan's work ethic. Jordan derived sheer joy in playing and was so obsessed with winning that he constantly pushed himself to work harder in practice than anyone else. Jordan was not only regarded as the greatest player of all time, he was also regarded as the greatest *practice player* of all time. He can be a model for all of us trying to bring out the best in ourselves.

MAINTAINING A BALANCED OFFENSIVE STANCE

With a well-balanced stance you are ready to move quickly, change direction, stop under control, and jump. In a well-balanced stance your head is over your waist and your back is straight. Your hands are above your waist with your elbows flexed, keeping your arms close to your body. Your feet are at least shoulder-width apart, the weight evenly distributed on the balls of your feet and your knees flexed so that you are ready to move (see Figure 1.1, left column).

MAINTAINING A BALANCED DEFENSIVE STANCE

For defense you must be able to quickly move in any direction and change direction while maintaining balance. The prerequisite is a well-balanced stance. Your defensive stance resembles your basic stance: Your head is over your waist, your back is straight, your chest is out. Having your head over your waist keeps the center of gravity over its base. Keep your feet wider apart than shoulder width and staggered, with one foot in front of the other. Distribute weight evenly on the balls of your feet and flex your knees so your body is low, ready to react in any direction.

Protect the Lead Foot

In the basic defensive stance—the feet staggered one in front of the other—the front foot is called the *lead foot*. It is easy to move back in the direction of the back foot: Moving back requires only a short step with the back foot as you start to move. To move back in the direction of the lead foot is much more difficult, requiring a vigorous *drop step* (reverse) with the lead foot while pivoting on your back foot as you start to move.

You must protect your lead foot as you establish your basic defensive stance. Position your lead foot outside your opponent's body and your back foot in line with the middle of your opponent's body. This position not only protects the weakness of your lead foot but also gives the impression of an opening toward your back foot or strength of your defensive stance.

Hand Position

There are three basic defensive hand positions. The first is keeping one hand up on the side of your lead foot to pressure the shooter and your other hand at your side to protect against passes. A second basic hand position is having both hands at waist level, palms up, to pressure the dribbler. This position allows you to flick at the ball with the hand that is nearer the direction in which your opponent is dribbling.

In the third basic hand position you keep both hands above your shoulders. This higher position has four advantages: It forces lob or bounce passes, which are more readily intercepted, readies the hands to block shots, prepares you to rebound with two hands, and helps prevent reaching fouls. If the opposition does not have the ball, one hand should point toward your opponent and the other should point toward the ball. When both hands are above your shoulders, use care that they do not spread away from your body, causing you to lose balance: Flex your elbows to keep your arms from reaching out. While you guard an opponent who has the ball, your eyes should be looking at your opponent's midsection (see Figure 1.1, right column).

Figure 1.1 **Keys to Success:** *Balanced Stances*

**Preparation
Phase**

Offensive Stance

Defensive Stance

1. Head over waist _____
2. See rim and ball _____
3. Back straight _____
4. Hands up above waist _____
5. Elbows flexed _____
6. Arms close to body _____
7. Feet staggered, shoulder-width apart _____
8. Weight even on balls of feet _____
9 Knees flexed _____
10. Ready to move _____

1. Head over waist _____
2. See opponent's midsection _____
3. Back straight _____
4. Hands up above shoulders _____
5. Elbows flexed _____
6. Wide base _____
7. Feet staggered, shoulder-width or wider apart _____
8. Weight even on balls of feet _____
9. Knees flexed _____
10. Ready to move _____

Detecting Errors in Stance

Errors in offensive and defensive stances vary with the individual. Tall players often have greater problems of balance than shorter players. Typically, a tall player does not spread or flex the knees enough to keep the center of gravity low.

ERROR   **CORRECTION**

Offensive Stance

1. Your balance is off in a forward direction. of the reach.

1. Flex your knees to get low, rather than bending at the waist, so you are ready to move backward as quickly as you can move forward. See Drill 1.

ERROR    **CORRECTION**

Offensive Stance

2. You easily lose balance to either side.

2. Spread your feet shoulder-width apart and flex the knees so you are balanced and ready to move in any direction.

Defensive Stance

1. You do not protect your lead foot.

1. Position your lead foot outside your opponent's body and align your back foot with the middle of your opponent's body.

2. You are susceptible to head fakes and ball fakes by your opponent.

2. Keep your eyes focused on your opponent's midsection—not on your opponent's head or the ball.

3. You reach away from your body with your arm, becoming off balance in the direction of the reach.

3. Your head should be over your waist, hands above your waist, and your elbows flexed, keeping your arms close to your body.

EXECUTING OFFENSIVE FOOTWORK

Moving with and without the ball is important to individual and team offense. As an offensive player you have an advantage over your defender in knowing what move you will make and when you will make it. Moving quickly with balance is the key. Once you have developed the skills, your footwork and fakes should allow you to keep your balance as you attempt to elude your defender, who will have difficulty reacting instantly to your moves. Moving continually with and particularly without the ball also demands superior physical condition. Successful players master the necessary skills and develop their physical condition to excel in this important part of the game.

There are eight basic offensive movements that you should master: (1) change of pace, (2) change of direction, (3) one-two stop, (4) jump stop, (5) front turn, (6) reverse turn, (7) two-foot jump, and (8) one-foot jump.

Change of Pace

The change of pace is a method of altering your running speed to deceive and elude your defender. Change from a fast running speed to a slower variable and then quickly back to fast, *without changing your basic running form.*

As you run, keep your head up so you can see the rim of the basket and the ball. Take your first step with your back foot, crossing it in front of your lead foot. Run on the balls of your feet, pointing your toes in the direction you are going. Lean your upper body slightly forward and pump your arms forward in opposition to your legs, keeping your elbows flexed. Completely extend your support leg. Get your knee up and thigh parallel to the floor as you bring it forward.

The effectiveness of your change of pace comes from deception and quickness in changing speed. To slow your speed, shorten your stride and decrease its speed. Use less force to push off your back foot: Do not completely extend your back knee. For better deception avoid leaning your head and shoulders back as you slow your pace.

To increase your speed, lengthen your stride to its maximum and increase its speed (see Figure 1.2).

To accelerate quickly to a faster speed push forcefully off the back foot. You have the advantage in changing your pace because *you* decide when to change speeds. With good deception and a forceful push off your back foot, you should be at least a step quicker than your defender immediately after the change to a faster speed.

Change of Direction

The change of direction underlies almost every basketball fundamental but it is particularly important for getting open to receive a pass. An effective change of direction depends on sharply cutting from one direction to another. To execute a change of direction step first with one foot and then the other *without crossing your feet*. Begin with a three-quarter step, rather than a full step. On your first step flex your knee as you plant your foot firmly to stop your momentum, turn on the ball of your foot, and push off in the direction you want to go. Shift your weight and take a long step with your other foot, pointing your toes in the new direction. After the change of direction get your lead hand up as a target to receive a pass.

A seemingly simple move, the change of direction takes concentrated practice to execute sharply and effectively. Concentrate on a two-count move: Changing from right to left, concentrate on a two-count *right—left*, and going from left to right, concentrate on a two-count *left—right* (see Figure 1.2).

Figure 1.2   Keys to Success: Change of Direction

Execution Phase

1. Three-quarter first step ____
2. Knee flexed ____
3. Turn on ball of foot ____
4. Push off in new direction ____
5. Shift weight ____
6. Long second step ____
7. Point toes in new direction ____
8. Lead hand up as target ____

One-Two Stop

Starting quickly is important, but so is stopping quickly. Inexperienced players often lose balance in trying to stop quickly. Learning two basic stops—the one-two stop and the jump stop—will help you stop under control.

In the *one-two stop* the back foot lands first followed by the other foot. If you execute the one-two stop while you receive a pass or on your last dribble, the foot that lands first becomes the pivot foot. The one-two stop is useful when you are running too fast to use the jump stop, when you are on the perimeter away from the basket, and especially when you are on the fast break.

In executing the one-two stop first hop before the stop to allow gravity to help slow your movement and then lean in the opposite direction. Land on your back foot first, and then on your lead foot with a wide base. The wider your base, the more balance you will have. Flex your back knee to lower your body to a "sitting" position on the heel of your back foot. The lower you get, the better your balance. Keep your head up (see Figure 1.3).

Jump Stop

In the *jump stop* both feet land simultaneously. As you catch the ball and land with a jump stop you can use either foot as a pivot. The jump stop is particularly advantageous when you are moving under control without the ball, especially when you receive a pass with your back to the basket in the low-post area (within 8 feet of the basket).

In executing the jump stop, like the one-two stop, hop before the stop to allow grav-ity to help slow your movement, lean back, and then stop with both feet landing simultaneously, shoulder-width apart, with your knees flexed. Shift your weight onto the back parts of your feet to keep your body from moving forward (see Figure 1.3).

Figure 1.3   Keys to Success: Two Basic Stops

**Execution
Phase**

One-Two Stop

1. Run ____
2. Hop before stop ____
3. Lean in opposite direction ____
4. Back foot lands first ____

5. Lead foot lands second ____
6. Wide base ____
7. "Sit" on back heel ____
8. Head up ____

Jump Stop

1. Short, quick steps ____
2. Hop before stop ____
3. Shoulders back ____
4. Land on both feet ____

5. Feet shoulder-width apart ____
6. Knees flexed ____
7. Shift weight to balls of feet ____
8. Head up ____

Pivoting

When you are in possession of the ball, the rules allow you to take as many steps as you need in any direction with one foot while *pivoting* (turning) on your other foot. The foot that you pivot with, or turn on, is called the *pivot foot*. Once you establish your pivot foot, you cannot lift it before you release the ball from your hand to dribble. When attempting a pass or shot, you may lift your pivot foot—providing you release the ball before your pivot foot again hits the floor. Once you have established one foot as your pivot, you cannot change to pivot on your other foot.

Pivoting often is an essential part of other basketball skills. To pivot well you need a balanced stance: head over your waist, back straight, and knees flexed. Keep your weight on the ball of the pivot foot and do not pivot on your heel.

The two basic pivots are for pivoting forward and for pivoting backward. These are called the *front turn*, or *forward pivot*, and the *reverse turn*, or *drop step*, and both are important to learn. Both pivots are used to move into an advanta-geous position against your opponent.

Front Turn (Forward Pivot)

Your chest leads the way when you make a front turn. Maintaining a balanced stance, keep your weight on the ball of your pivot foot and step forward with the nonpivot foot (see Figure 1.4, left column).

Reverse Turn (Drop Step)

Your back leads the way when you make a reverse turn. Maintaining a balanced stance, keep your weight on the ball of your pivot foot and drop your nonpivot foot back (see Figure 1.4, right column).

Figure 1.4   Keys to Success: *Pivots or Turns*

**Execution
Phase**

Front Turn   **Reverse Turn (Drop Step)**

____ 1. Balanced stance   ____
____ 2. Weight on ball of pivot foot   ____

3. Chest leads ____   3. Back leads ____
4. Pivot on ball of foot ____   4. Pivot on ball of foot ____
5. Step forward with other foot ____ 5. Drop other foot back ____

Jumping

Everyone recognizes the importance of jumping in basketball, including its role in rebounding, blocking shots, and shooting. Jumping is more than gaining height. How quickly and how often you jump are more important than jumping height. Timing, balance in the air, and landing are also important components of jumping.

There are two basic jumps: the two-foot jump and the one-foot jump.

Two-Foot Jump

Use the two-foot jump when you are not on the move, when it is important to land in balance (such as for shooting a jump shot), and for jumping in succession, such as in rebounding.

Start in a balanced stance (head over your waist, back straight, elbows flexed, arms close to your body, and weight on the balls of your feet). Before jumping flex your knees from 60 to 90 degrees, depending on your leg strength. If you can, take a short step before your takeoff. On your takeoff, push quickly and forcefully off both feet, extending your ankles, knees, and hips. The key to attaining maximum height is an explosive takeoff. The quicker and more forcefully you push against the floor, the higher you will jump. Lift both arms straight up as you jump. To increase the reach you have with one hand, at the top of your jump extend your nonreaching arm downward. A smooth, fluid action without tension results in a higher jump. Land in the same spot on the balls of your feet with your knees flexed to jump again or move (see Figure 1.5, left column).

One-Foot Jump

The one-foot jump is for jumping on the move: shooting a layup off a drive, moving to block a shot, and moving for an offensive rebound. When moving, it is quicker to jump off one foot than off two feet. Jumping off two feet takes time to stop and prepare for the jump. The one-foot jump's disadvantage is the difficulty of controlling your body in the air, which might cause a foul or even a collision with other players. It also is more difficult to land in balance after a moving one-foot jump and harder to change direction or make a quick second jump.

Start the one-foot jump from a run. To jump high you must gain speed on the last three or four steps of your approach but also be able to control that speed. The last step before your jump should be short, so you can quickly dip your takeoff knee. This will change forward momentum to upward momentum.

Your takeoff knee should flex from 60 to 90 degrees, depending on your leg strength. The takeoff angle should be as nearly vertical as possible. From a balanced stance push quickly and forcefully off your takeoff foot, extending your ankle, knee, and hip. Remember how vital the explosiveness of your takeoff is: The quicker and more forcefully your push against the floor, the higher you will jump. Lift your opposite knee and your arms straight up as you jump. As with the two-foot jump, to increase your reach, at the top of the jump extend your nonreaching arm downward; use a smooth fluid action without tension, and land in balance on the balls of your feet with your knees flexed (see Figure 1.5, right column).

Figure 1.5   Keys to Success: Jumping

**Execution
Phase**

Two-Foot Jump

One-Foot Jump

1. Stationary start ____

1. Running approach, increasing speed last few steps ____

____ 2. Short step before takeoff   ____
____ 3. Head over waist   ____
____ 4. Back straight   ____
____ 5. Elbows flexed   ____
____ 6. Arms close to body   ____

7. Balls of feet ____
8. Flex knees 60 to 90 degrees ____
9. Push quickly and forcefully off both feet ____
10. Extend both ankles, knees, and hips ____
11. Lift both arms straight up ____

7. Ball of takeoff foot ____
8. Flex takeoff knee 60 to 90 degrees ____
9. Push quickly and forcefully off takeoff foot ____
10. Lift non-takeoff knee; extend ankle, knee, and hip of takeoff foot ____
11. Reach high, extend nonreaching arm downward ____

____ 12. Land in same spot   ____

Detecting Errors in Offensive Footwork

ERROR

The most common errors in offensive footwork are listed here, along with suggestions to correct them.

CORRECTION

Change of Pace

1. You are not deceptive in changing your pace from fast to slow; you lean your head and shoulders back.

2. You do not make a quick change from slow to fast.

1. When changing your pace to a slower speed, keep your upper body leaning forward.

2. Push forcefully off your back foot to quickly accelerate.

Change of Direction

1. You are not deceptive; you slow your speed with short steps on your approach to the change of direction.

2. You circle your turn, rather than making a sharp cut.

3. You do not give a target with your lead hand.

1. Use normal running form and concentrate on a two-count move.

2. Use a three-quarter first step and flex your knee so you can pivot sharply and push off in the direction you want to go. Then shift your weight, and take a long second step.

3. After making the change of direction, get your lead hand up.

One-Two Stop

1. You slow your speed to make your stop using short steps on your approach.

2. You lose balance, going forward, causing you to drag your pivot foot.

1. Use normal running form. Hop before you stop so that gravity helps slow your movement.

2. Hop before you stop, allowing gravity to slow your forward momentum. Then lean back, land first on your back foot and then your front foot with a wide base and "sit" on the heel of your back foot. Keep your head up.

Jump Stop

1. One foot lands before the other.

2. With your weight on your toes you lose balance, taking an extra step forward.

1. Hop before your stop, lean back, keep your feet shoulder-width apart and your knees flexed.

2. See correction #1. Shift your weight to the back of your feet, keeping your head up and over your waist.

ERROR	CORRECTION

Pivoting

1. You do not understand the rules on pivoting.

2. You lose balance and lift or drag your pivot foot.

1. Once you establish one foot as your pivot, you may take any number of steps in any direction with your nonpivot foot. When you start to dribble, the ball must be released from your hand before you lift your pivot foot. When you attempt a pass or shot, you may lift your pivot foot if you release the ball before your pivot foot hits the floor.

2. Keep your weight on the ball of your pivot foot as you move your nonpivot foot and maintain a balanced stance.

Two-Foot Jump

1. You jump on a forward angle, rather than straight up. You bend forward at the waist, your head is down or leaning forward, and your arms are straight out in front of your body, so you are off balance in a forward direction.

2. You do not get an explosive takeoff, limiting the height of your jump.

3. After landing you are not ready to move or jump again.

1. Start in a balanced stance and keep your head up, with your eyes focused straight up in the direction of your jump.

2. Flex your knees between 60 and 90 degrees, depending on your leg strength: The stronger your legs, the more you can flex your knees. Through trial and error determine the correct angle for your strength and to produce a quick, forceful push against the floor.

3. Land in the same spot and on the balls of your feet with your knees flexed to prepare the next jump or move.

One-Foot Jump

1. You long-jump, rather than high-jump.

1. Shorten your last step before takeoff so you can quickly dip your takeoff knee and change forward momentum to upward momentum. On takeoff, lift your opposite knee straight up simultaneously with your arms. The combination of a forceful upward lift of your opposite knee and arms transfers momentum to lifting your body higher.

EXECUTING DEFENSIVE FOOTWORK

Moving your feet for defense is hard work that depends on desire, discipline, concentration, anticipation, and superior physical condition. Moving quickly with balance is the key to reacting to your opponent's moves and changing direction instantly.

To move on defense use short, quick steps with your weight evenly distributed on the balls of the feet. Push off the foot farther from where you are going and step with the closer foot. Do not cross your feet. Make an exception only when your opponent moves by your lead foot: Then you drop step to recover your defensive position. Your feet should not move closer than shoulder-width apart; keep them as close as possible to the floor.

Flex your knees and keep your body low, your upper body erect, and your chest out. Keep your head steady, avoiding up-and-down body movements. Hopping or jumping movements are slow and put you in the air, when you should be on the floor reacting to an opponent. Pressure the ball with quick flicks of whichever hand is closer to the direction your opponent is going, but do not reach or lean. Keeping your head over your waist, your arms close to your body, and your elbows flexed will help you maintain balance.

You should master these four basic defensive steps or movements:

1. Side step, or slide
2. Attack step
3. Retreat step
4. Reverse, or drop step

Each one starts from a defensive stance.

Side Step (Slide)

Maintain a balanced, defensive stance between your opponent and the basket. If your opponent moves to the side, quickly move your feet from a staggered stance to a parallel stance, with both feet in line with the direction you are going. Use short, quick steps with your weight evenly distributed on the balls of your feet. Push off the far foot and step with the foot closer to where you are going. Never cross your feet. Concentrate on keeping your balance to make quick changes of direction (see Figure 1.6).

Attack and Retreat

Attacking, or moving up on your opponent, is often referred to as *closing out*. It is not an easy skill: It requires good judgment and balance. You cannot close on your opponent so fast that you lose your balance and cannot change direction backward. Use short, quick attack steps, without crossing your feet, and

protect your lead foot by positioning it slightly outside your opponent's body.

If your opponent makes a move toward the basket on the side of your back foot, you should *retreat*, or move back, without losing balance. You cannot retreat so fast that you lose your balance and are unable to react quickly to get closer to your opponent. As with attacking, use short, quick retreat steps and do not cross your feet.

Attacks and retreats basically require the same footwork but in different directions. They both use short, quick steps, with one foot up and the other back. Keep your weight evenly distributed on the balls of your feet. Push off your back foot and step with your lead foot to attack; push off your front foot and step with your back foot to retreat. In attacking never cross your back foot in front of your lead foot, and in retreating never cross your front foot in front of your back foot. For both your attack and retreat strive for good defensive footwork (see Figure 1.6).

Reverse (Drop Step)

In the basic defensive stance your feet are staggered, one foot in front of the other. The weakness of this stance is in your lead foot: It is more difficult to move back in the direction of your lead foot than in the direction of your back foot. If an opponent dribbles toward the basket by your lead foot, quickly drop step with your lead foot while making a reverse pivot with your back foot. After making the drop step, use quick side steps to reestablish your intended defensive position with your lead foot forward. If you are not in position to do this, you must run and chase your opponent, and then turn into position with your intended lead foot forward.

Make your drop step in the direction of your opponent's move. Keep your head up over your waist and your eyes focused on your opponent. Do not turn in the opposite direction, taking your eyes off your opponent. As you reverse pivot, vigorously push off your back foot in the direction of your drop step. Your drop step should be straight back, moving your foot low to the floor. Do not circle or lift your lead foot high. For added momentum as you drop step, forcefully move the elbow on the side of your lead foot back close to your body (see Figure 1.6).

Figure 1.6   Keys to Success: Defensive Footwork

Execution Phase

Side Step (Slide)

1. Push off far foot ____
2. Step with foot closest to where you are going ____
3. Use short, quick steps ____
4. Lead foot continues outside opponent's body for protection ____
5. Back foot aligned with middle of opponent's body ____
6. Feet no closer than shoulder-width (never cross feet) ____
7. Move feet close to floor ____
8. Knees flexed, no hopping (up-and-down movements) ____

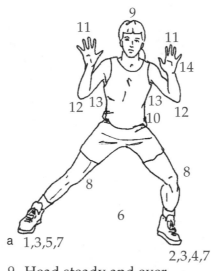
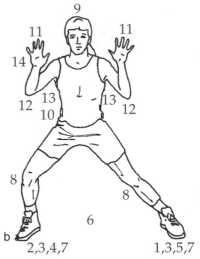

9. Head steady and over waist ____
10. Back straight (no leaning) ____
11. Hands up ____

12. Elbows flexed ____
13. Arms close to body ____
14. Pressure ball with quick flicking motion (do not reach) ____

Attack and Retreat

1. Attack by pushing off back foot ____
2. Retreat by pushing off front foot ____
3. Use short, quick steps ____
4. Lead foot continues outside opponent's body for protection ____
5. Back foot aligned with middle of opponent's body ____
6. Feet no closer than shoulder width (never cross feet) ____
7. Move feet close to floor ____
8. Knees flexed, no hopping (up-and-down movements) ____

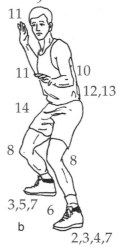

9. Head steady and over waist ____
10. Back straight (no leaning) ____
11. Hands up ____

12. Elbows flexed ____
13. Arms close to body ____
14. Pressure ball with quick flicking motion (do not reach) ____

Reverse (Drop Step)

Option 1: With Retreat Steps

Option 2: With Run

1. Opponent drives by lead foot ____
2. Reverse pivot on back foot ____
3. Drop step with lead foot ____
4. Drop step straight back, foot low to floor ____
5. Lead elbow moves back close to body ____
6. Eyes on opponent's midsection ____
7. Reestablish defensive position: (Option 1) Use retreat steps or (Option 2) run (when position cannot be established using retreat steps) ____
8. Front turn to reestablish intended lead foot ____
9. Ready to change direction ____

Detecting Errors in Defensive Footwork

The most common errors in defensive footwork are listed here, with suggestions to correct them.

ERROR **CORRECTION**

Side Step (Slide)

1. You hop or move your body up and down, causing you to move too slowly.

2. You cross your feet, preventing yourself from changing direction quickly.

3. You reach or lean, losing your balance.

1. Keep your head steady, knees flexed, and avoid up-and-down or hopping movements. Keep your feet moving as close as possible to the floor.

2. Never cross your feet or bring them closer together than shoulder-width apart.

3. Keep your head over your waist, hands up above your waist with your elbows flexed, and your arms close to your body.

Attack and Retreat

1. In attacking you cross your back foot in front of your front foot, and in retreating you cross your front foot in front of your back foot, preventing you from quickly changing direction.

2. You move up too fast on your attack, losing your balance (in a forward direction) so you cannot quickly change direction backward.

3. In attacking you hop forward with both feet parallel, preventing a quick change of direction backward.

4. In attacking you reach or lean forward, distributing your weight to your lead foot, which prevents you from quickly changing direction backward. In retreating you lean back with too much weight on your back foot, which prevents you from quickly changing direction forward.

1. To attack push off the back foot and step with your lead foot. To retreat push off your front foot and step with your back foot. Do not cross your feet or bring them closer together than shoulder-width apart.

2. Move up with control using short, quick attack steps. Do not cross your feet and keep them shoulder-width apart, your weight evenly distributed on the balls of your feet.

3. Keep your head steady, knees flexed, and use short, quick attack steps. Maintain a staggered stance with one foot in front of the other. Do not hop. Move with your feet close to the floor.

4. Concentrate on balance, keeping your weight evenly distributed on the balls of your feet.

Reverse (Drop Step)

1. You turn away from your opponent's move, losing sight of your opponent.

2. Your drop step is too slow.

3. After reversing you use retreat steps, rather than reestablishing your defensive position.

1. Drop step in the direction of your opponent's move, keeping your eyes on your opponent.

2. Make your drop step straight back and low to the floor. Do not circle your lead foot or lift it too high. Move your lead elbow back close to your body.

3. To reestablish your defensive position, judge whether to use side steps or, if necessary, to run and turn into position with your intended lead foot forward.

Quickness, Balance, and Footwork Drills

1. Stance Drill

First assume your offensive stance. Then shift your weight *too far back* on your heels. Next, lean *too far forward*, bending at the waist with your weight forward on your toes. Then correct the stance, positioning your head over your waist, raising your hands up and close to your body, distributing weight evenly on the soles of your feet, flexing your knees, and spreading your feet at least shoulder-width apart. Have a partner try to upset your balance in a backward direction by gently pushing you on your shoulder or pulling you forward by one of your hands.

Success Goal = 3 cycles in offensive stance without a partner being able to upset your balance backward or forward

Your Score = (#) _____ balanced stances

2. Footfire Drill

Have a partner give commands. On the command *stance!* quickly assume an offensive stance. On the command *go!* move your feet up and down as quickly as you can, maintaining your correct stance for 10 seconds or until you hear the command *stop!* Do three repetitions of 10 seconds each with 10-second rest intervals.

Success Goal = Feet hit the floor 40 to 50 times in each 10-second period

Your Score =
    a. (#) _____ times feet hit the floor, first 10-second period
    b. (#) _____ times feet hit the floor, second 10-second period
    c. (#) _____ times feet hit the floor, third 10-second period

3. Lane Defensive Slide

Start in the lane facing the foul line, with your right foot on the lane line to your right. Use a balanced defensive stance with your feet parallel and hands up. Using short, quick defensive side steps, move quickly to the lane line on your left, change direction, and move back to the lane line on your right. Continue as quickly as you can between left and right lane lines.

Success Goal = Touch 15 lines in 30 seconds

Your Score = (#) _____ lines touched

4. *Lane Defensive Attack and Retreat*

Start by facing the foul line, with your right foot on the defensive right box and your left foot forward and in the lane. Use a staggered defensive stance with your left foot forward at a 45-degree angle from your right foot and hands up. Use short, quick attack steps with your left foot forward as your lead foot until it touches the middle of the foul line. Quickly drop step with your left foot. Change to retreat steps, going until your left foot touches the defensive left box. Immediately change direction, switching to attack steps until your right foot touches the middle of the foul line. Then drop step and retreat to the right box. Continue from box to foul line and back to box as quickly as you can.

Success Goal = Touch a total of 15 lines and boxes in 30 seconds

Your Score = (#) _____ lines and boxes touched

5. *Lane Defensive Zigzag*

Start in the lane, facing the foul line with your right foot on the defensive right T (the intersection of the lane and foul lines). Be in a staggered defensive stance with your left foot back at a 45-degree angle. Use short, quick retreat steps to move back diagonally until your left foot touches the lane line on your left, just above the box. Quickly drop step with your right foot and use retreat steps until your right foot touches the intersection of the baseline and lane line to your right. Change quickly to offense and sprint diagonally to the defensive left T where you will change to a defensive stance with your left foot on the T. Use retreat steps until your left foot touches the lane line on your right, drop step with your left foot, and retreat until it touches the intersection of the baseline and lane line on your left. Change to offense and sprint to the defensive right T. Continue a defensive zigzag from T to lane line to the intersection of baseline and lane line, sprinting to the opposite T, as quickly as you can.

Success Goal = Touch 15 lines in 30 seconds

Your Score = (#) _____ lines touched

6. *Wave Drill*

Start in the middle of the halfcourt. Have a partner stand 20 feet in front randomly giving verbal commands and hand signals. On the command *defense!* quickly assume a defensive stance. On the command *slide!* move quickly to the side your partner signals by a hand wave. Your partner should also signal you to move up and back and to the other side. Use defensive side steps for moving to the side, and attack and retreat steps for moving up and back. Maintain a balanced defensive stance and execute good footwork with quick changes of direction.

   Variation: Have your partner randomly add the commands *rebound! loose ball!* and *fast break!* On the rebound command quickly execute a two-foot jump and simulate grabbing a rebound with two hands. On the loose ball command quickly assume a position with hands and feet on the floor, simulating going for a loose ball, and get back up just as fast. Sprint forward on the fast break command.

Success Goal = 30 seconds without stopping or making a mistake

Your Score = (#) _____ seconds without stopping or making a mistake

7. Jump Stops

Simulate being a low-post player with your back to the basket. Start at the dotted line in the 3-second lane, facing the foul line in a balanced offensive stance with your feet parallel and hands up above your waist. Use short side steps toward the offensive right box and make a balanced jump stop outside the lane and above the box. Again using short side steps, return to the dotted line and make a jump stop there. Now move to the offensive left box and make a jump stop outside the lane and above the box. Continue making jump stops, going from box to dotted line to box. Be sure to land on both feet simultaneously, coming to a complete stop.

Success Goal = 10 successful jump stops (A jump stop is successful when you come to a complete, balanced stop with both feet landing simultaneously.)

Your Score = (#) _____ successful jump stops

8. Fullcourt Offensive Footwork

This drill allows you to practice offensive footwork such as sprints, changing pace, changing direction, and making one-two stops. You will use a third of the floor width from lane line to sideline as you run between baselines.

a. Halfcourt Sprints. Start in an offensive stance, with your feet touching the baseline. Sprint to halfcourt, change pace to a trot, and continue to the opposite baseline. Return in the same manner.

b. Fullcourt Change of Pace. You will use a third of the floor width from lane line to sideline as you run between baselines changing pace. Start in an offensive stance, your feet behind the baseline. Run to the opposite baseline with at least three quick changes of pace from sprint to trot to sprint. Return in the same manner.

c. Fullcourt Change of Direction. You will use a third of the floor width from lane line to sideline as you run between baselines changing direction. Start in an offensive stance, with your left foot touching the intersection of the baseline and lane line on your left. Run diagonally at a 45-degree angle to the sideline on your right. Make a sharp 90-degree change of direction, from right to left, and run diagonally to the imaginary lane line extended on your left. Change directions, now making a sharp 90-degree change of direction from left to right. Continue changing direction at each sideline and imaginary lane line as you proceed to the opposite baseline. Return in the same manner.

d. Fullcourt One-Two Stops. You will use a third of the floor width from lane line to sideline as you run from baseline to baseline making one-two stops. Start in an offensive stance, your feet behind the baseline. Run to the opposite baseline, making four one-two stops. Alternate the foot you first land on for each one-two stop. Land first on your left foot for one stop, then land first on your right foot for the next stop. Return in the same manner.

Success Goal = 2 round-trips for each

Your Score =

a. (#) _____ round-trips (sprint)

b. (#) _____ round-trips (change of pace)

c. (#) _____ round-trips (change of direction)

d. (#) _____ round-trips (one-two stops)

9. *Fullcourt Defensive Footwork*

This drill allows you to practice defensive footwork such as the zigzag, attack and retreat, and reverse. In each variation you will use a third of the floor width from lane line to sideline.

a. Fullcourt Defensive Zigzag. Zigzag defensively from baseline to baseline. Start with your back to the far basket in a staggered defensive stance, your left foot forward and touching the intersection of the baseline and sideline on your left, and your right foot back at a 45-degree angle. Use defensive retreat steps to move diagonally back until your right foot touches the imaginary lane line extended on your right. Quickly drop step with your left foot to a 45-degree angle. Use retreat steps to move back diagonally until your left foot touches the sideline on your left. Quickly drop step with your right foot. Continue changing direction at each imaginary lane line extended and at each sideline as you proceed to the opposite baseline. Return in the same manner.

b. Fullcourt Defensive Attack and Retreat. Once again use a third of the floor width from lane line to sideline as you move defensively from one baseline to the other using attack and retreat steps. Imagine that you are guarding a dribbler. Start with your back to the far basket in a balanced defensive stance, your left foot forward and touching the baseline and your right foot spread directly back. Move backward to the halfcourt line, using defensive attack and retreat steps, until your right foot touches the halfcourt line. Quickly drop step, moving your left foot back. With your right foot forward, move backward to the baseline, using attack and retreat steps until your left foot touches the baseline. Vary your attack and retreat steps, avoiding a pattern as you move down the floor. Return in the same manner.

c. Fullcourt Defensive Reverse-Run-and-Turn. You will again use a third of the floor width from lane line to sideline as you move defensively from one baseline to the other. Imagine that a dribbler beats your lead foot, and you must recover by using a reverse-run-and-turn. Start with your back to the far basket in a staggered defensive stance, your left foot forward touching the baseline and your right foot spread directly back. Move backward using defensive attack steps, a quick reverse-run-and-turn. Reverse to the side of your lead foot, keeping your eyes on the imaginary dribbler. Run at least 3 steps before you turn back into position with your original foot up. From baseline to the halfcourt line make 2 reverse-run-and-turns, starting with your left foot forward. From halfcourt line to the opposite baseline make 2 reverse-run-and-turns, starting with your right foot forward. Return in the same manner.

Success Goal = 2 round-trips for each

Your Score =

a. (#) _____ round-trips (zigzag)

b. (#) _____ round-trips (attack and retreat)

c. (#) _____ round-trips (reverse)

10. Fullcourt One-on-One Cutter

Work with a partner. You will play defense against your partner, who will be a cutter on offense without the ball. Your partner will attempt to use quick starts, stops, and changes of pace and direction to get a head and shoulder by you. The offensive player must stay within a third of the floor width from lane line to sideline while moving down the floor from one baseline to the other. Once your partner gets a head and shoulder by you, both of you stop. As a defender you must stay within touching distance of the offensive player, attempting to draw an offensive foul by beating your partner to an intended spot in a set position.

   Get in a defensive stance facing each other and touch your partner's waist to start the drill. The offensive player gets a point each time a head and shoulder gets by you, and you get a point each time you gain an offensive foul. Continue the drill from whatever spot the point was gained, again starting with a defensive touch. When you reach the opposite baseline, switch roles for the return trip.

Success Goal = Score more points than your partner

Your Score = (#) _____ your points; (#) _____ partner's points

11. Two-Foot Vertical Jump Test

Chalk your fingertips, face a smooth wall, and make a mark at the height of your two-handed standing reach. Then stand with your shoulder to the wall. You are allowed one step before you jump. Make a standing two-foot jump as high as you can, touching the wall at the top of your jump with the fingertips of your near hand. Take three vertical jumps with 10 seconds between each for mental preparation. Measure the distance between the two chalk marks using a yardstick and record to the nearest half inch.

Success Goal = Your maximum two-foot vertical jump (measured to nearest half inch)

Your Score =
   a. (#) _____ inches on Trial 1
   b. (#) _____ inches on Trial 2
   c. (#) _____ inches on Trial 3

12. One-Foot Vertical Jump Training

This short drill consists of a set of 3 preliminary jumps and 5 to 10 all-out running, one-foot vertical jumps. Have a partner measure the height of your jumps at a net or backboard. The preliminary jumps should be progressive in effort but are running one-foot vertical jumps. On the approach use however many steps that will allow for your best jump.

   For your first jump try to touch the net or backboard about 12 inches below your best jumping height. On your second jump touch about 6 inches above your first jump and on your third try jump as high as possible. Then do five more, trying to improve on each succeeding jump. Take 10 seconds before each jump to mentally plan for it. If you still are improving with the fifth effort, continue on until you do not touch any higher on two successive attempts.

Stand under the net or backboard and reach with two hands. Have your partner use a yardstick to determine the difference between your two-handed standing reach and the mark at your highest running one-foot vertical jump, recording it to the nearest half inch.

Success Goal = Your maximum running one-foot vertical jump (measured to nearest half inch)

Your Score =

a. (#) _____ inches on first jump

b. (#) _____ inches on second jump

c. (#) _____ inches on third jump

d. (#) _____ inches on fourth jump

e. (#) _____ inches on fifth jump

f. (#) _____ inches on sixth jump

g. (#) _____ inches on seventh jump

h. (#) _____ inches on eighth jump

i. (#) _____ inches on ninth jump

j. (#) _____ inches on tenth jump

13. Jump Rope

Start in a balanced stance with your knees flexed and your weight on the balls of your feet. Hold the rope handles, your hands out to your sides at waist level and your elbows close to your body. Start with forward jumping, placing the rope behind your feet and swirling it over your head from back to front. Add variety by skipping, jumping on one foot, crossing arms, and backward jumping.

Success Goal = Your maximum number of jumps in 60 seconds; and 15 consecutive minutes of jumping rope

Your Score = (#) _____ jumps; (#) _____ consecutive minutes

Offensive and Defensive Footwork Checks

Footwork is the foundation for executing each of the fundamental skills with balance and quickness. You use offensive footwork and fakes to throw your defender off balance before making an offensive move.

Have a trained observer—your coach, teacher, or a skilled player—watch your offensive and defensive footwork. The observer can use the checklists in Figures 1.1 to 1.6 to evaluate your performance and provide corrective feedback.

Step 2   Shooting: Enhance Confidence, Mechanics, Rhythm, and Range

Shooting is the most important skill in basketball. The fundamental skills of passing, dribbling, defense, and rebounding may enable you to get a high percentage shot, but you must still be able to make the shot. In fact, good shooting can often overcome weaknesses in other fundamental skills.

WHY DEVELOPING AN ACCURATE SHOT IS IMPORTANT

The initial skill you must develop is an accurate shot. This forces your defender to play you tight and become vulnerable to a fake, allowing you to pass and drive as well as shoot. If you haven't developed an accurate shot, a defender can play back in anticipation of a drive or a pass and be less susceptible to your fake. When you do not have the ball, your defender can play further off you and be in better position to give defensive help to a teammate guarding another player. To be successful, a team must have players who can make the outside shot. A player who cannot shoot well must compensate by being outstanding in other areas to meet team needs.

DEVELOPING AN ACCURATE SHOT

A great shooter often is called a *pure shooter* because of a smooth, free-flowing shot or a soft touch. Some players think a pure shooter is naturally gifted—born that way. This is a misconception. Great shooters are made, not born.

A pure shooter, such as 1992 Olympic Dream Team member Chris Mullin, driving hard around an opponent and then effortlessly pulling up for a soft jump shot, appears to have been born a shooter. His thoughts are not on the mechanics of the shot but rather on the position and movement of teammates and defenders. A pure shooter considers faking the shot, delivering a pass, driving for the basket, or reversing direction to pull the ball out and reset the offense. For Mullin and other great shooters the skill is automatic: Like other talented people, pure shooters perform their skills to maximum level without conscious thought. Each was a beginner at one time, however, and each developed into a pure shooter through dedicated practice.

A commitment to practice leads to improved shooting skill, which in turn leads to enhanced confidence. Shooting confidence leads to success in games and renews commitment to practicing. It is a familiar cycle of success to those who have achieved greatness.

Shooting is a skill that you can practice by yourself. Once you understand correct mechanics, all you need is a ball, a basket, and an eagerness to improve. It is helpful, however, to also practice shooting under game conditions, including the pressure situations that occur late in the game. Practice with a partner providing the defensive pressure of an opponent. Remember that through practice you will develop shooting skill and confidence.

KEY WORDS TO ENHANCE SHOOTING CONFIDENCE, MECHANICS, RHYTHM, AND RANGE

Basketball is a mental, as well as a physical, game. Developing the mental aspect is a key to enhancing performance in all fundamentals, including shooting. You need confidence to shoot well: Being able to shoot under pressure distinguishes great shooters from the good shooters. The direct correlation between shooting confidence and shooting success is the most consistent factor we recognize in great shooters. Confident shooters control their thoughts, feelings, and shooting skill.

As important as confidence is, accurate shooting takes more than positive thinking: it also takes shooting skill. Neither mental confidence nor mechanics alone is enough. Success results from the integration of the mental and mechanical aspects of shooting.

When you think, you are in a sense talking to yourself. That talk can be either positive or negative. A technique called *positive self-talk* can help you integrate the mental and mechanical aspects of shooting, speeding the improvement of your shot. Positive self-talk uses key words to enhance performance.

Select words that help you learn correct mechanics, establish rhythm, and build confidence. The key words should be positive, concise (preferably one syllable), and personalized. A positive word that you associate with a successful shot is called an *anchor* word. Select your own personal anchor word that allows you to visualize your shot going in, such as *yes! net! face! whoosh! swish! in! through!*

Words that key the correct mechanics of your shot are called *trigger* words. Examples of trigger words are

- *legs* or *up*—to key the use of your legs,
- *hands*—to key the position of the shooting hand behind the ball,
- *catch*—to key catching the ball in position to shoot in one motion,
- *high*—to start your shot high and prevent lowering the ball,
- *front*—to start your shot in front and prevent throwing the ball,
- *in* or *side*—to set the ball on your shooting side with your elbow in,
- *loose* or *front*—to keep your shoulders relaxed and slightly forward,
- *straight*—to make your arm extend straight to the basket,
- *up*—to key a high arch,
- *finger*, *one*, or *touch*—to key the correct release of the ball off your index finger, and
- *through*—to key any part of your follow-through including shoulders, arm, wrist, and finger.

Identify two words that trigger the correct mechanics and one anchor word to reinforce shooting success. Sometimes a word can be both a trigger and an anchor word. For example, *through* as a trigger word can key the follow-through of your shoulders, arm, wrist, and fingers and it also can be an anchor word for the ball going through the basket.

Say your words in rhythm, from the time your shooting motion starts with your legs until you release the ball off your index finger. For example, if *legs* and *through* are your trigger words and *yes* is your anchor word, you would say in rhythm to your shot: *Legs—through—yes!* It works better to say your words aloud, rather than to yourself.

Saying your personalized key words in an even rhythm establishes the rhythm of your

shot and enhances your mechanics and confidence. Give time to mental, as well as physical, practice. Relax, mentally practice, saying your key words in the rhythm of your shot as you visualize shooting and seeing the ball go in the basket.

Your goal is to reduce conscious thought and promote automatic execution of your shot. Trigger words help make the mechanics of your shot automatic, and an anchor word, which reinforces a successful shot, helps build your confidence. As shooting improves one trigger word may suffice. Eventually, an anchor word may be all you need to trigger the automatic action of your shot.

LEARNING FROM THE REACTION OF YOUR SHOT ON THE RIM

Learn to shoot correctly and then practice intelligently each day. Develop an understanding of your own shot. You can always benefit from having an instructor or coach watch you shoot. Most of your practice, however, occurs when a coach is not present. Personal feedback (information about your performance) can help you determine what adjustments to make. Three basic sources of performance feedback are observing the reaction of your shot on the rim, internally feeling your shot, and video analysis of your shooting form.

Analyzing a shot's reaction on the rim can reinforce successful execution or reveal most shooting errors and their possible causes. For example, the ball goes where your shooting arm, hand, and shooting finger direct it. If you missed to the right (or left), your shooting arm, hand, and finger was pointed in that direction. Perhaps your body faced in the direction of the miss, rather than being square to the basket, or your elbow was out, causing your follow-through to go to the right.

If you see that the ball hits the right of the rim and rolls off to the left, you know you shot the ball with sidespin, which is generally caused by your shooting hand starting on the side of the ball and then rotating behind it. If you overrotate your shooting hand, the ball will hit the right rim with sidespin and roll left. If you underrotate, the ball will hit the left side of the rim and roll right. Sidespin is also caused by the ball sliding off your ring finger rather than your shooting finger.

Your sense of feel also yields clues: You might feel your shooting hand rotate to the right or the ball come off your ring finger (instead of your shooting finger). Both mistakes will give the ball sidespin. An excellent method to develop feel is to shoot free throws with your eyes closed. Have a partner rebound and tell you whether the shot was successful. After a miss your partner tells you the specific direction of the miss and the reaction of the ball on the rim. By analyzing your shot, you can detect and correct errors before they become bad habits.

BASIC MECHANICS AND THE ONE-HAND SET SHOT

Most players shoot seven basic shots: the one-hand set shot, free throw, jump shot, three-point shot, hook shot, layup, and runner. These shots all share certain basic mechanics, including sight, balance, hand position, elbow-in alignment, shooting rhythm, and follow-through. To develop your shot it is best to concentrate on only one or two mechanics at a time. The following basic mechanics for the one-hand set shot (see Figure 2.1), basically the same technique used for the free throw, can be applied to the other shots with some adjustments.

Sight

Focus your eyes on the basket, aiming just over the front of the rim for all except bank shots. Use a bank shot instead when you are at a 45-degree angle with the backboard. A 45-degree angle falls within the distance between the box and the middle hash mark on the lane line. The distance for the bank angle—called the *45-degree funnel*—widens as you move out. For shooting a bank shot aim for the top near corner of the box on the backboard.

Sight your target as soon as possible and keep your eyes focused on the target until the ball reaches the goal. Your eyes should never follow the flight of the ball or your defender's hand. Concentrating on the target helps eliminate distractions, such as shouting, towel waving, an opponent's hand, or even a hard foul.

Balance

Being in balance leads to power and rhythmic control in your shot. Your base, or foot position, is the foundation of your balance, and keeping your head over your feet (base) controls your balance.

Spread your feet comfortably to shoulder-width apart and point your toes straight ahead. Pointing your toes straight aligns your knees, hips, and shoulders to the basket. The foot on the side of your shooting hand (right foot for a right-handed shot) is forward. The toe of your back foot is aligned with the heel of the foot on your shooting side (toe-to-heel relationship).

Flex your legs at the knees. This gives crucial power to your shot. Beginning and fatigued players often fail to flex their knees, and then to compensate for the lack of power from not using their legs, they tend to throw the ball from behind the head or shove the ball from the hip—both actions produce errors.

Your head should be over your waist and feet. Your head controls your balance and should be slightly forward, inclining your shoulders and upper body forward toward the basket. Your shoulders should be relaxed.

Hand Position

Hand position is the most misunderstood part of shooting. It is important to place the shooting hand directly behind the ball. Placing the nonshooting hand under the ball for balance is also important. This position, with shooting hand behind and nonshooting hand under the ball, is called the *block-and-tuck*. It leaves your shooting hand free to shoot the ball, rather than having to balance *and* shoot the ball.

Place your hands fairly close together with both hands relaxed and the fingers spread comfortably. Keep the thumb of your shooting hand relaxed and not spread apart (to avoid tension in your hand and forearm). A relaxed hand position forms a natural cup, enabling the ball to contact the pads of your fingers and not your palm.

Place your nonshooting (balance) hand slightly under the ball: The weight of the ball balances on at least two fingers (the ring finger and the little finger). The arm of your balance hand is in a comfortable position, with the elbow pointing slightly back and to the side.

Place your shooting hand directly behind the ball, your index finger directly at its midpoint: The ball is released off your index finger. On a free throw there is time to align your index finger with the valve or other marking at the midpoint of the ball. Developing fingertip control and touch leads to a soft, accurate shot.

Elbow-In Alignment

Hold the ball comfortably in front of and above your shooting-side shoulder, between your ear and shoulder. Keep your shooting elbow in. When your shooting elbow is in, the ball is aligned with the basket. Some players do not have the flexibility to place the shooting hand behind the ball while keeping the elbow in. In this case, first put your shooting hand behind the ball, and then move the elbow in as far as your flexibility allows.

Shooting Rhythm

Shooting involves synchronizing the extension of your legs, back, shoulders, and shooting elbow and the flexion of your wrist and fingers. Shoot the ball with a smooth, evenly paced rhythmical lifting motion.

The initial force and rhythm for your shot comes from a down-and-up motion of your legs. Start with your knees slightly flexed: Bend your knees and then fully extend them in a down-and-up motion. As your legs reach full extension, your back and shoulders extend in a smooth, continuous upward direction.

As the shot starts the ball is tipped back from your balance hand to your shooting hand. A good guide when tipping back the ball is to drop your wrist back only until there is a wrinkle in the skin. This angle provides a quick release and consistent follow-through. Direct your arm, wrist, and fingers straight toward the basket at a 45- to 60-degree angle, extending your shooting arm completely at the elbow. The final force and control of your shot comes from flexing your wrist and fingers forward and down. Release the ball off your index finger with soft fingertip touch to impart backspin on the ball and soften the shot. Keep your balance hand on the ball until the point of release.

The amount of the force you should impart to the ball depends on the range of the shot. For short distances the arm, wrist, and fingers provide most of the force. Long-range outside shots require more force from your legs, back, and shoulder. Smooth rhythm and a complete follow-through will also improve long-range shooting.

An inside jump shot involves jumping and then shooting the ball at the top of your jump with your arm, wrist, and fingers applying most of the force. On a one-hand set shot, lift the ball simultaneously with the upward extension of your legs, back, and shoulder.

Follow-Through

After releasing the ball off the index finger, keep your arm up and fully extended with your index finger pointing straight to the target. The palm of your shooting hand should face down, and the palm of your balance hand should face up. Keep your eyes on your target. Hold your arm up in a complete follow-through position until the ball reaches the basket—then react to rebound or get into defensive position.

Figure 2.1   Keys to Success: *One-Hand Set Shot*

Preparation Phase

1. See target ____
2. Feet shoulder-width apart ____
3. Toes straight ____
4. Knees flexed ____
5. Shoulders relaxed ____
6. Nonshooting hand under ball ____
7. Shooting hand behind ball ____
8. Thumb relaxed ____
9. Elbow in ____
10. Ball between ear and shoulder ____

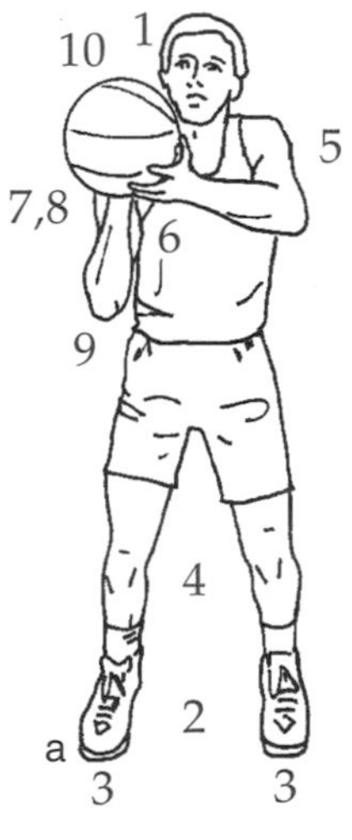

**Execution
Phase**

b

**Follow-Through
Phase**

c

1. See target ____
2. Extend legs, back, shoulders ____
3. Extend elbow ____
4. Flex wrist and fingers forward ____
5. Release off index finger ____
6. Balance hand on ball until release ____
7. Even rhythm ____

1. See target ____
2. Arm extends ____
3. Index finger points to target ____
4. Shooting hand palm down ____
5. Balance hand palm up ____

Detecting Errors in Shooting

The most common errors in shooting the one-hand set shot and the jump shot (see page 41) are listed here, along with suggestions to correct them.

🚫

ERROR

CORRECTION

1. Your shot is short.

1. The cause of a shot being short usually is not using your legs, not following-through, or having a slow or uneven rhythm. Using neural feedback—through feeling—determines whether you need more force from your legs, follow-through (keeping your arm up until the ball reaches the basket), or a quicker or more even-paced rhythm.

ERROR	CORRECTION
2. Your shot is long.	2. Your shooting arm extends on too flat a trajectory (less than 45 degrees), your shoulders lean back, or your hands are too far apart on the ball, preventing you from lifting it. Move your shoulders to a relaxed forward position, move your hands closer together, or raise your shooting arm higher to put a higher arc on your shot.
3. Your shot is inconsistently short or long.	3. You probably use incomplete and inconsistent elbow extension: Extend your arm completely for every shot.
4. Your shot hits the right side of the rim (right-handed shot).	4. You are not squared up facing the basket or you start with the ball in front of your head and your elbow out, your arm extending to the right on the shot. Square your body to the basket. Set the ball on the shooting side of your head between your ear and shoulder, with your elbow in so you can extend your arm straight to the basket.
5. Your shot hits the left side of the rim (right-handed shot).	5. You are not squared up facing the basket or you start with the ball on your right hip or too far to your right, shoving the ball from right to left as you shoot. Shoving the ball results from not using your legs for power. Square your body to the basket, setting the ball on the shooting side of your head between your ear and shoulder with your elbow in. Make your shooting arm, wrist, and finger go straight through to the basket.
6. Your shot lacks range, control, and consistency. You miss short, long, or to either side.	6. You probably lower the ball, bring it behind your head or shoulder, or throw the ball to the basket with an inconsistent follow-through, faults resulting from not using your legs for power. Start your shot with the ball high in front of your ear and shoulder. Emphasize force from your legs and complete the follow-through by keeping your arm up until the ball reaches the basket.

ERROR   **CORRECTION**

7. Your shot hits the rim and circles out or skims from front to back and out, rather than hitting the rim and dropping in.

7. You are starting your shot with your shooting hand on the side of the ball and rotating the hand behind the ball as you shoot, or releasing the ball off your ring finger instead of your shooting finger. Both mistakes give the ball sidespin instead of backspin. Start your shot with your hands in block-and-tuck position, your shooting hand behind the ball, and your balance hand under the ball. Release the ball off your index finger.

8. Your mechanics appear to be correct, but the shot lacks control and the ball hits hard on the rim.

8. You probably rest the ball on your palm. Relax the thumb of your shooting hand and set the ball on your finger pads with your palm off the ball. Then you can release the ball off your index finger with backspin, control, and a soft touch.

9. Your mechanics appear to be correct, but you still miss the basket.

9. Have someone watch your eyes as you shoot. You probably do not concentrate your eyes on the target. Concentrate on the target—not on the ball's flight—until the ball reaches the basket.

FREE THROW

Success in free throw shooting requires sound mechanics, a routine, relaxation, rhythm, concentration, and confidence. Routine, relaxation, and rhythm contribute to concentration and confidence.

Confidence is the single most important part of free throw shooting. Think positively: You always shoot from the same place on the line. No one is guarding you. Three and a half balls can fit through the basket. With confidence—and sound mechanics—you cannot miss.

Develop a sound routine for the free throw to check preshot mechanics. A routine also helps you relax, focus, and shoot with rhythm. Most importantly, using a routine will enhance your confidence. The routine can include a set number of dribbles, checking mechanics, using visualization to practice your free throw mentally just before shooting it, and taking a deep breath to relax. Adopt a

sound routine and stay with it: It is a mistake to copy fads or repeatedly change the routine.

Most players use the one-handed shot for a free throw, having time to control each of the basic mechanics: sight, balance, hand position, elbow-in alignment, shooting action, and follow-through. Here is a sample routine that you can adjust to fit you. Stand a few feet behind the free throw line until the official hands you the ball. You will stay more relaxed there. If you hear negative remarks from the crowd or recognize your own negative thought, interrupt it with the word *stop*. Take a deep breath and let go of the negative thought as you exhale. Replace it with a positive statement of affir-mation, such as "I'm a shooter," "Nothing but net," or "Count it!" Once you receive the ball, position your feet making certain to line up the ball (not your head) with the middle of the basket. Use the small indentation mark in the floor at the exact middle of the free throw line that was used to mark the free throw circle. Set your shooting foot slightly to the outside of this mark, lining up the ball with the middle of the basket.

Set up in a balanced stance. Some players bounce the ball a certain number of times to help them relax. Use a relaxed hand position and line up your index finger with the valve on the ball. Next check your elbow-in alignment. Take a deep breath to relax. Before shooting, visualize a successful shot: Visualization just before you shoot can produce a more free-flowing, smooth rhythm and increase confidence. Focus on the target and shoot. Exaggerate your follow-through, keeping your eyes on the target and your shooting arm up until the ball reaches the basket.

Relaxation may be the biggest problem in shooting free throws: A free throw allows you more time to think than other shots do. Trying too hard may bring undue physical or emotional tension. Place your mind and body in a state of relaxation with deep breathing. For a free throw you should particularly relax your shoulders: Take a deep breath and let your shoulders drop and loosen. Do the same for your arms, hands, and fingers. Learn to relax other parts of your body. Controlling your breathing and relaxing your muscles are especially useful in a free throw routine.

Use personalized key words to help establish a smooth, sequential rhythm for free throw shooting. Say your words in the rhythm of your shot. For example, if your trigger words are *legs* and *through* and your anchor word is *yes*, put them together—*legs, through, yes!*—saying them in rhythm with your shot, from the start of your shot until the ball is released. Using personalized key words this way establishes your rhythm, enhances your mechanics, and builds confidence.

Confidence and concentration go together. Using affirmation statements can promote confident thoughts about yourself and your ability to shoot. For example, you can state to yourself "I am a shooter" or remind yourself of past successes.

The most important step before initiating the free throw motion, however, is to eliminate all distractions from your mind, focusing on the basket. Concentrate on shooting a successful shot and let go of the shot that missed or what you might do wrong. Stay in the present. Visualize shooting a successful free throw while you emphasize your anchor word: *yes! net! in! through!* Most of all, enjoy the moment. Focus on your target just over the front of the rim. See it, shoot it, *count it!* (see Figure 2.2).

Figure 2.2 Keys to Success: Free Throw

Preparation Phase

1. Positive affirmations off line ____
2. Set shooting foot slightly outside mark ____
3. Perform routine ____
4. Balanced stance ____
5. Nonshooting hand under ball ____
6. Shooting hand behind ball ____
7. Thumb relaxed ____
8. Elbow in ____
9. Ball between ear and shoulder ____
10. Shoulders relaxed ____
11. Deep breath, relax ____
12. Visualize successful shot ____
13. Concentrate on target ____

Execution Phase

1. See target ____
2. Say key words in rhythm ____
3. Extend legs, back, shoulders ____
4. Extend elbow ____
5. Flex wrist and fingers forward ____
6. Release off index finger ____
7. Balance hand on ball until release ____

Follow-Through Phase

1. See target ____
2. Arm extends ____
3. Index finger points to target ____
4. Shooting hand palm down ____
5. Balance hand palm up ____
6. Keep arm up until ball goes through net ____

Detecting Errors in Shooting the Free Throw

The most common errors in free throw shooting are listed here, along with suggestions to correct them.

ERROR

CORRECTION

1. You repeatedly change your free throw routine or copy fads.

2. You feel tense before and during your free throw.

1. Adopt a sound free throw routine and stay with it.

2. Use deep breathing to release your mind and body to a state of relaxation. Breathe in deeply and exhale fully. Relax your shoulders, letting them drop and loosen. Do the same for your arms, hands, and fingers. Learn to relax other parts of your body as necessary.

ERROR 🚫

3. You use a more uneven or slower rhythm shooting your free throw than shooting from the field.

4. You lack confidence and are easily distracted, especially by negative thoughts and comments.

5. Your free throw is short because you step off the line to get back on defense.

CORRECTION

3. Say your key words in the even rhythm of your shot, timing them from the start of your shot until the ball is released.

4. Concentrate. When you hear a negative statement or recognize your own negative thought, eliminate it immediately with the word *stop* and replace it with a positive affirmation, such as "I am a shooter." Visualize a successful free throw while saying your personal anchor word. Focus on the target.

5. Exaggerate your follow-through by keeping your arm up and staying on the line until the ball reaches the basket.

JUMP SHOT

A jump shot is similar to shooting a one-hand set shot except for two basic adjustments. In a jump shot you align the ball higher and shoot after jumping, rather than shooting with the simultaneous extension of your legs. Because you jump first and then shoot, your upper body, arm, wrist, and fingers must generate more force.

Align the ball between your ear and shoulder but raise the ball, sighting the target below the ball (rather than above the ball as you would in a one-hand set shot). Place your forearm at a right angle to the floor and your upper arm parallel to the floor, or higher. Jump straight up off both feet, fully extending your ankles, knees, back, and shoulders: Do not float forward, backward, or to the side.

The height of your jump should depend on the range of the shot. On an inside jump shot, when you are closely guarded, your legs should generate enough force to jump higher than the defender. You shoot at the top of your jump; therefore, your arm, wrist, and fingers provide most of the force. You may feel as though you are hanging in the air as you release the ball.

On most long-range outside jump shots you have more time. Therefore, it is not necessary to jump higher than your defender. You will be able to use more force from your legs for shooting the ball, rather than for gaining height on the jump. You will feel that you are shooting the ball *as* you jump, rather than at the top of your jump. Strive for a balanced jump that enables you to shoot without straining. Balance and control are more important than gaining maximum height on your jump. Smooth rhythm and complete follow-through also are important components of long-range jump shooting.

Land in balance in the same spot as your takeoff (see Figure 2.3).

Figure 2.3 Keys to Success: Jump Shot

Preparation Phase

1. Feet shoulder-width apart ____
2. Toes straight ____
3. Knees flexed ____
4. Shoulders relaxed ____
5. Nonshooting hand under ball ____
6. Shooting hand behind ball ____
7. Thumb relaxed ____
8. Elbow in ____
9. Ball high between ear and shoulder ____
10. See target ____

Execution Phase

1. Jump, then shoot ____
2. Jump height depends on range ____
3. Extend legs, back, shoulders ____
4. Extend elbow ____
5. Flex wrist and fingers forward ____
6. Release off index finger ____
7. Balance hand on ball until release ____
8. Even rhythm ____
9. See target ____

Follow-Through Phase

1. Arm extends ____
2. Index finger points at target ____
3. Shooting hand palm down ____
4. Balance hand palm up ____
5. See target ____
6. Land in balance (in same spot as takeoff) ____

THREE-POINT SHOT

For a three-point shot, set up far enough behind the line to avoid concern about stepping on the line and to focus your sight on the basket. Use a balanced jump shot, shooting the ball without straining as you jump.

The longer the shot, the more important are correct mechanics, sequence, and rhythm. On three-point shots you usually have time and do not need much height on your jump. You can use more force from your legs and may generate additional force by stepping into your shot. You can benefit also from the sequential buildup of force from your back and shoulders. It feels as if you are shooting the ball as you jump, rather than at the top of your jump (as with outjumping your defender on a closely guarded inside shot).

Strive for a balanced jump that enables you to shoot without straining. Balance and control are more important than maximum height. Smooth rhythm and a complete follow-through help long-range jump shooting and on three-point shots, as in all jump shots, you should land in balance in the same spot as your takeoff.

Successful three-point shooters excel in (a) smooth, even rhythm, (b) the sequential use of legs, back, and shoulders, (c) correct mechanics, such as hand position and elbow-in alignment, and (d) complete follow-through (see Figure 2.4).

Figure 2.4   Keys to Success: Three-Point Shot

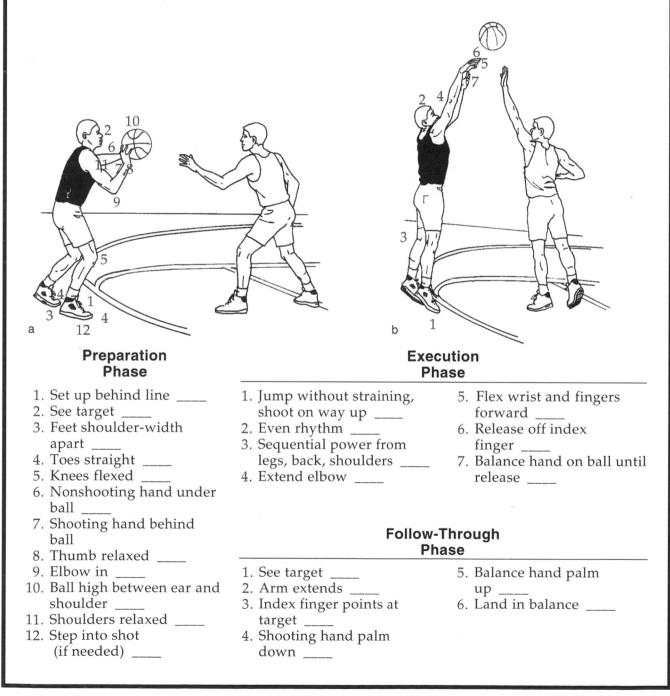

Preparation Phase

1. Set up behind line ____
2. See target ____
3. Feet shoulder-width apart ____
4. Toes straight ____
5. Knees flexed ____
6. Nonshooting hand under ball ____
7. Shooting hand behind ball
8. Thumb relaxed ____
9. Elbow in ____
10. Ball high between ear and shoulder ____
11. Shoulders relaxed ____
12. Step into shot (if needed) ____

Execution Phase

1. Jump without straining, shoot on way up ____
2. Even rhythm ____
3. Sequential power from legs, back, shoulders ____
4. Extend elbow ____
5. Flex wrist and fingers forward ____
6. Release off index finger ____
7. Balance hand on ball until release ____

Follow-Through Phase

1. See target ____
2. Arm extends ____
3. Index finger points at target ____
4. Shooting hand palm down ____
5. Balance hand palm up ____
6. Land in balance ____

Detecting Errors in Three-Point Shooting

The most common errors in shooting the three-pointer are listed here, along with suggestions to correct them.

ERROR

CORRECTION

1. You look down to find the three-point line, losing sight of the target.

2. Your shot is short.

1. Set up well enough behind the line that you do not have to worry about stepping on the line. Focus your sight on the target.

2. A three-point shot is usually short because you do not use your legs, back, and shoulders; do not follow-through; or you have a slow or uneven rhythm. Determine through feel whether to emphasize force from your legs, back, and shoulders; to complete the follow-through by keeping your arm up until the ball reaches the basket; or to increase the speed of your rhythm or pace it more evenly.

HOOK SHOT

The advantage of the hook shot is that it is difficult to block, even for taller opponents. The hook shot generally is limited to an area close to the basket—a range of 10 to 12 feet. Learning the hook shot with either hand will greatly increase your effectiveness in the lane area. Well executed, the hook forces your opponent to overplay you, and a fake hook can create an opening in the opposite direction for a power move, drive, or pass. Contrary to popular belief, it is not difficult to learn the hook shot and with practice you can use your weak, as well as your strong, hand for hook shooting.

Start in a balanced stance with your back to the basket, feet spread shoulder-width apart and knees flexed. Sight your target by looking over your shoulder in the direction you will turn to shoot. Within a 45-degree angle of the backboard (above the box and below the middle hash mark on the lane line) accuracy is aided by using the backboard to soften the shot. When banking the shot, aim for the top near corner of the backboard. If

you aren't at a 45-degree angle, aim just over the rim.

In most instances, you will make a ball fake in the opposite direction of your intended shot. After your fake, move your shooting hand under and your balance (nonshooting) hand behind and slightly on top of the ball. This is called the *hook shot position*. Flex the elbow of your shooting arm and position it at your hip, keeping the ball in direct alignment with your shooting shoulder.

Using the foot opposite your shooting side, step away from your defender. As you step, hold the ball back and protect it with your head and shoulders, rather than leading with the ball. As you step, pivot in, turning your body toward the basket. Lift the knee on your shooting side and jump off your pivot foot.

Shoot by lifting the ball to the basket with a hook motion as you extend your shooting arm in an ear-to-ear direction. Flex your wrist and fingers toward the target and release the ball off your index finger, keeping the balance hand on the ball until the release. Land in balance, ready to rebound any missed shot with two hands and score using a power move. A missed hook shot should be considered as a pass to yourself: A defender attempting to block your hook shot will not be in position to box out and prevent your getting the rebound (see Figure 2.5).

Figure 2.5 Keys to Success: *Hook Shot*

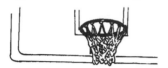
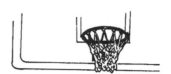

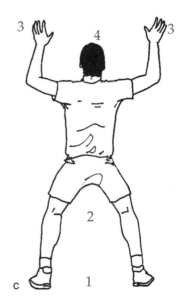
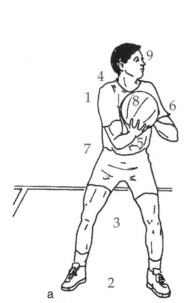

Preparation Phase

1. Back to basket ____
2. Feet shoulder-width apart ____
3. Knees flexed ____
4. Shoulders relaxed ____
5. Shooting hand under ball ____
6. Nonshooting hand behind ball ____
7. Elbow at hip ____
8. Ball back, protected by head and shoulders ____
9. See target ____

Execution Phase

1. Step and pivot in ____
2. Lift ball in ear-to-ear direction ____
3. Extend elbow ____
4. Flex wrist and fingers ____
5. Release off index finger ____
6. Balance hand on ball until release ____
7. Even rhythm ____
8. See target ____

Follow-Through Phase

1. Land in balance ____
2. Knees flexed ____
3. Both hands up ____
4. Ready to rebound ____

Detecting Errors in the Hook Shot

ERROR

The most common errors in shooting the hook shot are listed here, along with suggestions to correct them.

CORRECTION

1. Your shot is inconsistently short or long.

1. You probably have incomplete and inconsistent elbow extension: Extend your arm completely on every shot.

2. Your shot hits the right side of the rim (right-handed shot).

2. Your arm goes in front of your head on the follow-through. Start by holding the ball in the hook shot position, your shooting elbow aligned with your hip, allowing you to extend your arm with an ear-to-ear motion straight to the basket.

3. Your shot hits the left side of the rim (right-handed shot).

3. Your arm goes behind your head on your follow-through. Start by holding the ball in the hook shot position, your shooting elbow aligned with your hip, allowing you to extend your arm with an ear-to-ear motion straight to the basket.

4. Your shot hits the rim and rather than pulling in, it circles out or skims from front-to-back and out.

4. This indicates side rotation on the ball: You are starting with your hands on the side of the ball and rotating them to the side as you shoot or you are releasing the ball off your ring finger instead of your index finger. Both mistakes produce sidespin instead of backspin. Start in hook shot position, your shooting elbow aligned with your hip. Set your shooting hand under the ball and your balance hand slightly behind and on top of the ball. Release the ball off your index finger to get backspin, and the ball will pull in if it hits the rim.

5. You lose protection and control of the ball as you shoot.

5. You are taking your balance hand off the ball too soon: Keep your balance hand on the ball until your release.

LAYUP

The layup shot is used near the basket after a cut or drive. To jump high on layup you must have speed on the last three or four steps of your cut or drive, but you also must control your speed. Step with your opposite foot. The step before your layup should be short, so you can quickly dip your takeoff knee to change forward momentum to upward momentum. Lift your shooting knee and the ball straight up as you jump, bringing the ball between your ear and shoulder. Direct your arm, wrist, and fingers straight to the basket at an angle between 45 degrees and 60 degrees and release the ball off your index finger with a soft touch. Keep your balance hand on the ball until the release.

Follow through by keeping your arm up and fully extended at the elbow, your index finger pointing straight at the target and the palm of your shooting hand facing down (see Figure 2.6).

RUNNER (EXTENDED LAYUP)

The runner (extended layup shot) is used away from the basket when a quick shot is needed off a cut or drive. Shoot the runner the same way as the layup except for the takeoff position being farther from the basket. When shooting the runner, emphasize smooth rhythm and a complete follow-through (see the previous directions for a layup; also see Figure 2.6).

Figure 2.6   Keys to Success: Layup and Runner

**Preparation
Phase**

Layup	Runner		
____	____	1.	See target
____	____	2.	Short step
____	____	3.	Dip knee
____	____	4.	Shoulders relaxed
____	____	5.	Nonshooting hand under ball
____	____	6.	Shooting hand behind ball
____	____	7.	Elbow in
____	____	8.	Ball between ear and shoulder

**Execution
Phase**

Layup	Runner		
____	____	1.	Lift shooting knee
____	____	2.	Jump
____	____	3.	Extend leg, back, shoulders
____	____	4.	Extend elbow
____	____	5.	Flex wrist and fingers forward
____	____	6.	Release off index finger
____	____	7.	Balance hand on ball until release
____	____	8.	Even rhythm

**Follow-Through
Phase**

Layup   Runner

____   ____ 1. See target
____   ____ 2. Land in balance
____   ____ 3. Knees flexed
____   ____ 4. Hands up

Detecting Errors in Shooting the Layup and Runner

The most common errors in shooting the layup and runner are listed here, along with suggestions to correct them.

ERROR

CORRECTION

1. On the takeoff you use a long jump (floating forward or to the side), rather than a high jump.

2. Before shooting you swivel the ball to the side, allowing it to be blocked or stolen.

3. You lose protection and control of the ball as you shoot because you take your balance hand off the ball too soon.

4. Your shooting hand rotates from the side, giving the ball sidespin so it rolls off the rim.

5. The ball hits low on the backboard and then goes up. With slight contact on your arm, the shot falls short.

6. After shooting the layup you are not ready to get back on defense or rebound the ball on a miss.

1. Keep your head up and focus on your target. Make the step before your takeoff short so you can quickly dip your takeoff knee and create upward momentum. On your takeoff lift your opposite knee straight up simultaneous with lifting the ball to the basket. The combination of this forceful upward lift of your opposite knee and arms transfers the momentum to lift your entire body higher.

2. Lift the ball straight up as you shoot.

3. Keep your balance hand on the ball until your release.

4. Shoot with your hand directly behind the ball to give it backspin and have it pull in the basket.

5. Shoot the ball high above the backboard box so it drops into the basket. Even if fouled on your layup, the ball will still have a chance to go in.

6. Land in same spot—on the balls of your feet with your knees flexed, ready to rebound.

Shooting Drills

1. *Shooting Warm-Up*

Shooting close to the basket as a warm-up helps to develop confidence and correct form and rhythm. Start in a balanced stance about 9 feet in front of the basket with the ball in good shooting position in front of your shooting shoulder. Shoot, leaving your arm up on your follow-through until the ball hits the floor. A correct hand position—your shooting hand behind the ball—and release off your index finger will impart backspin, enabling the ball to bounce back to you.

Say your personalized key words in rhythm with your shot from its start to the release of the ball. If you miss, visualize a successful shot in good form, again saying your key words. If you have not selected key words, start with the words *legs—through—yes!* Get feedback from the feel of your shot and reaction of the ball on the rim. Emphasize the key word you feel will produce a successful shot. For example, if your shot was short, and you felt that the miss came from not using your legs, emphasize "legs" as you say *legs—through—yes!*

Your goal is to make 5 consecutive shots and then increase the distance. Once you make the 5 consecutive shots from 9 feet, increase your distance to 12 feet. When you make 5 consecutive shots from 12 feet, move back to the foul line (15 feet from the backboard).

Success Goal = 5 consecutive shots made at each distance

Your Score =

   a. (#) _____ consecutive shots made at 9 feet

   b. (#) _____ consecutive shots made at 12 feet

   c. (#) _____ consecutive shots made at 15 feet (free throw distance)

2. *On-Your-Back Shooting*

The on-your-back shooting drill focuses on your shooting hand behind the ball, elbow-in alignment, correct release off your index finger, follow-through, and catching the ball in position to shoot. Lying on your back, start with the ball above your shooting shoulder. Place your shooting hand behind the ball with your index finger at the midpoint of the ball. Check for elbow-in alignment. Shoot the ball up into the air with complete follow-through (full elbow extension), aiming to have the ball return straight back to your shooting position without your having to move your hands on the catch. Say your personalized key words in rhythm with your shot. If the ball does not return to your starting position, visualize a successful shot in good form, again saying your key words, and use feedback from the feel of your shot and direction of the ball. Emphasize whichever key word you feel will produce a successful shot. For example, if your shot was off to the side, you might concentrate on making your arm go straight and say *straight!* or if the ball went off the wrong finger, producing sidespin, you might say *finger!* or *one!* If you catch the ball with your hands on its side, consider using *hands!* or *catch!*

Your goal is making 5 consecutive shots (with complete follow-through) that return straight back to your shooting position so you don't have to move your hands on the catch. Once you make these 5 consecutive shots, increase the height of each shot.

Success Goal = 5 consecutive shots with complete follow-through (full elbow extension) that return straight back to your shooting hand position

Your Score = (#) _____ consecutive shots with complete follow-through that return straight back to your shooting hand position

3. Wall Shooting

The wall shooting drill focuses on your shooting hand behind the ball, elbow-in alignment, release off the index finger, follow-through, and catching the ball in position to shoot. Facing a wall or backboard, pick a spot on it at least 10 feet high to serve as your target: A spot on the side of the backboard is excellent for fostering a straight shot. Starting with the ball in shooting position above your shooting shoulder, place your shooting hand behind the ball with your index finger at the ball's midpoint. Check for elbow-in alignment. Shoot the ball, with complete follow-through (full elbow extension), to the wall or backboard target, making it return to your shooting position without your moving your hands on the catch. Say your personalized key words in rhythm from the start of your shot to the release of the ball. If the ball does not return to your starting position, jump behind the ball and catch it in position to shoot. After an incorrect shot visualize a successful shot in good form, again saying your key words. Use feedback from the feel and direction of the ball. Some key words might be *straight!* if you felt the miss was because your arm went to the side; *one!* or *finger!* if the ball went off the wrong finger producing sidespin; and *hands!* if you catch with your hands on the side of the ball.

Success Goal = 5 consecutive shots that hit the spot on the wall and 5 consecutive catches from shooting position without moving your hands on the catch

Your Score =
    (#) _____ consecutive shots that hit the target
    (#) _____ catches from shooting position

4. Shooting From a Chair

Shooting from a chair fosters consistency in lifting the ball to the basket and extending your elbow completely on your follow-through. This drill develops the shooting range and helps a player who has a tendency to throw the ball. Sitting in a chair necessitates using your back, shoulders, and full arm extension to provide force for the shot.

Set the chair 9 feet in front of the basket. Shooting from a chair you will practice centering yourself, the process of balancing yourself mentally and physically. When you are centered you are in a state of readiness: Your muscles relax and you breathe a little deeper and more slowly than normal. Being centered also involves balancing your weight evenly for the skill you will be performing, which is particularly helpful for gaining power. You center yourself with confident thoughts, controlled breathing, and your weight evenly balanced. By centering you can raise your center of gravity and transfer your force from back to shoulders to generate full power for your shot.

Place your shooting hand behind the ball, with your index finger at the ball's midpoint. Check for elbow-in alignment. Work for the sequential buildup of force from your back, shoulders, arm, wrist, and fingers as you shoot. Say your personalized key words in the rhythm of your shot from its start to the release of the ball. Again, visualize a successful shot with good form, saying your key words. Use feedback from your shot's feel, distance, direction, and reaction on the rim to tell you which key word to emphasize. If your shot was short, *through!* is a good key word. To increase the shot's distance try using *back—shoulders—through!* for the sequential buildup of force.

Success Goal = 5 consecutive shots made at each distance, shooting from a chair

Your Score =

    a. (#) _____ consecutive shots made at 9 feet

    b. (#) _____ consecutive shots made at 12 feet

    c. (#) _____ consecutive shots made at 15 feet (free throw distance)

    d. (#) _____ consecutive shots made at 18 feet

5. *One-Hand Shooting*

One-hand shooting is excellent for developing your ability to shoot with your weak hand. This drill is particularly beneficial if your nonshooting hand tends to interfere with your shot (e.g., thumbing the ball with your nonshooting hand). The one-hand shooting drill allows you to focus on your shooting hand position behind the ball, elbow-in alignment, and lifting the ball to the basket with a short stroke.

    Start about 9 feet from the basket. Keeping your nonshooting hand down behind your back, balance the ball in your shooting hand, which should face the basket with your index finger at the ball's midpoint. Check that your forearm is up at a right angle from the floor and that it forms an L with your upper arm: This position helps you lift the ball to the basket, rather than throw it. Check for elbow-in alignment to keep the ball in front of and above your shooting shoulder. Use your personalized key words in rhythm with your shot or when you are correcting your shot. If you tend to bring the ball back and throw it, rather than lift it, to the basket, consider using *front!* or *lift!* as a key word. If you feel your shot misses because your elbow is out, consider saying *in!* as a key word.

Success Goal = 5 consecutive shots made with each hand

Your Score =

    a. (#) _____ consecutive shots made from 9 feet with strong hand

    b. (#) _____ consecutive shots made from 9 feet with weak hand

6. *Jump Shot Warm-Up*

The objectives of this drill are to develop jump-shooting confidence, form, rhythm, and range. Start in a balanced stance about 9 feet in front of the basket. For a jump shot the ball is held higher than for a one-hand set shot. The height of your jump depends on the range: Close to the basket, you should release the ball at the top of your jump with your arm, wrist, and fingers providing most of the force. On long-range outside jump shots you will not need to jump high, allowing you to use more of your legs' force for the shot. Strive for a balanced jump so you can shoot without strain and land in balance in the same spot as your takeoff. Leave your arm up on your follow-through until the ball hits the floor. Say your three personalized words in rhythm from the start of your shot to the release of the ball.

Your goal is to make 5 consecutive shots and then increase your distance. After making 5 consecutive shots from 9 feet, move to 12 feet. After you make 5 consecutive shots from 12 feet, move back to the foul line (15 feet from the backboard). Continue to increase your distance by 3 feet, going to 18 feet, then to college 3-point range (21 feet from the backboard), then to NBA 3-point range.

Success Goal = 5 consecutive shots made at each distance

Your Score =

    a. (#) _____ consecutive shots made at 9 feet

    b. (#) _____ consecutive shots made at 12 feet

    c. (#) _____ consecutive shots made at 15 feet (free throw distance)

    d. (#) _____ consecutive shots made at 18 feet

    e. (#) _____ consecutive shots made at 21 feet (college 3-pointer)

    f. (#) _____ consecutive shots made at 24 feet (NBA 3-pointer)

7. Bank Jump Shot Warm-Up

The bank jump shot warm-up drill is the same as the regular jump shot warm-up drill except that you shoot from a 45-degree angle on each side of the basket. Start in a balanced stance at a 45-degree angle with the backboard, which is within the distance between the box and the middle hash mark on the lane. The distance of the bank angle, which widens as you move out, is called the *45-degree funnel*. With bank shots aim for the top near corner of the box on the backboard, saying your key words in rhythm from the start of your shot to the release of the ball.

Success Goal = 5 consecutive bank jump shots made at each distance

Your Score =

    a. (#) _____ consecutive bank jump shots made from 9 feet

    b. (#) _____ consecutive bank jump shots made from 12 feet

    c. (#) _____ consecutive bank jump shots made from 15 feet

    d. (#) _____ consecutive bank jump shots made from 18 feet

8. Hook Shot Warm-Up

This warm-up consists of standing under the front of the rim and shooting hook shots, first with your strong hand and then with your weak hand. Start with your head under the front of the rim, facing the sideline in a balanced stance. Hold the ball with your shooting elbow at your side, your shooting hand under the ball, and your balance hand slightly behind and on top of the ball. This is called *hook shot position*. Shoot the hook by lifting the ball to the basket in an ear-to-ear motion, keeping your balance hand on the ball until the release. Use two hands to catch the ball as it comes through the basket or to rebound on a missed shot: Consider a missed shot as a pass to yourself.

Success Goal = 5 consecutive hook shots made with each hand

Your Score =
   a. (#) _____ consecutive hook shots made with strong hand
   b. (#) _____ consecutive hook shots made with weak hand

9. *Hook Shot Warm-Up with Crossover Step*

Use the hook shot warm-up with a crossover step after you have made 5 consecutive warm-up hook shots with each hand. Starting with your head under the front of the rim, face the sideline with the ball in *hook shot position*. Make a crossover step toward the foul line with your inside (closer-to-basket) foot and shoot a hook shot. When you cross over, pivot toward the basket on your step and lift your shooting-side knee as you shoot.

Success Goal = 5 consecutive hook shots with crossover steps made with each hand

Your Score =
   a. (#) _____ consecutive hook shots made with strong hand
   b. (#) _____ consecutive hook shots made with weak hand

10. *Alternate Hand Hook Shooting*

This drill alternates shooting right-handed and left-handed bank hook shots using a crossover step. Your first shot will be with your right hand. Start under the rim facing the right sideline. Hold the ball in the hook shot position with your right hand under the ball. Crossover step with your inside foot at a 45-degree angle, pivoting toward the basket on your step and lifting your right knee as you shoot. Shoot a right-handed bank hook shot, aiming for the high near corner of the box on the backboard. Catch the ball with two hands after either a good shot or a rebound. Placing the ball in the hook shot position, with your left hand under the ball, face the left sideline and make a crossover step with your right foot at a 45-degree angle. Pivot and shoot a left-handed bank hook shot, catching the ball with two hands. Continue the drill, alternately shooting right- and left-handed hook shots.

Success Goal = 10 consecutive, alternate hand hook shots

Your Score = (#) _____ consecutive, alternate hand hook shots made

11. Free Throw Practice

You should shoot a set number of free throws each day. Practice sets of 10 free throws after other drills. Only on rare occasions does a player shoot more than two free throws in a row during a game: Likewise, in this drill never take more than two successive free throws without moving off the line.

Practice under pressure. Use imagination and compete against yourself. For example, imagine that time is out and that making the free throw will win the game. Record the number of free throws that you make out of 100 attempts and constantly challenge your own record. Do the same with consecutive free throws.

Be confident. Use positive affirmation statements before you go to the line, and visualize a successful shot just before shooting. Having a routine helps build confidence for free throws. Use deep breathing and muscle relaxation techniques. The final step before shooting is to eliminate all distractions and focus on the basket. Say your personalized key words in rhythm from the start of your free throw to the release of the ball. If you miss, visualize a successful free throw with good form, again saying your key words.

Success Goal = Improve your record of free throws made out of 100 attempts and the number of consecutive free throws made

Your Score = (#) _____ free throws made; (#) _____ free throws attempted; (#) _____ consecutive free throws made

12. Free Throw Shooting With Eyes Closed

Research has shown that combining free throw practice with your eyes closed and normal (eyes open) free throw practice improves shooting more than normal free throw practice alone. Shooting with closed eyes removes vision as your dominant sense, heightening your other senses—particularly the kinesthetic (feel of body movement) and tactile (touch).

Visualize a successful shot and focus on the basket immediately before closing your eyes to shoot. Use a partner to rebound and give feedback on each shot, including the reaction of your shot on the rim. Use the feedback and your kinesthetic and tactile senses to adjust your shot as necessary.

Success Goal = Improve your record of free throws made with eyes closed out of 10 attempts and the number of consecutive free throws made

Your Score = (#) _____ free throws made eyes closed; (#) _____ free throws attempted eyes closed; (#) _____ consecutive free throws made eyes closed

Shooting Checks

Shooting is the most important skill in basketball and is, to a great degree, mental: You must have confidence in yourself to shoot well. As important as confidence is to shooting, you also need shooting skill. It's the integration of the mental and mechanical aspects of shooting that fosters shooting success.

You can always benefit from having a trained observer—your coach, teacher, or a skilled player—watch you shoot. The observer can use the checklists in Figures 2.1 to 2.6 to evaluate your performance and provide corrective feedback. Most of your shooting practice will occur when a coach or teacher is not present, however, so learn to analyze your shot's reaction on the rim to reinforce successful execution or reveal shooting errors and their possible causes.

Step 3 Passing and Catching: Make Your Teammates Better

At its best basketball is a game where five players *move the ball as a team.* Good passing and catching are the essence of team play, the skills that make basketball such a beautiful team sport.

Passing is the most neglected fundamental of the game: Players tend not to want to practice passing. Perhaps because of the attention that fans and media give the players who score, not enough notice is given the players who make the assist (the passes that lead to a score). The best players make their teammates better. They are always a threat to the defense because of their ability to pass to any teammate at any time. Developing your ability to pass and catch makes you a better player and helps make your teammates better.

WHY PASSING AND CATCHING ARE IMPORTANT

Two basic reasons for passing are to move the ball for good shots and to maintain possession of the ball and, thereby, to control the game.

Deceptive, timely, and accurate passes create scoring opportunities for your team. To be in range for a shot the ball must be moved up the court into the scoring area through passing or dribbling. A pass travels many times faster than a dribble. Once in the scoring area, quick, accurate passes from the ball-side of the court to the off-side open up offensive opportunities. Moving the ball keeps defenders on the go and less able to give defensive help or to double-team the player with the ball.

A team that controls the ball with good passing and catching provides few opportunities for the opposition to score. Knowing when and where to pass under pressure not only provides your team a chance to score, but also keeps your team from losing the ball through interceptions—which often result in your opponent getting easy scores.

Specific uses of the pass are to

- get the ball out of a congested area (e.g., after a rebound or when being double-teamed),
- move the ball quickly up the court on a fast break,
- set up offensive plays,
- pass to an open teammate for a shot, and
- pass and cut to get your own shot.

KEY PRINCIPLES

Understanding principles for passing and catching improves your judgment, anticipation, timing, faking, deception, accuracy, force, and touch—all factors that affect your ability as a playmaker. These principles will help you on different levels of play.

1. See the rim. This allows you to use peripheral vision to see the court, including open teammates, and whether a defender is playing you for the pass, shot, or drive.

2. Pass before you dribble. A pass travels many times faster than a dribble.

3. Know your teammates' strengths and weaknesses. Recognize the position to which your teammate is moving and the next move he or she is likely to make. Pass the ball to your teammate when and where your teammate can do some good.

4. Time lead passes. Anticipate your teammate's speed on a cut to the basket, and make a well-timed lead pass, slightly ahead of your teammate, to the open area.

5. Use deception. Fake before you pass but do not telegraph the pass by looking in its direction. See your target without looking at your receiver. Use the surprise element.

6. Draw and kick. Draw your defender to you with a fake shot or dribble before passing. Do not attempt to pass by a sagging defender, who will have more time and distance to react and intercept or deflect the pass.

7. Make passes quick and accurate. Eliminate wasted motion: Do not wind up to pass or start the pass behind the plane of your body.

8. Judge the force of your pass. Pass forcefully for longer distances and use touch when you're close to the receiver.

9. Be sure about your pass. It is better not to pass than to risk a pass that cannot be completed. A good pass is one that is caught. Do not force a pass into a crowd or before you have an open teammate.

10. Pass away from the defender. When your teammate is closely guarded, pass to the side away from the defender. When you receive the pass but are not in position to shoot, keep your hands above your waist, meet the pass, and catch the ball with relaxed hands, in position to make another pass.

11. Pass to open shooter's far hand. When a teammate is open and in position to shoot, pass the ball to the shooter's far hand. The shooter should not have to move his hands or change body position because the pass is off target. When you are open in position to shoot and receive the pass, let the ball come to you. Jump behind the ball, catching it with your hands relaxed in block-and-tuck position—ready to shoot. (See page 65, Catching the Ball in Position to Shoot.)

Basic moves include the chest pass, bounce pass, overhead pass, sidearm pass, baseball pass, and behind-the-back pass. Practice to make each of these fundamental passes automatic. Then learn to determine and apply the correct pass for different court situations. You can practice with a partner or by yourself to develop quickness and accuracy in passing. For practicing alone you need a ball and a level wall or tossback. You learn decision making in passing by practicing in competitive group drills and in game experience.

EXECUTING THE CHEST PASS

The chest pass is the most common pass in basketball because it can be used with quickness and accuracy from most positions on the floor. Start in a balanced stance. Hold the ball with two hands in front of your chest, keeping your elbows in. Your hands should be slightly behind the ball in a relaxed position. See your target without looking at it: Look away or fake before passing. Step in the direction of your target, extending your legs, back, and arms. Force your wrists and fingers "through" the ball. Emphasize forcing your weak hand through the ball—the strong hand tends to dominate. The ball will go where your fingers direct it. Releasing it off the first and second fingers of both hands imparts backspin and gives the ball direction. Follow through by pointing your fingers at the target with the palms facing down (see Figure 3.1).

EXECUTING THE BOUNCE PASS

When a defender is between you and the target, one option is to use a bounce pass under the defender's arms. The bounce can move the ball to a wing on the end of a fast break or to a player cutting to the basket. It is slower than the chest pass because of bouncing off the floor.

Execute the bounce pass like the chest pass. Pass the ball so that it bounces off the floor at a distance allowing it to be received about waist level. To judge the correct distance aim for a spot two thirds of the way or a few feet in front of the target. Bouncing the ball too close to you results in a high, slow bounce that is easily intercepted, but bouncing the ball too close to the receiver makes it too low to handle. Remember—the ball will go where the fingers direct it. Follow through by pointing your fingers at the target with the palms of your hands facing down (see Figure 3.1).

Figure 3.1   Keys to Success: Chest and Bounce Passes

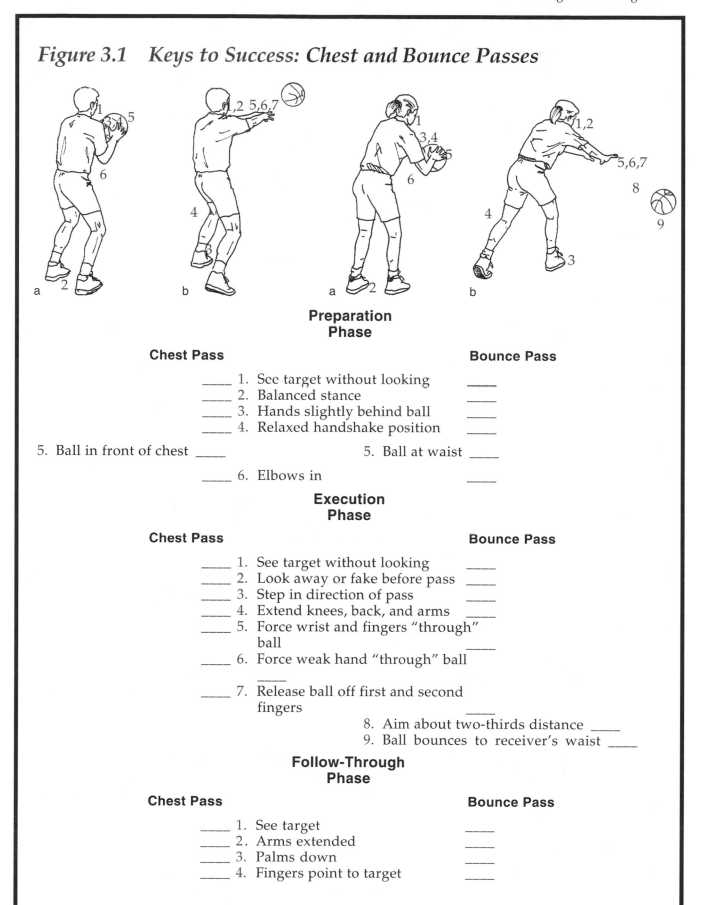

Preparation Phase

Chest Pass   **Bounce Pass**

____ 1. See target without looking   ____
____ 2. Balanced stance   ____
____ 3. Hands slightly behind ball   ____
____ 4. Relaxed handshake position   ____

5. Ball in front of chest ____   5. Ball at waist ____

____ 6. Elbows in   ____

Execution Phase

Chest Pass   **Bounce Pass**

____ 1. See target without looking   ____
____ 2. Look away or fake before pass ____
____ 3. Step in direction of pass   ____
____ 4. Extend knees, back, and arms   ____
____ 5. Force wrist and fingers "through" ball   ____
____ 6. Force weak hand "through" ball   ____
____ 7. Release ball off first and second fingers   ____

8. Aim about two-thirds distance ____
9. Ball bounces to receiver's waist ____

Follow-Through Phase

Chest Pass   **Bounce Pass**

____ 1. See target   ____
____ 2. Arms extended   ____
____ 3. Palms down   ____
____ 4. Fingers point to target   ____

Detecting Errors in the Chest and Bounce Passes

The most common errors in the chest and bounce passes are listed here, along with suggestions to correct them.

ERROR

CORRECTION

Chest Pass

1. You telegraph your pass by looking at your receiver.

2. You pass with your dominant hand, rather than with two hands.

3. Your chest pass lacks force.

4. Your pass is not accurate.

Bounce Pass

1. Your pass bounces too high and is too slow.

2. Your pass bounces too low.

3. Your bounce pass lacks force.

1. See your target without looking at your receiver. Look away or fake before passing.

2. Emphasize forcing your weak hand through the ball to keep your strong hand from dominating.

3. Start your pass with your elbows in and force your wrists and fingers through the ball.

4. Point your fingers at the target: The pass will go where your fingers direct it.

1. Start the pass from waist level and aim the ball's bounce closer to your receiver.

2. Start the pass from your waist level and aim it to bounce farther from your target so the receiver can catch the ball at waist level.

3. Start your pass with your elbows in and force your wrists and fingers through the ball.

EXECUTING THE OVERHEAD PASS

The overhead pass is used when you are closely guarded and have to pass over your defender; that is, as an outlet pass to start a fast break against pressing defenders and as a lob pass to a player cutting backdoor to the basket. Like the sidearm bounce pass, the overhead pass is an option for feeding the low post. Start in a balanced stance, holding the ball above your forehead with your elbows in and flexed about 90 degrees. Do not bring the ball behind your head from where it takes longer to execute the pass or allows the ball to be stolen. Step in the direction of the target, getting maximum power by extending your legs and back. Quickly pass the ball, extending your arms and flexing your wrists and fingers. Release the ball off the first and second fingers of both hands. Follow through by pointing your fingers at the target, palms down (see Figure 3.2).

EXECUTING THE SIDEARM PASS

The sidearm pass is used when you are closely guarded and have to pass around your defender. Like the overhead pass, a sidearm bounce pass is an option for feeding the low post. Except for the start, its execution is similar to the overhead pass. In the sidearm pass start by moving the ball to one side—between your shoulder and hip—as you step to that side. Do not bring the ball behind your body from where it takes longer to execute the pass and the ball can also be stolen. Follow through by pointing your fingers toward the target, palms to the side.

You can use two hands for the sidearm pass, as in the overhead pass, or one hand. With one hand, place your passing hand be-

hind the ball. Keep your nonpassing hand in front and on the ball until the point of release so you can stop and make fakes when needed. You should practice the sidearm pass as a one-handed pass with your weak, as well as strong, hand (see Figure 3.2).

Figure 3.2 Keys to Success: Overhead and Sidearm Passes

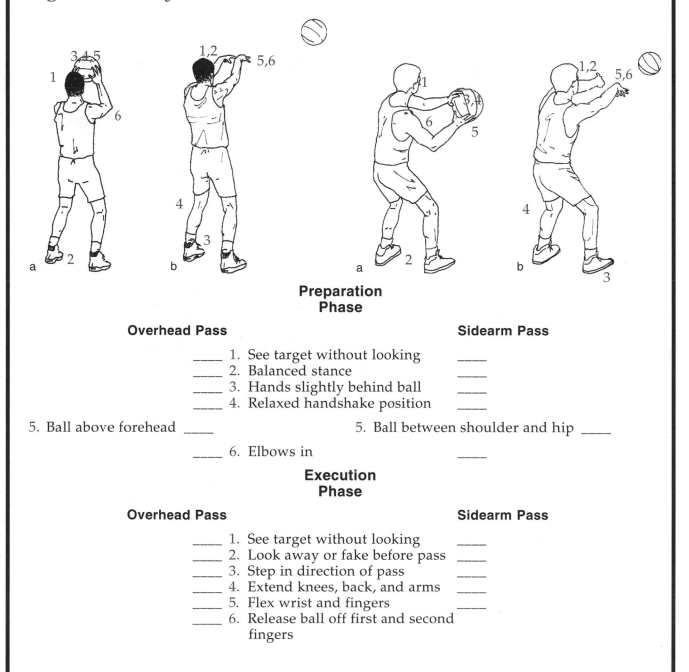

Preparation Phase

Overhead Pass   **Sidearm Pass**

____ 1. See target without looking   ____
____ 2. Balanced stance   ____
____ 3. Hands slightly behind ball   ____
____ 4. Relaxed handshake position ____

5. Ball above forehead ____   5. Ball between shoulder and hip ____

____ 6. Elbows in   ____

Execution Phase

Overhead Pass   **Sidearm Pass**

____ 1. See target without looking   ____
____ 2. Look away or fake before pass ____
____ 3. Step in direction of pass   ____
____ 4. Extend knees, back, and arms ____
____ 5. Flex wrist and fingers   ____
____ 6. Release ball off first and second fingers

**Follow-Through
Phase**

Overhead Pass   **Sidearm Pass**

_____ 1. See target   _____
_____ 2. Arms extended   _____

3. Palms down _____   3. Palms to side _____

_____ 4. Fingers point to target   _____

Detecting Errors in Overhead and Sidearm Passes

The most common errors in the overhead and sidearm passes are listed here, along with suggestions to correct them.

ERROR   **CORRECTION**

Overhead Pass

1. At the start of your overhead pass, you bring the ball behind your head, which causes a slow release and gives the defender time to intercept or deflect it.

1. Start the overhead pass from a position _above_ your forehead: The pass is quicker if you do not break the plane of your body. Get power by keeping your elbows in, flexing your wrists and fingers, and extending your legs, back, and arms.

2. Your overhead pass lacks force and accuracy.

2. See if you are bringing the ball back behind your head, which tends to force your elbows out, leading to an incomplete follow-through. Do not break the plane of your body. Get force by keeping your elbows in, flexing your wrists and fingers, and extending your legs, back, and arms. Get accuracy by pointing the first and second fingers of each hand toward the target.

Sidearm Pass

1. At the start of your sidearm pass, you bring the ball back behind your body. This causes a slow release and gives the defender time to intercept or deflect it.

1. Start the sidearm pass from _beside_ your body, between your shoulder and hip. The pass is quicker if you do not break the plane of your body. Get power by keeping your elbows in, flexing your wrists and fingers, and extending your legs, back, and arms.

ERROR

CORRECTION

2. Your sidearm pass lacks force and accuracy.

2. See if you are bringing the ball back behind your body, which tends to force your elbows out and lead to an incomplete follow-through. Do not break the plane of your body. Get force by keeping your elbows in, flexing your wrists and fingers, and extending your legs, back, and arms. Get accuracy by pointing the first and second fingers of each hand toward the target.

EXECUTING THE BASEBALL PASS

When you want to make a long pass, you will often select the baseball pass; that is, for making an outlet pass to start a fast break, throwing a long lead pass to a teammate cutting toward the basket, or inbounding the ball. Start in a balanced stance. Pivot on your back foot, turning your body to your passing-arm side. Bring the ball up to your ear with your elbow in, passing hand behind, and your balance hand in front of the ball (like a catcher starting to throw a baseball). As you pass the ball, shift your weight from your back to your front foot. Extend your legs, back, and passing arm forward toward the target. Flex your wrist forward as you release the ball off your fingertips. Follow through by pointing your fingers at the target with the palm of your passing hand down. Although this is a one-handed pass, keep your nonpassing hand on the ball until the release so you can stop and fake if necessary (see Figure 3.3).

EXECUTING THE BEHIND-THE-BACK PASS

At an advanced level you may be able to pass behind the back, especially when a defender comes between your teammate and you on a two-on-one fast break. Pivot on the ball of your back foot, turning your body to your passing-arm side. Move the ball with two hands to a position behind your hip. You should hold the ball with your passing hand behind the ball and your nonpassing hand in front. Shift your weight from your back to your front foot as you pass the ball behind your back and toward the target. Extend your passing arm and flex your wrist and fingers, releasing the ball off your fingertips. Follow through by pointing your fingers at the target with your passing hand palm up and passing arm contacting your back. Practice this pass also with your weak hand (see Figure 3.3).

Figure 3.3   Keys to Success: Baseball and Behind-the-Back Passes

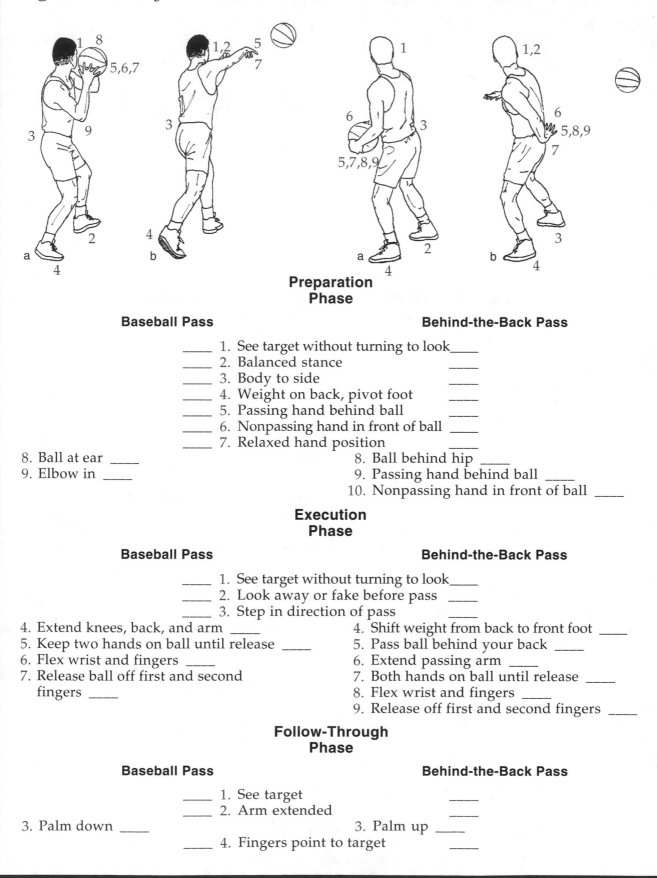

Preparation Phase

Baseball Pass   **Behind-the-Back Pass**

____ 1. See target without turning to look ____
____ 2. Balanced stance   ____
____ 3. Body to side   ____
____ 4. Weight on back, pivot foot   ____
____ 5. Passing hand behind ball   ____
____ 6. Nonpassing hand in front of ball   ____
____ 7. Relaxed hand position   ____

8. Ball at ear ____   8. Ball behind hip ____
9. Elbow in ____   9. Passing hand behind ball ____
                                     10. Nonpassing hand in front of ball ____

Execution Phase

Baseball Pass   **Behind-the-Back Pass**

____ 1. See target without turning to look ____
____ 2. Look away or fake before pass ____
____ 3. Step in direction of pass   ____

4. Extend knees, back, and arm ____   4. Shift weight from back to front foot ____
5. Keep two hands on ball until release ____   5. Pass ball behind your back ____
6. Flex wrist and fingers ____   6. Extend passing arm ____
7. Release ball off first and second   7. Both hands on ball until release ____
   fingers ____   8. Flex wrist and fingers ____
                                       9. Release off first and second fingers ____

Follow-Through Phase

Baseball Pass   **Behind-the-Back Pass**

____ 1. See target   ____
____ 2. Arm extended   ____

3. Palm down ____   3. Palm up ____
____ 4. Fingers point to target   ____

Detecting Errors in the Baseball and Behind-the-Back Passes

The most common errors in the baseball and behind-the-back passes are listed here, along with suggestions to correct them.

ERROR 🚫

CORRECTION

Baseball Pass

ERROR

1. Your pass is too slow and not deceptive.

2. Once you start the pass, you are unable to stop and fake.

3. Your pass lacks force.

4. The pass curves.

CORRECTION

1. Start the baseball pass from a position by your ear with both hands on the ball. Do not wind up. Keep both hands on the ball until the release in order to stop and fake at any time.

2. You are starting the pass with one hand on the ball or taking the nonpassing hand off too soon. Start the baseball pass from a position by your ear with both hands on the ball and keep two hands on the ball until the release.

3. You are not using your legs or not following through. Start with your weight on your back foot, shifting it to your front foot as you step toward the target. Forcefully extend your legs, back, and arm and follow through by forcing your wrist and fingers through the ball.

4. Keep your passing hand directly behind the ball—not to the side—and point your fingers at the target. Your pass will go where your fingers direct it.

Behind-the-Back Pass

ERROR

1. Once you start the behind-the-back pass, you are unable to stop and fake.

2. Your pass lacks force.

3. Your pass lacks accuracy.

CORRECTION

1. You do not start the pass with both hands on the ball or you take your nonpassing hand off too soon. Start the pass from behind your hip with both hands and keep two hands on the ball until the release.

2. You are not using your legs or not following through. Start with your weight on your back foot and shift it to your front foot as you step, forcefully extending your legs, back, and arm. Follow through by forcing your wrist and fingers through the ball.

3. Point your fingers at the target. Your pass will go where your fingers direct it.

CATCHING A PASS AWAY FROM THE SCORING AREA

When you are away from your scoring area and closely guarded, give the passer a good target and *meet the pass* (go to the ball). Catching the ball requires keeping your hands soft. Catch the ball with your hands in a relaxed position, forming a natural cup with your palm off the ball and your thumb and fingers relaxed—not spread. Give with the ball as you catch it, bringing your arms and hands into position in front of your chest. After receiving the pass, land with a one-two stop, see the rim, and be ready to pass upcourt (see Figure 3.4).

Figure 3.4   Keys to Success: Catching a Pass Away From the Scoring Area

Preparation Phase

1. See ball ____
2. Balanced stance ____
3. Feet shoulder-width apart ____
4. Knees flexed ____
5. Back straight ____
6. Hands up at ball distance ____
7. Thumb and fingers relaxed ____

Execution Phase

1. Come to meet ball ____
2. Two-handed catch ____
3. Thumb and fingers relaxed ____
4. Give with ball on catch ____
5. One-two stop ____

Follow-Through Phase

1. Bring ball to front of chest ____
2. Elbows out ____
3. See rim of basket ____
4. Feet shoulder-width apart ____
5. Knees flexed ____
6. Back straight ____
7. Ready to pass upcourt ____

Detecting Errors in Catching a Pass Away From the Scoring Area

The most common errors in catching a pass away from the scoring area are listed here, along with suggestions to correct them.

ERROR

CORRECTION

ERROR	CORRECTION
1. You are not ready to receive a pass.	1. Get in a balanced stance with your hands up and your eyes on the ball. Be in position to see the ball, the rim, and your defender.
2. When closely guarded, you do not go to the ball.	2. Meet the pass to keep your defender from stepping into the passing lane and intercepting the ball.
3. You fumble the ball as you receive it.	3. Keep your hands up. See the ball all the way into your hands. Keep your hands relaxed and give with the ball as you catch it.
4. After receiving the pass, you tend to bounce the ball before looking.	4. When you receive the pass, land with a one-two stop, see the rim, and be ready to pass upcourt to an open teammate.

CATCHING THE BALL IN POSITION TO SHOOT

The basic objective in basketball is to score, and the best pass is one that enables you to catch the ball within your shooting range and in position to shoot. Your shooting range is the distance within which you can consistently make the outside shot. If you are open to shoot the ball within your shooting range, give a good target with your hands up and in shooting position. As the pass is thrown, jump behind the ball facing the basket in position to shoot. Let the ball come to your hands: Do not reach for the ball.

Catch the ball with your hands in a relaxed position, giving with the ball as it is caught. Use the *block-and-tuck* method to catch the ball; that is, in shooting position with your shooting hand behind the ball and your nonshooting hand under the ball. Never catch the ball with your hands on the sides, rotating it into position, because when rushed you'll put sidespin on the ball. Block the ball with your far hand, then tuck your nonshooting hand under and place your shooting hand behind the ball. The passer should aim for your far hand, which will block the pass.

When you receive a pass from in front (inside out), block the ball with your shooting (far) hand, tucking your nonshooting hand under the ball (see Figure 3.5). When you receive a pass from your strong-hand side, block the ball with your nonshooting (far) hand, placing your shooting hand behind and resetting your nonshooting hand under the ball (see Figure 3.5). If a pass comes from your weak-hand side, block the ball with your shooting (far) hand, tuck your nonshooting hand under, and then adjust your shooting hand behind the ball (see Figure 3.5).

Figure 3.5   Keys to Success: Catching the Ball in Position to Shoot

From in Front

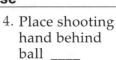

a

b

Preparation Phase

Execution Phase

1. Face basket ____
2. See passer and basket ____
3. Feet shoulder-width apart ____
4. Toes straight ____
5. Knees flexed ____
6. Shoulders relaxed ____

7. Elbow in ____
8. Hands high between ear and shoulder ____
9. Nonshooting hand facing up ____
10. Shooting hand facing basket ____

1. Jump behind ball in position to shoot ____
2. Arms in, not reaching ____
3. Block ball with shooting hand ____
4. Tuck nonshooting hand under ball ____

From Strong-Hand Side

a

b

c

Preparation Phase

Execution Phase

1. Face basket ____
2. See passer and basket ____
3. Feet shoulder-width apart ____
4. Toes straight ____
5. Knees flexed ____
6. Shoulders relaxed ____

7. Elbow in ____
8. Hands high between ear and shoulder ____
9. Nonshooting hand facing passer ____
10. Shooting hand facing basket ____

1. Jump behind ball in position to shoot ____
2. Arms in, not reaching ____
3. Block ball with nonshooting hand ____

4. Place shooting hand behind ball ____
5. Reset nonshooting hand under ball ____

From Weak-Hand Side

a   b   c

Preparation Phase

1. Face basket ____
2. See passer and basket ____
3. Feet shoulder-width apart ____
4. Toes straight ____
5. Knees flexed ____
6. Shoulders relaxed ____
7. Elbow in ____
8. Hands high between ear and shoulder ____
9. Nonshooting hand facing up ____
10. Shooting hand facing passer ____

Execution Phase

1. Jump behind ball in position to shoot ____
2. Arms in, not reaching ____
3. Block ball with shooting hand ____
4. Tuck nonshooting hand under ball ____
5. Take shooting hand off ball ____
6. Reset shooting hand behind ball ____

Detecting Errors in Catching the Ball in Position to Shoot

The most common errors in catching the ball in position to shoot are listed here, along with suggestions to correct them.

ERROR

CORRECTION

1. When you receive a pass from the side, you face the passer and reach for the ball, slowing your release.

1. Face the basket, turn your head to see the pass, and let the ball come to you. Jump behind the ball, and catch and shoot in one motion.

2. You catch the ball with your hands on the side and rotate the ball into position causing sidespin.

2. Block with your far hand and tuck your nonshooting hand under the ball. Your shooting hand should always be behind the ball before you shoot. When you receive a pass from the side of your strong hand, your nonshooting hand is your far hand: After catching the ball, reset your nonshooting hand under the ball. When you receive a pass from the side of your weak hand, your shooting hand is your far hand: After catching the ball, adjust by taking your shooting hand off the ball and placing it behind the ball for the shot.

3. You receive a pass but have a slow release due to lowering the ball before shooting it.

3. Catch the ball in position to shoot, keeping it high and shooting in one motion.

Passing and Catching Drills

1. Ball-Handling Warm-Up

This warm-up drill consists of passing and catching the ball, going from one hand to the other. The six parts of the ball-handling drill are (a) over your head, (b) around your head, (c) around your waist, (d) around one leg, (e) around your other leg, and (f) figure eight through your legs.

Start in a balanced stance. Pass and catch the ball from one hand to the other forcefully by flexing your wrist and fingers. To improve your weak hand, emphasize forcing it through the ball. Follow through completely on each pass, pointing your fingers at your catching hand. Work for force and control, not only for quickness. On each part of the drill pass the ball 10 times in one direction, reverse direction, and pass the ball 10 times in the other direction.

Success Goal = 3 minutes with a maximum of 3 errors

Your Score = (#) _____ minutes; (#) _____ errors

2. Tossback (or Wall) Passing

The tossback drill consists of passing to a tossback or wall (if a tossback is unavailable) to develop quickness, accuracy, and confidence in passing. In this drill you will execute the chest, bounce, overhead, sidearm, baseball, and behind-the-back passes. Start in a balanced stance 12 feet in front of a tossback or wall, with the ball in good passing position. Pass and catch the ball as quickly and accurately as you can. Correct fingertip release will impart backspin and direct the ball straight back to you. Leave your arms up on your follow-through until the ball hits the tossback.

Success Goal = 30 passes made in 30 seconds at 12 feet with each pass—except bounce pass: 20 passes in 30 seconds

Your Score =

a. (#) _____ chest passes

b. (#) _____ overhead passes

c. (#) _____ sidearm passes

d. (#) _____ baseball passes

e. (#) _____ behind-the-back passes

f. (#) _____ bounce passes

3. Tossback (Wall) Passing on the Move

Practicing this drill to a tossback or to a wall while moving from side to side develops quickness, accuracy, and confidence. Place the tossback in the middle of the lane. Start 12 feet away from it with your outside foot touching the lane line to your left. Use the chest pass when passing and catching on the move. Starting in good passing position, pass and catch the ball as quickly and accurately as you can while moving laterally, taking short, quick side steps and not crossing your feet. Move laterally until your outside foot touches the lane line to your right. Change direction and move back to the lane line to your left, passing and catching on the move. Keep moving laterally as you pass and catch, changing direction each time you touch the line. You can modify this drill by running, making a one-two stop as you catch each pass. If a tossback is unavailable, use a wall. Mark the lines with tape 12 feet apart to serve as lane lines.

Success Goal = 30 chest passes made in 30 seconds at 12 feet while moving from lane line to lane line

Your Score =

a. (#) _____ passes while moving with short, quick steps

b. (#) _____ passes while running and making a one-two stop as you catch each pass

4. Partner Passing

This drill uses a partner to develop quickness, accuracy, and confidence in passing—executing the chest, bounce, overhead, sidearm, baseball, and behind-the-back passes. With the ball in good passing position, start in a balanced stance 15 feet in front of a tossback or wall. Pass and catch the ball as quickly and accurately as you can, using fingertip release to impart backspin and accuracy. Point your fingers in the direction of the pass, exaggerating your follow-through by leaving your arms up until the pass is caught. When you catch, be in a balanced stance with your hands up as a target and ready to move to meet each pass.

Success Goal =

a. 30 passes made in 30 seconds at 15 feet for the chest, overhead, sidearm, and behind-the-back passes

b. 20 passes made in 30 seconds at 15 feet for the bounce pass

c. 20 passes made in 30 seconds at 20 feet for the baseball pass

Your Score =

a. (#) _____ chest passes at 15 feet

b. (#) _____ bounce passes at 15 feet

c. (#) _____ overhead passes at 15 feet

d. (#) _____ sidearm passes at 15 feet

e. (#) _____ baseball passes at 20 feet

f. (#) _____ behind-the-back passes at 15 feet

5. Line Passing (Pass and Follow)

This drill, performed with several teammates, is challenging, competitive, and fun. Divide into two lines 12 feet apart, with the first players in each line facing each other. The free throw circle or center circle can be used as measures of spacing 12 feet apart. The first player in line has a ball and passes to the first person in the other line and then follows the pass by running to the right behind the line of the player who receives the pass. The receiver catches the ball and then passes it to the second player in the first line, following the pass by running over to the right behind the player who received the pass. The drill continues with each player catching, passing, and following the pass with quickness and accuracy.

Success Goal =

a. 60 passes made in 60 seconds at 12 feet for the chest, overhead, sidearm, and behind-the-back passes

b. 40 passes made in 60 seconds at 12 feet for the bounce pass

c. 40 passes made in 60 seconds at 20 feet for the baseball pass

Your Score =

a. (#) _____ chest passes at 12 feet

b. (#) _____ bounce passes at 12 feet

c. (#) _____ overhead passes at 12 feet

d. (#) _____ sidearm passes at 12 feet

e. (#) _____ baseball passes at 20 feet

f. (#) _____ behind-the-back passes at 12 feet

6. Star Passing

Another challenging, competitive, and fun drill, star passing is performed with at least 10 players. Set up in a star formation with five lines 12 feet apart around the free throw circle or center circle. The first player in one of the lines has a ball and passes to the first person two lines away to the right (in the line to the right not immediately next to his or her line) and then follows the pass by running to the right behind the line of the receiver. The player receiving the pass then passes the ball to the first person two lines farther away (the line to the right not immediately next to his or her line) and follows the pass, running to the right behind the second receiver. The drill continues with each player catching, passing, and following the pass with quickness and accuracy.

Success Goal =

a. 60 passes made in 60 seconds at 12 feet for the chest, overhead, sidearm, and behind-the-back passes

b. 40 passes made in 60 seconds at 12 feet for the bounce pass

c. 40 passes made in 60 seconds at 20 feet for the baseball pass

Your Score =

a. (#) _____ chest passes at 12 feet

b. (#) _____ bounce passes at 12 feet

c. (#) _____ overhead passes at 12 feet

d. (#) _____ sidearm passes at 12 feet

e. (#) _____ baseball passes at 20 feet

f. (#) _____ behind-the-back passes at 12 feet

7. Bull in the Ring

This is another fun passing drill with five players on offense and one player on defense. Four teammates and you spread out equidistant around the center circle or foul circle. One of you has a ball, and one defender, placed in the middle of the circle (the bull in the ring), tries to intercept, deflect, or touch a pass. The player with the ball may fake and use any type pass to any player in the circle except the closest player to either side. The passer may not hold the ball longer than 2 seconds (counts). If the defensive player touches the ball or if the passer makes a bad pass or violation, the passer becomes the defender in the middle, with the defender going to offense.

Success Goal = 5 consecutive passes made without a deflection, bad pass, or violation

Your Score = (#) _____ consecutive passes without error

8. *Give-and-Go Speed Layup*

The give-and-go speed layup drill is a challenging combination of passing and shooting layups that you perform with two teammates. It consists of alternately passing and cutting from each elbow, or T (the intersection of the foul line and lane line), and shooting layups with your right hand when cutting right or with your left hand when cutting left.

One of your teammates is positioned 12 feet to the right side of the lane and halfway between the elbow and basket. Your other teammate stands 12 feet to the left side of the lane halfway between the elbow and basket. You start in a balanced stance with your left foot forward and your right foot back on the elbow. Pass to your teammate on your right and cut to the basket (give-and-go). Receive a return pass and shoot a right-handed layup. Catch the ball as it comes through the net or on its rebound.

Pass to your teammate on the other side of the lane and cut to the left elbow. Receive a return pass and place your inside (left) foot on the left elbow, or T. Pass back to your teammate, change direction, and cut to the basket. Receive a return pass and shoot a left-handed layup, catching the ball as it comes through the net or on its rebound. Continue the drill, alternately passing, cutting, and shooting layups on each side of the basket.

Success Goal = 5 to 6 layups in 30 seconds is good; 7 to 8 layups in 30 seconds is excellent

Your Score = (#) _____ layups made in 30 seconds

9. *Catch and Shoot on Pass From in Front (Inside Out)*

Work with a partner. In this drill you will shoot from 5 outside spots—the wing and corner positions on each side and the top. Start at the top directly in front of the basket. Face the basket in position to catch and shoot within your shooting range. Your partner starts at the inside low-post area with a ball by making a chest pass to your far (shooting) hand. Catch and shoot in one motion. You get 1 point each time you make a successful shot. Continue the drill after each attempted shot, with your partner going for a two-handed rebound and passing back out to you. Take 10 shots and then switch positions with your partner. After you shoot at the top, the drill continues with you and your partner taking 10 shots each at each of the other positions.

Success Goal = 7 baskets out of 10 attempts on pass from in front (inside out)

Your Score =
   a. (#) _____ baskets; (#) _____ shots attempted from top
   b. (#) _____ baskets; (#) _____ shots attempted from right wing
   c. (#) _____ baskets; (#) _____ shots attempted from left wing
   d. (#) _____ baskets; (#) _____ shots attempted from right corner
   e. (#) _____ baskets; (#) _____ shots attempted from left corner

10. *Catch and Shoot on Pass From Strong-Hand Side*

Work with a partner. In this drill the pass will come from your strong-hand side. You will shoot from 3 spots—the elbow (the intersection of the foul and lane lines), wing, and corner positions on your weak-hand side. Start at a spot above your weak-hand side elbow within your shooting range. Face the basket, ready to catch and shoot in one motion. Your partner starts at the elbow on your strong-hand side by making a chest pass to your far (nonshooting) hand. When you receive the pass, block the ball with your nonshooting hand and place your shooting hand behind the ball, then reset your nonshooting hand under the ball. You get 1 point each time you make a basket. Continue the drill after each attempted shot, with your partner going for a two-handed rebound and dribbling out to the elbow before passing to you. Take 10 shots and then switch positions with your partner. Continue the drill by taking 10 shots each from the wing and corner positions on your weak-hand side, with the pass coming from your strong-hand side elbow.

Success Goal = 7 baskets out of 10 attempts on pass from your strong-hand side

Your Score =

   a. (#) _____ baskets; (#) _____ shots attempted from elbow
   b. (#) _____ baskets; (#) _____ shots attempted from wing
   c. (#) _____ baskets; (#) _____ shots attempted from corner

11. Catch and Shoot on Pass From Weak-Hand Side

Work with a partner. In this drill the pass will come from your weak-hand side. You will shoot from the elbow, wing, and corner positions on your strong-hand side and start at a spot above your strong-hand side elbow within your shooting range; your partner begins at the elbow on your weak-hand side by making a chest pass to your far (shooting) hand. When you receive a pass from your weak-hand side, block the ball with your far (shooting) hand, tuck your nonshooting hand under the ball, and then adjust your shooting hand behind the ball. For scoring, follow the pattern of the previous drill.

Success Goal = 7 baskets out of 10 attempts on pass from your weak-hand side

Your Score =

   a. (#) _____ baskets; (#) _____ shots attempted from elbow
   b. (#) _____ baskets; (#) _____ shots attempted from wing
   c. (#) _____ baskets; (#) _____ shots attempted from corner

Passing and Catching Checks

Passing and catching are the essence of team play, the skills that make basketball such a beautiful team sport. Developing your ability to pass and catch makes you a better player and helps make your teammates better.

Have a trained observer—your coach, teacher, or a skilled player—watch you pass and catch. The observer can use the checklists in Figures 3.1 to 3.5 to evaluate your performance and provide corrective feedback. Also, ask your coach to evaluate your decision making in passing.

Step 4   Dribbling: Master Your Weak Hand

Dribbling is an integral part of basketball and vital to individual and team play. Like passing, it is a way of moving the ball. To maintain possession of the ball while you move you have to dribble (tap or bounce the ball to the floor). At the start of the dribble the ball must leave your hand before you lift your pivot foot from the floor. While dribbling you may neither touch the ball simultaneously with both hands nor allow it to come to a rest in your hand.

The ability to dribble with your weak hand as well as your strong hand is a key to advancing your level of play. If you only dribble well with your strong hand, you can be overplayed to that side and be made virtually ineffective. To protect the ball in dribbling you keep your body between your defender and the ball. In other words, when you drive to your weak-hand side (to your left if you are right-handed), you dribble with the weak (left) hand to protect the ball with your body.

WHY DRIBBLING IS IMPORTANT

Dribbling allows you to move the ball by yourself. By dribbling you can advance the ball up the court and evade pressure by defenders. Every team needs at least one skilled dribbler who can advance the ball up the court on a fast break and protect it against defensive pressure.

Some specific uses of the dribble are to

- move the ball out of a congested area when passing to a teammate is impossible (such as after a rebound or when being double-teamed),
- advance the ball up the court when receivers are not open, especially against pressure defenses,
- move the ball up the court on a fast break when teammates are not open in position to score,
- penetrate the defense for a drive to the basket,
- draw defender to you to create an opening for a teammate,
- set up offensive plays,

- improve your position or angle before passing to a teammate, and
- create your own shot.

HOW TO DRIBBLE

Dribbling is the most misused fundamental of the game. It is important to understand when—and when not—to dribble. A pass travels many times faster than a dribble, so before you dribble look to pass to open teammates. If you dribble too much, your teammates will tend to not move, making the defense's job easier. Excessive dribbling can destroy teamwork and morale.

Learn to minimize the use of the dribble. It should have a purpose: The dribble should take you somewhere. Do not waste it.

The tendency to bounce the ball automatically the moment you receive it can become a bad habit. By dribbling unnecessarily you may miss the opportunity to pass to an open teammate or you may pick up your dribble (stop your dribble) before you have an open teammate. When you immediately dribble the ball once or twice and then pick it up, you have made it easier for your defender to apply pressure against your shot. Your teammates will be more easily denied receiving a pass as you are no longer a threat to drive. Once you start to dribble, remember not to stop until you have an open teammate to receive your pass.

To be an effective playmaker you must become skilled at dribbling with either hand. Strive to feel that the ball is an extension of your hand. Keep your head up to see the entire court and make the right decision at the right time. How well you dribble—your control, timing, deception, and quickness—determines in great measure your progress as a playmaker.

The basic dribble moves to learn include control dribble, speed dribble, footfire dribble, change-of-pace dribble, retreat dribble, crossover dribble, inside-out dribble, reverse dribble, and behind-the-back dribble. Practice to make dribbling skills so automatic that you do not think about dribbling but devote full attention to the different situations taking place on the court. Learn how quickly you can dribble and still have control. In practice, strive to improve your ability but in games, know your limitations. Dribbling is a skill that you can practice by yourself: All you need are a ball, a level spot, and an eagerness to improve.

EXECUTING THE CONTROL DRIBBLE

Use the control dribble when you are closely guarded and must keep the ball protected and under control. A well-balanced stance, basic to the control dribble, makes you a triple threat to shoot, pass, or drive. It allows you to move quickly, change direction, change pace, and stop under control, while keeping the ball protected. Keep your head up and see the rim of the basket so you can see the entire court—open teammates and defenders. Learn to dribble without looking at the ball. Keep your head over your waist and your back straight. Your feet should be at least shoulder-width apart, your weight evenly distributed on the balls of your feet, and your knees flexed, preparing you to move. Keep the elbow of your dribbling hand close to your body. Your dribbling hand should be in a re-

laxed position, your thumb relaxed and your fingers comfortably spread. Dribble the ball off your finger pads with fingertip control, flexing your wrist and fingers to impart force to the ball. Do not pump your arm. Dribble the ball no higher than knee level and close to your body. Keep the nondribbling hand in a protective position close to the ball. Position your body between your defender and the ball (see Figure 4.1).

EXECUTING THE SPEED DRIBBLE

The speed dribble is useful when you are not closely guarded, when you must move the ball quickly on the open floor, and when you have a quick drive to the basket. For speed dribbling use a high dribble at waist level, keep your head up, and see the rim of the basket so you can see the entire court—open teammates and defenders. Start by throwing the ball out several feet and running after it. Remember: The ball must leave your hand before you lift your pivot foot. Push the successive dribbles out at waist level, flexing your wrist and fingers to put force on the ball. Dribble the ball off your finger pads with fingertip control (see Figure 4.1).

Figure 4.1 Keys to Success: *Control and Speed Dribbles*

Execution Phase

Control Dribble

Speed Dribble

_____ 1. Head up, see the rim _____

2. Dribble ball close to body _____

3. Dribble knee level or lower _____

2. Throw ball out several feet, run after it _____

3. Push dribble forward at waist level _____

_____ 4. Ball leaves hand before lifting pivot foot _____

_____ 5. Dribble ball off finger pads _____

_____ 6. Strong wrist and finger flexion _____

_____ 7. Body, nondribbling hand protect ball _____

Detecting Errors in the Control and Speed Dribbles

The most common errors in the control and speed dribbles are listed here, along with suggestions to correct them.

ERROR 🚫

CORRECTION

Control Dribble

ERROR	CORRECTION
1. You look at the ball when you are dribbling.	1. Keep your head up, see the rim.
2. You do not protect the ball while dribbling: You dribble too high and far away from your body.	2. Protect the ball by keeping your non-dribbling hand up and your body between the ball and your defender. Dribble the ball at knee level and close to your body.
3. You have trouble controlling the dribble.	3. Use your fingertips for control.
4. You do not get enough force on the dribble.	4. Flex your wrist and fingers completely, rather than pumping your arm.

Speed Dribble

ERROR	CORRECTION
1. The first dribble is too close to you.	1. Throw the first dribble out several feet and run after it.
2. You take too many dribbles.	2. Push each dribble out at waist level and run after it, keeping the number of dribbles to a minimum.

EXECUTING THE ONE-TWO STOP AT THE END OF A SPEED DRIBBLE

Speed dribbling is important but so is stopping quickly with balance. After dribbling at full speed, inexperienced players often lose balance and control as they try to stop quickly. The one-two stop can prevent dragging your pivot foot and traveling when you stop after speed dribbling, and it is especially important on a fast break.

In the one-two stop your back foot lands first, followed by your other foot. When the one-two stop is executed on your last dribble, the foot that first lands becomes your pivot foot.

In executing the one-two stop, hopping before the stop allows gravity to help you slow your movement. Lean in the opposite direction and land with a wide base. The *wider* your base, the more *stable* you will become. Flex your back knee to lower your body to a "sitting" position on the heel of your back foot: The *lower* you get, the more you will be in *balance*. Keep your head up (see Figure 4.2).

EXECUTING THE FOOTFIRE DRIBBLE

The footfire dribble is a method of stopping while keeping the dribble alive as you approach a defensive player in the open court. Especially at the end of a fast break it enables you to gain balance and see (read) the defender's positioning while you become a triple threat to shoot, pass, or drive as you dribble.

To execute the footfire you quickly change from a speed dribble to a control dribble, coming to a stop while keeping your dribble alive. Dribbling in place, face the basket with feet shoulder-width apart. Move your feet up and down as rapidly and as close to the floor as you can—as if they were on a hot surface. This rapid footfire movement helps you gain complete balance while also temporarily freezing your defender. The effectiveness of your footfire dribble comes from gaining complete balance and control, reading your defender's position, and faking before you make your next move to shoot, pass, or drive (see Figure 4.2).

Figure 4.2   Keys to Success: Gaining Control After the Speed Dribble

One-Two Stop

Preparation Phase

1. Head up, see rim ____
2. Speed dribble, waist level ____

Execution Phase

1. Hop before stop ____
2. Lean back ____
3. Catch ball off last dribble ____
4. Land first on back foot ____
5. Land second on lead foot ____
6. Wide base ____
7. Head up, see rim ____
8. Ready to pass or shoot ____

Footfire Dribble

a

**Preparation
Phase**

1. Head up, see rim ____
2. Speed dribble, waist
   level ____

b

c

**Execution
Phase**

1. Change to control
   dribble ____
2. Continue dribbling ____
3. Footfire (rapid movement
   of feet) ____

4. Head up, see rim ____
5. Be a triple threat to shoot,
   pass, or drive ____
6. Head fake before next
   move ____

Detecting Errors in the One-Two Stop
and the Footfire Dribble

The most common errors in the one-two stop
and footfire dribble are listed here, along with
suggestions to correct them.

ERROR ⦸

CORRECTION

One-Two Stop

1. You slow your dribbling speed with short
   steps on your approach to make your stop.

2. You lose balance forward, causing you to
   drag your pivot foot.

1. Use speed dribble. Hop before you stop to
   allow gravity to help slow your movement.

2. Hop before you stop to allow gravity to
   help slow your momentum, lean back, land
   first on your back foot and then your front
   foot, with a wide base for stability and "sitting" on the heel of your back foot. Keep
   your head up.

Footfire Dribble

1. You are unstable during the footfire dribble.

2. You rush your next move.

1. Emphasize complete balance and control
   with your feet shoulder-width apart and
   knees flexed.

2. While you execute the footfire dribble, be in
   a triple-threat position facing the basket, and
   head fake before you shoot, pass, or drive.

EXECUTING THE CHANGE-OF-PACE DRIBBLE

The change-of-pace dribble is useful to deceive and elude your defender. To execute the change-of-pace, change your dribble method from speed to control and quickly back to speed. The effectiveness of your change-of-pace depends on your deception and quickness. Push the dribble out to change quickly from a slower to a faster speed. In changing your pace you have the advantage because *you* decide when to change speeds. With good deception and a forceful push of the dribble to quickly increase speed, you should be at least a step ahead of your defender just after changing pace from the control dribble to speed dribble (see Figure 4.3).

EXECUTING THE RETREAT DRIBBLE

The retreat dribble is used to beat trouble when being pressured by defenders. It is often combined with a front change-of-direction and speed dribble to elude being trapped by two defenders. By first retreating backward with your dribble, you can gain space for a front change-of-direction and speed dribble to get by the trap. To execute the retreat dribble use short, quick retreat steps while dribbling in a backward direction. As you retreat keep the ball protected and maintain a balanced stance: you want to make a controlled change-of-direction dribble and be able to explode past the defenders with a speed dribble. Keep your head up and your eyes on the rim to see and pass to open teammates (see Figure 4.3).

Figure 4.3   Keys to Success: *Beat Trouble With a Change-of-Pace or Retreat Dribble*

Change-of-Pace Dribble

a

b

c

Preparation Phase

1. Head up, see rim ____
2. Control dribble at knee level ____
3. Body and nondribbling hand protect ball ____

Execution Phase

1. Head up, see rim ____
2. Change to speed dribble at waist level ____
3. Push dribble out and run after it ____

4. Change to control dribble at knee level ____
5. Body and nondribbling hand protect ball ____

Retreat Dribble

a

b

c

**Preparation
Phase**

1. Head up, see rim ____
2. Control dribble at knee
   level ____
3. Body and nondribbling
   hand protect ball ____

**Execution
Phase**

1. Head up, see rim ____
2. Change to retreat dribble
   at knee level ____
3. Short, quick retreat
   steps ____
4. Body and nondribbling
   hand protect ball ____

5. Change to speed dribble at
   waist level ____
6. Push dribble out and run
   after it ____

Detecting Errors in the Change-of-Pace and Retreat Dribbles

The most common errors in the change-of-pace and retreat dribbles are listed here, along with suggestions to correct them.

ERROR

CORRECTION

Change-of-Pace Dribble

1. You do not make a quick change from control dribble to speed dribble.

2. You do not control the dribble in changing from speed dribble to control dribble.

1. Emphasize pushing out your first speed dribble and running after it.

2. Widen your base and flex your knees to gain balance. Dribble the ball at knee level or lower.

Retreat Dribble

1. You have trouble retreating quickly.

1. Do not lean forward, maintain your balance, and use short, quick retreat steps.

EXECUTING THE CROSSOVER DRIBBLE (FRONT CHANGE-OF-DIRECTION DRIBBLE)

The crossover dribble is important in the open court on a fast break, to get open on your drive to the basket, and to create an opening for your shot. Effectiveness in the crossover dribble is based on how sharply you change your dribble from one direction to another. To execute a crossover dribble cross the ball in front of you at a backward angle, switching the dribble from one hand to the other. Dribble the ball close to you, at knee level or lower with a control dribble and at waist level with a speed dribble. When you make the change of direction, get your nondribbling hand up and change your lead foot and body position for protection (see Figure 4.4).

EXECUTING THE INSIDE-OUT DRIBBLE (FAKE CHANGE-OF-DIRECTION DRIBBLE)

The inside-out dribble is a fake change-of-direction dribble off a control or footfire dribble. It is a deceptive dribble for getting open on a drive to the basket or for a shot. You set up the deception by faking a change of direction with a head fake to the opposite side. In executing the inside-out dribble start by crossing the ball in front of you. Instead of releasing the ball and changing the dribble to your other hand, however, rotate your hand over the ball and dribble the ball outside your base back to the side from which you started. Dribble close to your body at knee level. Protect the ball with your body and nondribbling hand up (see Figure 4.4).

Figure 4.4   Keys to Success: *Changing Direction and Faking a Change of Direction*

Crossover Dribble (Front Change of Direction)

a   b   c

Preparation Phase

Execution Phase

1. Head up, see rim ____
2. Control dribble at knee level ____
3. Body and nondribbling hand protect ball ____

1. Head up, see rim ____
2. Cross ball in front at backward angle ____
3. Dribble close to body ____

4. Switch hands ____
5. Control dribble at knee level ____
6. Body and nondribbling hand protect ball ____

Inside-Out Dribble (Fake Change of Direction)

 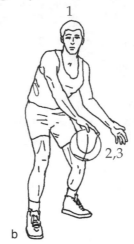 

a   b   c

**Preparation
Phase**

1. Head up, see rim ____
2. Control dribble at knee level ____
3. Body and nondribbling hand protect ball ____

**Execution
Phase**

1. Head up, see rim ____
2. Fake crossing ball in front ____
3. Quickly rotate hand over ball ____

4. Dribble ball back to same side outside base ____
5. Control dribble at knee level ____
6. Body and nondribbling hand protect ball ____

Detecting Errors in the Crossover and Inside-Out Dribbles

The most common errors in changing direction or faking a change of direction are listed here, along with suggestions to correct them.

ERROR   **CORRECTION**

Crossover Dribble

1. You dribble the ball too high or wide when changing direction.

1. Dribble at knee level and close to your body.

2. You do not protect the ball as you dribble.

2. Protect the ball with your body and by keeping your nondribbling hand up.

ERROR **CORRECTION**

Inside-Out Dribble

1. You make an extra dribble in toward your opposite hand before dribbling back to the same side.

2. Your inside-out dribble does not go out enough on the return to the same side.

3. Your inside-out dribble is not deceptive.

1. Rotate your hand over the ball and make your inside-out dribble out to the same (first) side, rather than in toward your opposite hand.

2. Rotate your hand over the ball so that your inside-out dribble goes outside your base on the same (first) side.

3. Make a head fake in the opposite direction.

EXECUTING THE REVERSE DRIBBLE (SPIN DRIBBLE)

The reverse dribble keeps your body between the ball and your defender for protection as you change direction. It has the disadvantage, however, of temporarily taking your eyes off other defenders who may attempt a blind-sided steal of the ball. The reverse dribble is best used as an offensive move to counter a strong defensive overplay to your dribbling side: It enables you to create your own shot in the opposite direction.

This is a two-dribble move. First dribble *backward* and then pivot backward on your opposite foot while turning your shoulders back toward your dribbling-hand side. Bring your back foot forward as you pull a second dribble *forward* and close to your body using your same hand. After completing the reverse dribble move, change hands for your next dribble (see Figure 4.5).

EXECUTING THE BEHIND-THE-BACK DRIBBLE

The behind-the-back dribble keeps your body between the ball and your defender for pro-

tection as you change direction. It is best used on the open floor when there is a defensive player in front who is overplaying you to your dribbling side. Although developing the behind-the-back dribble takes more practice than other dribble moves, it is well worth the effort, having advantages over the front change-of-direction and the reverse dribbles. Compared with the front change-of-direction dribble, it is better because you can keep your body between the ball and a defender. Compared with the reverse dribble, its advantage is allowing you to change direction without taking your eyes off the rim or other defenders. The behind-the-back dribble is much quicker than the reverse dribble and almost as quick as the front change-of-direction dribble.

Like the reverse dribble, this is a two-dribble move. Again, dribble backward. Then move your pelvis forward as you pull a second dribble behind your back and close to your body, in a forward direction to your other hand. After your second dribble, change hands. Use your body and nondribbling hand for protection (see Figure 4.5).

Figure 4.5   Keys to Success: Advanced Changes of Direction

Reverse Dribble (Spin Dribble)

Preparation Phase

Execution Phase

1. Head up, see rim ____
2. Dribble ball back behind body ____
3. Body and nondribbling hand protect ball ____

1. Head up, see rim ____
2. Reverse pivot on front foot ____
3. Step through with back foot ____
4. Pull second dribble forward ____

5. Switch hands ____
6. Control dribble at knee level ____
7. Body and nondribbling hand protect ball ____

Behind-the-Back Dribble

Preparation Phase

Execution Phase

1. Head up, see rim ____
2. Dribble ball back behind body ____
3. Body and nondribbling hand protect ball ____

1. Head up, see rim ____
2. Move pelvis forward ____
3. Pull second dribble behind back and then forward ____

4. Switch hands ____
5. Control dribble at knee level ____
6. Body and nondribbling hand protect ball ____

Detecting Errors in the Reverse and Behind-the-Back Dribbles

The most common errors in the reverse dribble and the behind-the-back dribble are listed here, along with suggestions to correct them.

ERROR ⊘

CORRECTION

Reverse Dribble

1. You do not understand which foot and direction to take when executing the reverse dribble.

2. You change hands on your dribble as you reverse, causing you to dribble too wide.

1. Pivot backward on your opposite foot, turning your shoulders toward your dribbling hand side.

2. First dribble backward. As you reverse pivot, emphasize pulling the ball forward and close to your body using your same hand.

Behind-the-Back Dribble

1. You cannot dribble the ball behind your back.

2. You dribble too wide.

1. Make the first dribble back and move your pelvis forward.

2. Emphasize pulling the ball forward and close to your body on the second dribble, using your same hand.

SHOOTING OFF THE DRIBBLE

When open, dribble to the front of your shooting knee and pick the ball up facing the basket in position to shoot: Do not reach for the ball. Pick the ball up in front of your shooting knee with your knees flexed to gain balance for your shot and prevent floating forward, backward, or to the side.

Pick the ball up with your shooting hand on top of the ball and your nonshooting hand under the ball. As you bring the ball up to shoot, your shooting hand will be positioned behind the ball, enabling you to shoot with backspin. Never pick up the ball with your hands on the sides and rotate it into position because when you are rushed you'll put sidespin on the ball when you shoot.

When dribbling to your strong-hand side, jump behind your last dribble and pick the ball up in front of your shooting knee. When dribbling to your weak-hand side, use a crossover dribble on your last dribble to pick the ball up in front of your shooting knee (see Figure 4.6).

Figure 4.6   Keys to Success: Shooting Off the Dribble

Dribbling to Strong-Hand Side

**Execution
Phase**

1. Dribble with strong hand ____
2. Control dribble to front of shooting knee ____

3. Jump behind ball facing basket ____
4. Pick up ball with shooting hand on top ____
5. Place nonshooting hand under ball ____

6. Shoot jump shot ____

Dribbling to Weak-Hand Side

**Execution
Phase**

1. Dribble with weak hand ____

2. Crossover dribble to front of shooting knee ____

3. Jump behind ball facing basket ____
4. Pick up ball with shooting hand on top ____
5. Place nonshooting hand under ball ____

6. Shoot jump shot ____

Detecting Errors in Shooting Off the Dribble

The most common errors in shooting off the dribble are listed here, along with suggestions to correct them.

ERROR

CORRECTION

ERROR	CORRECTION
1. When shooting off the dribble, you reach to the side for the ball, and start your shot from the side of your body, causing you to miss to either the right or left side of the basket.	1. When open, dribble to the front of your shooting knee, and pick the ball up facing the basket in position to shoot: Do not reach for the ball.
2. You pick up the ball off the dribble with your hands on the side and rotate the ball into position causing sidespin on your shot.	2. Pick the ball up in front of your shooting knee with your shooting hand on top of the ball and your nonshooting hand under the ball. As you bring the ball up to shoot your shooting hand will then be positioned behind the ball enabling you to shoot with backspin.
3. When shooting off the dribble, you float forward, back, or to the side.	3. Pick the ball up in front of your shooting knee with your knees flexed to gain balance for your shot and prevent floating forward, back, or to the side.

Dribbling Drills

1. Dribble Warm-Up

The dribble warm-up develops ability and confidence in dribbling with either your strong or weak hand. The drill's five parts are crossover, figure eight, one knee, sitting, and lying down.

   a. Crossover. In a balanced stance change the ball from one hand to the other, dribbling it below your knees and not wider than your knees. Keep your nondribbling hand up as a guard hand for protection. Also change the position of your feet and body to protect the ball with your body. Alternating from right to left and left to right, complete 20 repetitions (10 crossover dribbles with each hand).

   b. Figure Eight. Dribble the ball in a figure eight from back to front through the middle of your legs. Change from one hand to the other after the ball goes through your legs. After 10 repetitions change direction and dribble the ball in a figure eight from front to back through the middle of your legs for 10 more repetitions.

   c. One Knee. Continue to dribble the ball as you kneel down on one knee. Starting in front of your knee, dribble around to one side and under your raised knee. Change hands and dribble behind your back leg. Again change from one hand to the other and continue to the starting point in front of your knee. Dribble in a figure eight for 10 repetitions in one direction; reverse and dribble in a figure eight for 10 repetitions in the opposite direction.

    d. Sitting. Continue dribbling as you sit down. Dribble for 10 repetitions on one side while sitting. Raise your legs, dribble the ball under them to your other side, and dribble on that side for 10 repetitions.

    e. Lying Down. Continue dribbling as you lie down on your back. While lying down dribble for 10 repetitions on one side. Sit up, raise your legs, dribble the ball under your legs to the other side, lie down, and dribble for 10 repetitions.

Success Goal = 10 repetitions without error in each direction for each part of the drill

Your Score =

    a. (#) _____ crossover dribbles in 20 attempts

    b. (#) _____ figure eight dribbles in 10 attempts starting to the left

       (#) _____ figure eight dribbles in 10 attempts starting to the right

    c. (#) _____ one-knee figure eight dribbles in 10 attempts starting to the left

       (#) _____ one-knee figure eight dribbles in 10 attempts starting to the right

    d. (#) _____ right-hand sitting dribbles in 10 attempts

       (#) _____ left-hand sitting dribbles in 10 attempts

    e. (#) _____ right-hand lying down dribbles in 10 attempts

       (#) _____ left-hand lying down dribbles in 10 attempts

2. *One-Knee Crossover Dribble*

In addition to being a valuable offensive maneuver, the crossover dribble is an exciting move. To improve confidence and skill in making a crossover dribble with either the strong or weak hand, many players—including some in the NBA—now use the one-knee crossover dribble drill. Kneel down on one knee. Crossover dribble under your other, raised knee back and forth between hands. On each crossover dribble use as much force and quickness as possible. Flex your wrist and fingers to gain power, and point your fingers at your receiving hand to improve accuracy. Because you are dribbling the ball with as much force as possible, use a relaxed hand position to control the ball as it is received. Crossover dribble for 30 seconds, kneeling on your left knee and dribbling under your right. Then do it for 30 seconds kneeling on your right knee and dribbling under your left. You may want to cushion the knee you kneel on with a towel, especially if you plan on using this drill for more than 1 minute.

Success Goal = 60 crossover dribbles with 3 or less errors for each set of 30 seconds under the knee

Your Score =

    a. (#) _____ crossover dribbles under your right knee; (#) _____ errors

    b. (#) _____ crossover dribbles under your left knee; (#) _____ errors

3. *Two-Ball Dribble*

Dribbling two balls is fun and will develop dribbling ability and confidence with both your strong and weak hands. There are six parts to this drill: together, alternate one up and one down, crossover, inside-out, through the legs, and a side-pull forward and back. Each part includes dribbling two balls simultaneously. If a ball gets away, keep dribbling with the other while you recover it.

a. Together. Dribble two basketballs below knee level simultaneously.

b. Alternate One Up and One Down. Dribble two basketballs simultaneously, so that one ball is up while the other is down.

c. Crossover. Change the balls from one hand to the other by crossing them back and forth in front of you, keeping them low and close to your body. Mix how you make the changes, rather than executing each crossover with the same hand going in front.

d. Inside-Out. An inside-out dribble is a fake change of direction. Start the ball in but then rotate your hand over the ball to dribble it outside your base on the same side. Perform the inside-out dribble alternating hands and then with both hands simultaneously.

e. Through Your Legs. Dribble first one ball, then the other, and then both balls through the legs.

f. Side-Pull Forward and Back. Start by dribbling a ball on each side of your body. Then dribble them back and forward by flexing your wrists and fingers in an action that is similar to pulling the balls back and forward.

Success Goal = 20 dribbles without error on each part of the drill

Your Score =

a. (#) _____ together dribbles

b. (#) _____ alternate one-up and one-down dribbles

c. (#) _____ crossover dribbles

d. (#) _____ inside-out dribbles with right hand; (#) _____ left hand; (#) _____ hands together

e. (#) _____ through-your-leg dribbles with right hand; (#) _____ left hand; (#) _____ both balls going through together

f. (#) _____ side-pull forward and back dribbles

4. *Moving Two-Ball Dribble*

After dribbling two balls in a stationary position, a greater challenge is to dribble two balls while moving. The moving two-ball dribble will improve your weak-hand and strong-hand dribbling ability and, thus, your confidence. This drill also has six parts: zigzag, attack and retreat, stop and go, change of pace, reverse, and fake reverse.

a. Zigzag. Dribble two balls up the court in a zigzag manner; that is, dribbling diagonally to one side and then the other. Change direction by crossing both balls in front.

b. Attack and Retreat. Dribble two balls up the court using an attack and retreat; that is, by dribbling forward and then back without crossing your feet. Alternate the lead foot each time you attack and retreat.

c. Stop and Go. Dribble two balls up the court using a stop-and-go dribble. Speed dribble, pushing both balls forward; stop sharply, your body under full control; keep dribbling as you stop.

d. Change of Pace. Dribble two balls up the court changing pace (speed to control and control to speed). Use imagination to add deception, accelerating at various speeds.

e. Reverse. Dribble two balls zigzagging up the court, changing direction by using a reverse pivot. Dribble both balls back to one side, then reverse pivot on your opposite (lead) foot while pulling both balls close (to where your body was before your reverse pivot).

f. Fake Reverse. Dribble two balls zigzagging up the court. Use a fake reverse before changing direction by dribbling both balls back to one side and turning your head and shoulders back. Then quickly turn your head and shoulders forward as you dribble both balls forward again.

Success Goal = 2 fullcourt trips with maximum 1 error on parts a and b, and 3 errors on remaining parts

Your Score=

  a. (#) _____ fullcourt zigzag trips; (#) _____ errors

  b. (#) _____ fullcourt attack-and-retreat trips; (#) _____ errors

  c. (#) _____ fullcourt stop-and-go trips; (#) _____ errors

  d. (#) _____ fullcourt change-of-pace trips; (#) _____ errors

  e. (#) _____ fullcourt reverse trips; (#) _____ errors

  f. (#) _____ fullcourt fake-reverse trips; (#) _____ errors

5. Dribble Cones

Set up five cones, one each at the baseline, halfway between the baseline and halfcourt, at the halfcourt, halfway between halfcourt and the opposite baseline, and at the opposite baseline. The drill has three parts: crossover, behind-the-back, and retreat dribble and crossover. Dribble full speed during each.

a. Crossover Dribble. Start at the baseline cone. Dribble at full speed with your strong hand. After passing the next cone, immediately make a crossover dribble and change the ball in front to your weak hand. Speed dribble with your weak hand and as soon as you go by the next cone, make a crossover dribble back to your strong hand. Continue to the opposite baseline and return, continuing to dribble at full speed and making a crossover dribble after you pass each cone.

b. Behind-the-Back Dribble. You execute this part of the drill the same way except that you make a full-speed behind-the-back dribble after you pass each cone.

c. Retreat Dribble, Crossover Dribble, and Speed Dribble. Speed dribble to each cone, then use a retreat dribble. Make at least three retreat dribbles back and then a crossover dribble before resuming your speed dribble.

Success Goal=

  a. 10 cones passed in 30 seconds using crossover dribble

  b. 8 cones passed in 30 seconds using behind-the-back dribble

  c. 6 cones passed in 30 seconds using retreat dribble and crossover dribble

Your Score =

    a. (#) _____ cones passed using crossover dribble

    b. (#) _____ cones passed using behind-the-back dribble

    c. (#) _____ cones passed using retreat dribble and crossover dribble

6. Knock the Ball Out of the Circle

This drill develops your ability to dribble with your head up and to protect the ball against pressure. Select another player as an opponent. You will each have a basketball and dribble within either the free throw circle or center circle, each of you trying to deflect the other's basketball out of the circle. To vary the drill you and your opponent can dribble with your weak hand only. Another variation is allowing more contact than normal to work on dribbling under severe defensive pressure.

Success Goal = You receive 1 point each time you knock your opponent's ball out of the circle, with 5 points winning the game

Your Score =

    a. (#) _____ your points; (#) _____ partner's points on strong- or weak-hand dribble

    b. (#) _____ your points; (#) _____ partner's points on weak-hand dribble

    c. (#) _____ your points; (#) _____ partner's points on allowing additional contact

7. Dribble Tag

Dribble tag is a game that develops ability to dribble with the head up and to change direction quickly. Select five or more players to participate with you. Each of you will have a basketball and dribble within the halfcourt area. Designate one player as "it." The other players try to avoid being tagged by the designated player and a player becomes the next "it" when tagged. A variation is to have each player dribble only with the weak hand. The time limit for each game is 2 minutes.

Success Goal = You receive 1 point if you are not tagged within the time limit, with 3 points winning the game

Your Score =

    a. Strong- or weak-hand dribble; (#) _____ your points

    b. Weak-hand dribble only; (#) _____ your points

8. *One-Dribble Layup Drill*

This drill is a lead-up for shooting strong- and weak-hand layups off the dribble. First practice with your strong hand, starting in a balanced stance at the middle hash mark on the lane off your strong side. Use your strong-side foot as the pivot foot: It should be back and your weak-side foot forward. Dribble with your strong hand and then take a short step with your weak-side foot. Pick up the ball at your strong-side knee, with your balance hand under and your shooting hand behind the ball in block-and-tuck position. Jump straight up and shoot a strong-hand layup high above the box on the backboard. Land in balance and catch the ball with two hands after either making a shot or a rebound.

Next, practice the same way with your weak hand. Now your weak-side foot should be back and your strong-side foot forward. Reverse the previous practice by dribbling with your weak hand, taking the short step with your strong-side foot, picking up the ball at your weak-side knee, and shooting a weak-hand layup.

Success Goal = 5 consecutive one-dribble layups made with each hand

Your Score =

    a. (#) _____ consecutive one-dribble layups made with strong hand

    b. (#) _____ consecutive one-dribble layups made with weak hand

9. *One-Dribble Runner*

This drill is a lead-up for shooting strong- and weak-hand runners off the dribble. Start the practice with your strong hand in a balanced stance 9 feet in front of the basket. Your strong-side foot should be back and your weak-side foot forward, with your back foot used for pivoting. The routine is like the one-dribble layup. Dribble with your strong hand, take a short step with your weak-side foot picking up the ball at your strong-side knee with your balance hand under and your shooting hand behind the ball in block-and-tuck position. Jump straight up and shoot a strong-hand runner. Land in balance, ready to rebound or get back for defense.

Then practice the same way with your weak hand. Your weak-side foot should be back and your strong-side foot forward. Dribble with your weak hand, step with your strong-side foot, picking up the ball at your weak-side knee, jumping straight up, and shooting a weak-hand runner. Land in balance, ready to rebound or get back for defense.

Your goal is to make 5 consecutive runners and then increase the distance. After 5 consecutive runners from 9 feet, increase the distance to 12 feet. When you make 5 consecutive shots from 12 feet, move back to the foul line (15 feet from the backboard).

Success Goal = 5 consecutive one-dribble runners made with each hand

Your Score =

    a. (#) _____ consecutive one-dribble runners made with strong hand at 9 feet

    b. (#) _____ consecutive one-dribble runners made with weak hand at 9 feet

    c. (#) _____ consecutive one-dribble runners made with strong hand at 12 feet

    d. (#) _____ consecutive one-dribble runners made with weak hand at 12 feet

    e. (#) _____ consecutive one-dribble runners made with strong hand at 15 feet

    f. (#) _____ consecutive one-dribble runners made with weak hand at 15 feet

10. Speed Dribble Layup

This challenging alternate hand layup drill combines the use of the strong- and weak-hand speed and reverse dribbles. The drill consists of alternately driving from each elbow, or T (the intersection of the foul line and lane line), and shooting layups with your right hand when dribbling right and your left hand when dribbling left.

Start in a balanced stance with your left foot forward and right foot back at the right elbow, or T. Drive to the basket using a speed dribble with your outside (right) hand and shoot a right-handed layup. Catch the ball with two hands and speed dribble out to the left elbow, or T, using your outside (right) hand. Place your inside (left) foot on the left T and reverse dribble, pulling the ball back toward the basket with your outside (right) hand.

Drive to the basket using a speed dribble with your outside (left) hand and shoot a left-handed layup. Catch the ball with two hands and speed dribble out to the right T, using your outside (left) hand. Place your inside (right) foot on the T and reverse dribble, pulling the ball back toward the basket with your outside (left) hand. Continue the drill, alternately driving and shooting layups on each side of the basket.

Success Goal = 5 or 6 layups in 30 seconds is good and 7 or 8 layups is excellent

Your Score = (#) _____ layups made in 30 seconds

11. Chase the Dribbler

This drill develops your ability to speed dribble and make a driving layup while protecting the ball against a pursuing defensive player. Select another player as your opponent. Start at halfcourt on your strong-hand side facing the sideline. Your opponent, who will be a defensive chaser, will start one step behind you. Your opponent's lead foot will be touching your back foot. The drill starts when you initiate a drive to the basket using a speed dribble. The chaser should provide as much defensive pressure as possible, trying to deflect your dribble or pressure your shot. You get 1 point each time you make a successful shot. After each attempted shot, continue the drill, switching roles as offense and defense. A variation is to start on your weak-hand side and drive only with your weak hand.

Success Goal = More points than your partner with each of you taking 5 shots on each side

Your Score =

    a. (#) _____ your points; (#) _____ partner's points on strong-hand drive

    b. (#) _____ your points; (#) _____ partner's points on weak-hand drive

Dribbling Checks

Dribbling is vital to individual and team play. However, it is the most misused fundamental of the game. It is important to understand when—and when not—to dribble. Excessive dribbling can destroy teamwork and morale. Look to pass before you dribble, then dribble only when you need it to take you somewhere. Dribbling is a skill that you can practice by your-self. All you need are a ball, a level spot, and an eagerness to improve.

Have a trained observer—your coach, teacher, or a skilled player—watch your dribbling skills. The observer can use the checklists in Figures 4.1 to 4.6 to evaluate your performance and provide corrective feedback. Also, ask your coach to evaluate your decisions in using the dribble.

Step 5 Rebounding: Want the Ball

Rebounding is the one game fundamental that you cannot do too often. You can shoot too often, dribble too much, pass too much, and try too often to steal the ball or block shots but you can never rebound too much. Possession of the ball comes more often from missed shots than any other way. The team that controls the backboards usually controls the game.

WHY REBOUNDING IS IMPORTANT

Successful team play depends on both offensive and defensive rebounding. Offensive rebounding adds to your team's scoring opportunities, and defensive rebounding limits your oppo-nent's scoring opportunities.

Attacking the offensive glass for rebounds enables your team to create second shot scoring opportunities. More often than not, these second shots are high percentage inside shots and many result in 3-point plays. Offensive rebounding takes desire and effort, and gaining possession of the ball by getting an offensive rebound often inspires your team.

Gaining possession of the ball through defensive rebounding, however, is even more valuable. Controlling the defensive backboard provides your opponent fewer opportunities to gain second shots that often result in easy scores and 3-point plays. Not only does defensive rebounding limit your opponent's second chance scoring opportunities but it also creates the most opportunities of any method for starting fast breaks.

WHAT IT TAKES TO REBOUND

The factors that determine a good rebounder are emotional, mental, physical, and skill.

Emotional

Desire. Wanting the ball is the most important factor in rebounding. Assume that every shot will be missed and add to this the attitude that you will go after every rebound. Since many rebounds are not obtained by the first player to touch the ball, second effort is truly needed. The difference between good and great rebounders is that the great ones go after more rebounds.

Courage. The physical contact of rebounding demands courage. Your greatness as a rebounder can be measured by the amount of physical contact you can take. To be a great rebounder you must be eager to get into the battle of the boards. Often there is no glory in rebounding, just victory.

Mental

Anticipation of missed shots. Check the rims, backboards, and bracing to determine how hard or soft the ball will rebound. Know your teammates' shooting techniques and study your opponents' shooting to anticipate where shots will rebound. Observe the angle and distance of shots: Most shots rebound to the opposite side, and 3-point shot attempts tend to rebound longer.

Knowledge of your opponent. Know your individual opponent's height, strength, jumping ability, quickness, aggressiveness, block-out technique, and second effort.

Physical

Quickness. Move! On offense, move quickly around your opponent and go for the ball. On defense, move quickly to block out your opponent and then go for the ball.

Jumping. Work continually to improve your jump—not only to improve the height but also the quickness and explosiveness of your jump. A quick second jump is a great asset for rebounding.

Muscular endurance. Improve muscular endurance in your legs: It is not just how high you jump but how often you jump.

Strength. Use a conditioning program to improve your total body strength so you can withstand the body contact under the boards.

Height. You cannot change how tall you are but you can control all the other qualities that determine your success as a rebounder.

Skill

Vision. Use peripheral vision to see the total picture, including the ball and your opponent. When you play defense, after the shot watch your opponent, block out, and go for the ball. When you play offense, after the shot determine how your opponent blocks out, use the correct method to get by the block out, and go for the ball.

Balance. Maintain a balanced stance to counter such physical play as bumping, shoving, and pushing. Be on the balls of your feet, with the feet shoulder-width apart, knees flexed, back straight, head up, and hands above your shoulders.

Position. Anticipate your opponent's move, and work to establish inside position.

Hands up. Move both hands to a position above your forehead, placing your hands ball-width apart.

Timing. Time your jump to reach the ball at the maximum height of your jump.

Jump often. In rebounding it is not how high but how often you jump that is crucial for success.

Two-hand catch. Catch the ball with two hands and aggressively protect it in front of your forehead and away from your opponent.

Spread-eagle. After gaining possession and while still in the air, spread your legs and keep your elbows out to protect the ball.

Land in balance. Come down in a balanced stance. On offense, be ready to score with a power move or to pass out to a teammate. On defense, be ready to pivot and use a quick outlet pass to start a fast break.

HOW TO GET DEFENSIVE REBOUNDS

The key to defensive rebounding is getting inside position on your opponent and going for the ball. When playing defense you usually have the inside position between your opponent and the basket, giving you the early advantage in the ensuing battle for the rebound.

There are two coaching strategies for defensive rebounding. The most commonly used philosophy is to *block out* (often called *box out*) your opponent. Blocking out involves first blocking your opponent's path to the

ball—by putting your back to your opponent's chest—and then going for the ball. The other philosophy, espoused by John Wooden (the great UCLA coach of 10 NCAA championship teams), is simply to step in your opponent's path and go for the ball. Wooden's method, called the check-and-go, might be best when your quickness and leaping ability are highly superior to your opponent's. Blocking out is recommended for most players.

There are two methods of blocking out: the front turn and the reverse turn. Putting your back on your opponent's chest and going for the ball are more important than which block out method you use.

The *front turn* method is best for blocking out the shooter. After the shot, you simply step into the shooter. The *reverse turn* is best when you are defending a player without the ball. After the shot, you first observe your opponent's cut and then reverse turn, dropping your foot backward and away from your opponent's cut. Guarding the player without the ball, you take a defensive stance that allows you to see the ball and your opponent.

To guard a player on the ball side of the basket (also called the strong side), you would take a denial stance—one hand and one foot up in the passing lane. To guard a player on the opposite side of the basket (called the help side or weak side), you would take a defensive stance several steps away that allows you to see the ball and the player you are guarding. When you defend a player off the ball and a shot is taken, first observe your opponent's cut and then reverse turn, dropping the foot backward, away from your opponent's cut. Block out and get the rebound (see Figure 5.1).

You must develop the attitude that you are going to go after every ball. Always try to catch the ball with two hands, but if you cannot make a two-hand catch then use one hand to try to keep it alive until you or a teammate can grab it.

Figure 5.1   Keys to Success: Defensive Rebounding Methods

Front Turn

Preparation Phase

1. See ball and opponent ____
2. Defensive stance ____
3. Hand up in passing lane ____

1. Front pivot on back foot ____
2. Step toward opponent ____

Execution Phase

3. Back on opponent's chest ____
4. Wide base ____
5. Hands up ____

6. Go for ball ____
7. Catch ball with two hands ____
8. Spread eagle ____
9. Protect ball in front of forehead ____
10. Land in balance ____

Reverse Turn

Preparation Phase

1. See ball and opponent ____
2. Defensive stance ____
3. Hand up in passing lane ____
4. Watch opponent's cut ____

1. Reverse pivot on foot closest to opponent's cut ____
2. Drop other foot back ____

Execution Phase

3. Back on opponent's chest ____
4. Wide base ____
5. Hands up ____

6. Go for ball ____
7. Catch ball with two hands ____
8. Spread eagle ____
9. Protect ball in front of forehead ____
10. Land in balance ____

HOW TO GO FOR OFFENSIVE REBOUNDS

The key to offensive rebounding is to move. Develop the attitude—and will—to move and go after every ball. Move to outmaneuver the defender, who is usually between you and the basket. Make a quick, aggressive move to get by your defender and jump to get the ball, always trying to catch it with two hands. If you cannot catch the ball with two hands, then using one hand, try to tip it into the basket or keep it alive until you or a teammate can grab it. To avoid being blocked out keep moving.

If you are blocked out, use every effort to get around the block out. Even great rebounders get blocked out, but they keep moving to outmaneuver it. It is not a mistake to be blocked out, but it is a mistake to stay blocked out.

Four methods of moving by the block out are the straight cut, fake-and-go, spin, and step-back. Use the *straight cut* when your opponent blocks you out with a front turn: You quickly cut by before the block out can be set (see Figure 5.2). Use the *fake-and-go* when your opponent blocks you out with a reverse turn: Fake in the direction of your opponent's reverse step and cut by the other side (see Figure 5.2). Use the *spin* when your opponent blocks you out and holds your body. Place your forearm on your opponent's back, reverse pivot on your lead foot, hook your arm over your opponent's arm for leverage, and cut by (see Figure 5.2). Use the *step-back* when your opponent leans back on you while blocking out. Simply step back so your opponent loses balance, then cut by and go for the ball (see Figure 5.2).

Figure 5.2   Keys to Success: *Offensive Rebounding Methods*

Straight Cut

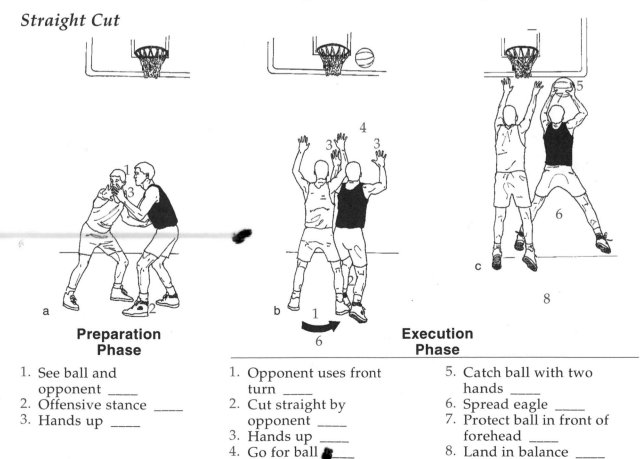

Preparation Phase

1. See ball and opponent ____
2. Offensive stance ____
3. Hands up ____

Execution Phase

1. Opponent uses front turn ____
2. Cut straight by opponent ____
3. Hands up ____
4. Go for ball ____

5. Catch ball with two hands ____
6. Spread eagle ____
7. Protect ball in front of forehead ____
8. Land in balance ____

Fake-and-Go

Preparation Phase

1. See ball and opponent ____
2. Offensive stance ____
3. Hands up ____

Execution Phase

1. Opponent uses reverse turn ____
2. Fake in direction of opponent's reverse step ____

3. Cut to opposite side ____
4. Hands up ____
5. Go for ball ____
6. Catch ball with two hands ____

7. Spread eagle ____
8. Protect ball in front of forehead ____
9. Land in balance ____

Spin

Preparation Phase

1. See ball and opponent ____
2. Offensive stance ____
3. Hands up ____

Execution Phase

1. Opponent holds you ____
2. Place forearm on opponent's back ____

3. Reverse pivot ____
4. Hook arm over opponent's arm ____
5. Go for ball ____

6. Catch ball with two hands ____
7. Spread eagle ____
8. Protect ball in front of forehead ____
9. Land in balance ____

Step-Back

a

b

c

d

Preparation Phase

1. See ball and opponent ____
2. Offensive stance ____
3. Hands up ____

1. Opponent leans on you ____

Execution Phase

2. Step back ____
3. Opponent falls ____
4. Go for ball ____

5. Catch ball with two hands ____
6. Spread eagle ____
7. Protect ball in front of forehead ____
8. Land in balance ____

Detecting Errors in Rebounding

The most common errors in rebounding are listed here, along with suggestions to correct them.

ERROR

CORRECTION

ERROR	CORRECTION
1. You watch the ball, and your opponent cuts by you.	1. Locate your opponent first, get inside position, block out or check, and then go for the ball.
2. You lose balance when your opponent fakes.	2. Use a wide base, and keep moving on the balls of your feet.
3. You hold your opponent, and your opponent hooks an arm over yours for leverage.	3. Keep your hands up.
4. You have trouble holding onto rebounds.	4. Catch the ball with two hands.
5. After gaining the rebound, you have it stripped by an opponent.	5. Keep the ball protected above your forehead, with your elbows out and away from your opponent.

Rebounding Drills

1. Backboard Rebounding

Starting in a balanced stance 8 feet in front of the backboard and to the side of the rim, make a two-handed chest pass, aiming high on the backboard. Rebound the ball with two hands and land in balance. Protect the ball above your forehead with elbows out, and do not lower the ball.

Success Goal = 8 out of 10 successful rebounds where you catch the rebound with two hands, the ball no lower than your forehead, and land in a balanced stance

Your Score = (#) _____ rebounds

2. Superman or Wonder Woman Rebounding

Start in a balanced stance with one foot outside the lane line and above the box. Make a strong two-handed chest pass, aiming high on the opposite corner of the backboard. You should pass the ball so that it rebounds above the box to the opposite side of the lane. Rebound the ball with two hands and land in balance, at least one foot outside the lane and above the box. Protect the ball above your forehead with elbows out.

Success Goal = 10 successful rebounds in 30 seconds, catching the rebound with two hands, the ball no lower than your forehead, while landing in a balanced stance outside the lane and above the middle hash mark

Your Score = (#) _____ rebounds

3. One-Versus-Two Offensive Rebound and Score

Start in a balanced stance 8 feet in front of the backboard and to the side of the rim. Two players will take positions on either side of you. Make a two-handed chest pass, aiming high on the backboard. Rebound the ball with two hands and land in balance. Without lowering the ball below your forehead and keeping your elbows out, try to score with a power move (strong two-handed shot). The other players will give you some resistance by slightly bumping your arms, trying to knock the ball out of your hands after your rebound and during your scoring attempt.

Success Goal = 6 out of 10 successful rebounds and scores

Your Score = (#) _____ rebounds and scores

4. Tipping

Stand in front of the backboard to the side of the rim in a balanced stance. Using only one hand shoot the ball high and softly on the backboard. Time the shot to tip the ball at the top of your jump with one hand. Using your strong hand, tip the ball high on the board 5 times in succession and then score into the basket. Use your weak hand next, tipping the ball 5 times in succession and then into the basket.

Success Goal =

    a. 5 successive strong-hand tips and a score

    b. 5 successive weak-hand tips and a score

Your Score =

    a. (#) _____ successive strong-hand tips and a score

    b. (#) _____ successive weak-hand tips and a score

5. Alternate Hand Tipping

Stand in front of the backboard to the side of the rim. In a balanced stance use your weak hand and shoot the ball high and softly on the backboard, so it rebounds to the opposite side. Move quickly to the other side of the basket, jump, and tip the ball using your strong hand, so it again rebounds to the opposite side. Now move quickly back to the first side of the basket, jump, and tip the ball using your weak hand. Continue tipping the ball high across the board, alternating hands as you tip, and then score on your last tip.

Success Goal = 3 successive, alternate hand tips and then a score

Your Score = (#) _____ successive, alternate hand tips and a score

6. Circle Rebounding

For this drill you need three players and a ball placed inside the free throw or center circle. Start as a defensive player. Assume a rebounding stance outside the circle facing the ball. An offensive player gets in a balanced stance behind you. The third player gives commands. On the command *go!* the offensive player will use an offensive rebounding method to try to get the ball while you block out, trying to keep the offensive player from getting the ball for 3 seconds. The command *stop!* should be given after the 3 seconds. Follow this with 4 repetitions (3 seconds each) with 10-second rest intervals in between. Players then rotate, going from defense to offense to giving commands.

Success Goal =

    a. 3 block outs in 5 attempts   b. 3 offensive rebounds in 5 attempts

Your Score = (#) _____ block outs; (#) _____ offensive rebounds

7. *Circle Rebounding With Front Turn*

This is similar to the previous drill. Here, though, the defense starts in a *defensive* stance *facing* the offensive player (whom you assume to be the shooter). On the command *go!* block out the offensive player, using a front turn. The opponent will again use an offensive rebounding method to try to get the ball, while you block out, trying to keep the offensive player from getting the ball for 3 seconds. The *stop!* command should be given after the 3 seconds, followed by 4 repetitions (3 seconds each) with 10-second rest intervals in between. Players then rotate, going from defense to offense to giving commands.

Success Goal =

    a. 3 block outs in 5 attempts   b. 3 offensive rebounds in 5 attempts

Your Score = (#) _____ block outs; (#) _____ offensive rebounds

8. *Circle Rebounding With Reverse Turn*

Here is another similar drill, where the defense, however, starts in a defensive stance from a *denial* position—with one foot and hand to the side of the offensive player whom you assume to be *without* the ball. On the command *go!* use a reverse turn, dropping the outside foot to block out the offensive player. That opponent will use an offensive rebounding method to try to get the ball while you block out, trying to keep the offensive player from getting the ball for 3 seconds, after which the *stop!* command will be given. Follow this with 4 repetitions (3 seconds each) with 10-second rest intervals in between. Again the procedure is to rotate from defense to offense to giving commands.

Success Goal =

    a. 3 block outs in 5 attempts   b. 3 offensive rebounds in 5 attempts

Your Score = (#) _____ block outs; (#) _____ offensive rebounds

9. *Block-Out-the-Shooter Rebounding*

For this drill you need one partner. You begin as a defensive player and the partner starts as a shooter. The shooter starts outside the free throw line with the ball, while you take a defensive stance facing your partner. Allow the shot and then use a front turn to block out the shooter and get the rebound of a missed shot. Meanwhile, the shooter will be trying to get an offensive rebound and, if successful, that player can shoot again from the spot of the rebound. Continue until you rebound, following this pattern for 5 missed shots with 10-second rest intervals in between shots. Rotate then from defense to offense.

Success Goal =

    a. 4 defensive rebounds from 5 missed shots   b. 2 offensive rebounds from 5 missed shots

Your Score = (#) _____ defensive rebounds; (#) _____ offensive rebounds

10. Block-Out-the-Player-Without-the-Ball Rebounding

This drill requires three players. You will be a defensive player rebounding against an offensive player without the ball, while a third player will be a shooter only. On one side of the floor (from at least 15 feet) the shooter intentionally tries to miss. On the opposite side of the basket (help side or weak side) you take a defensive stance that allows you to see the ball and the player without the ball whom you are guarding.

On the shot first observe your opponent's cut and then reverse turn, dropping the foot away from your opponent's cut in a backward direction. Block out and get the rebound. The offensive player will try to get an offensive rebound of a missed shot. If successful, that player can shoot again from the spot of the rebound. Continue until you rebound, following this pattern for 5 missed shots with 10-second rest intervals in between. Then rotate roles from defense to offense to shooter.

Success Goal =

a. 4 defensive rebounds in 5 missed shots   b. 2 offensive rebounds in 5 missed shots

Your Score = (#) _____ defensive rebounds; (#) _____ offensive rebounds

11. Three Players, Two Balls, Shooting, Passing, and Rebounding

This drill uses three players and two balls. There are three shooting areas with two shooting spots in each: right corner to right T (elbow), right T to left T, and left T to left corner.

The *shooter* (S) starts at one spot with a ball, shoots, and moves to the other spot. The rebounder (R) is positioned at the opposite side of the basket and the passer (P) at the opposite T or corner.

The shooter (S) starts, shooting the ball first in the right corner and then moving to the right T to receive the next ball. Face the basket to shoot, catching and shooting in one motion. Jump behind the ball if the pass is off target. Follow through until the ball reaches the basket before moving to the next spot.

After the shooter moves to the next shooting spot, the passer (P) starts with a ball at the opposite T and passes to the shooter. Be in triple-threat position to pass, facing the basket, and fake before passing to the shooter's far hand—without telegraphing the pass.

The third player (rebounder, R) rebounds the ball and passes it to the passer. Using two hands rebound without letting the ball hit the floor, land in balance keeping the ball high above your forehead, and fake before making a two-hand overhead outlet pass. Continue for 25 seconds (see Diagram a). After that you have 5 more seconds to rotate: The shooter (S) rotates to rebounder (R), the rebounder rotates to passer (P), and the passer rotates to shooter. After 90 seconds change to the second shooting area (see Diagram b), and after 3 minutes change to the third shooting area (see Diagram c). The drill takes 4-1/2 minutes, with each player getting at least 30 shots, 30 rebounds, and 30 passes. As a variation of the drill have one or more additional players or coaches put a hand up on the shooter, apply pressure to the passer, or knock the ball out of the rebounder's hand if the rebounder lowers the ball below forehead level.

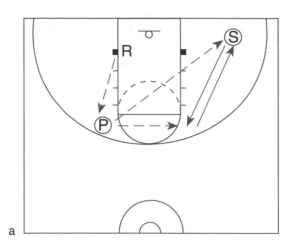
a

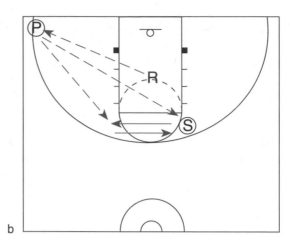
b

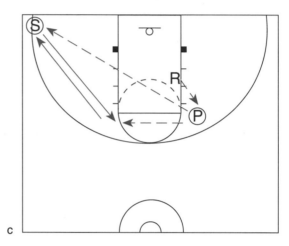
c

Success Goal =

a. 20 shots in 30 attempts

b. 24 accurate passes (to shooter's far hand) in 30 attempts

c. 24 two-hand rebounds in 30 attempts

Your Score =

a. (#) _____ shots made in
(#) _____ attempts

b. (#) _____ accurate passes in
(#) _____ attempts

c. (#) _____ two-hand rebounds in
(#) _____ attempts

Rebounding Checks

The team that controls the backboards usually controls the game. Wanting the ball is the most important factor in rebounding. The key to defensive rebounding is to *block out* your opponent and go for the ball. The key to offensive rebounding is to move.

Have a trained observer—your coach, teacher, or a skilled player—watch your defensive rebounding skills. Your observer can use the checklists in Figure 5.1 (to evaluate your defensive rebounding) and Figure 5.2 (to evaluate your offensive rebounding) and provide corrective feedback. Also, ask your coach to evaluate your rebounding in competition, paying particular attention to your desire to go after every rebound.

Step 6   Offensive Moves: Be a Triple Threat

Basketball is a team game. By playing together and complementing each other's talents, a team with less individual talent can beat a team with greater individual talent. This does not mean there is no place for one-on-one opportunities. On the contrary, they arise throughout basketball games.

Some players can score only when they receive open shots. Better players develop offensive moves and become triple threats—to shoot, pass, or drive. To be a triple threat you must be able to make the outside shot, pass to an open teammate in better scoring position, and drive to the basket and finish the play with a shot or a pass to an open teammate for the score.

WHY OFFENSIVE MOVES ARE IMPORTANT

Every time you receive the ball, you have the opportunity to use offensive moves with the ball against your defender in a one-on-one confrontation. You can help or hurt your team depending on what you do with the situation.

A selfish one-on-one player guns the ball or drives into trouble. Team defense where players off the ball give help to their teammate defending the ball prevent the selfish player from succeeding. As a team one-on-one player you can gain an advantage over your defender with a solid fake or penetrating drive that forces defensive help from another defender and creates an opening that enables you to pass to your teammate for a score. This concept of one-on-one basketball, called *draw and kick*, is an integral part of team play. There is no greater offensive play than drawing another defensive player to react to stop you and then passing to your open teammate who is spotting up for an easier shot. This concept of unselfish one-on-one basketball that creates openings for teammates is team basketball at its best. All-time greats Bob Cousy, Julius Erving, Magic Johnson, Larry Bird, and Michael Jordan were unselfish one-on-one players who used offensive moves to draw and kick to open teammates to score.

CLASSIFICATION OF MOVES

Offensive moves with the ball may be classified as low post (inside back to the basket) and one-on-one (outside facing the basket). The low post is the area close to the basket—inside the middle hash marks on the lane and below the dotted semicircle line in the lane. There are four basic low-post moves: drop-step baseline power move, drop-step middle hook, front-turn baseline bank jump shot, and front-turn baseline crossover and hook. There are six basic one-on-one moves:

1. drive-step jump shot
2. straight drive
3. crossover drive
4. straight-drive one-dribble jump shot
5. crossover-drive one-dribble jump shot
6. step-back one-dribble jump shot

GETTING OPEN TO RECEIVE A PASS IN THE LOW POST

When you are in the low post, try to seal (keep to one side) your defender by using your back, shoulder, and upper arm on that side. Do not allow your defender to get a foot in front of your foot. Your strategies will vary, depending on whether you want to get open when denied or when fronted.

Receiving a Pass When Denied

If your defender is in a denial position with a foot and hand in the passing lane between you and the ball, move a few steps away from the passer. Quickly cut back on one side of your defender toward the ball. Work to get open—using short, quick steps—and get position with a strong balanced stance, your feet spread at least shoulder-width apart, knees flexed, back straight, and hands up at ball-width apart for a target.

On the pass meet the ball, catching it with two hands. Use a jump stop landing outside the lane and above the box. The feet land at the same time on a jump stop, enabling you to use either one as a pivot foot. To keep from stepping forward after the catch, land with your weight initially back on your heels.

After the landing transfer your weight forward to the balls of your feet to get the balance you need to react and make an offensive move. Use a wide base and flex your knees. Protect the ball by keeping it in front of your forehead with your elbows out (see Figure 6.1).

Receiving a Pass When Fronted

If a defender completely fronts you, take your defender high by moving up the lane with short, quick steps to a position above the middle hash mark. Quickly cut to the basket, looking to receive a high lob, or alley-oop, pass. Cutting behind your defender toward the basket is called a *backdoor cut* (see Figure 6.1).

Figure 6.1   Keys to Success: Getting Open to Receive a Pass in the Low Post

When Denied

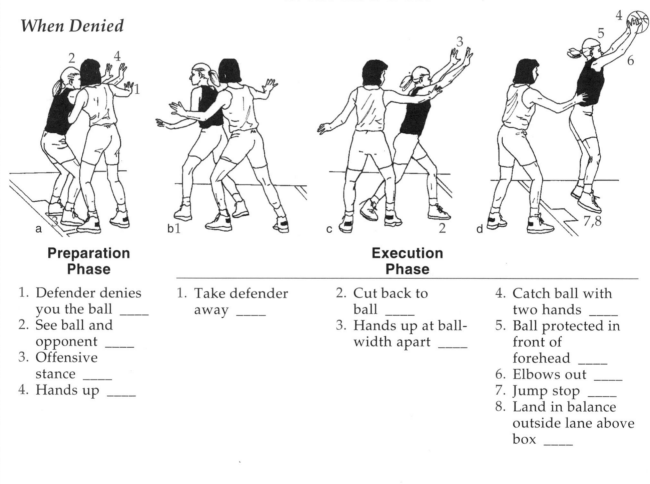

Preparation Phase

1. Defender denies you the ball ____
2. See ball and opponent ____
3. Offensive stance ____
4. Hands up ____

1. Take defender away ____

Execution Phase

2. Cut back to ball ____
3. Hands up at ball-width apart ____

4. Catch ball with two hands ____
5. Ball protected in front of forehead ____
6. Elbows out ____
7. Jump stop ____
8. Land in balance outside lane above box ____

When Fronted

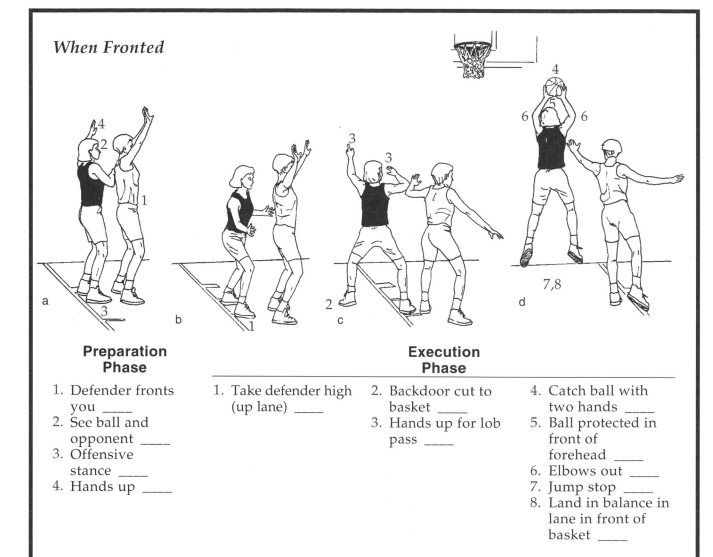

Preparation Phase

1. Defender fronts you ____
2. See ball and opponent ____
3. Offensive stance ____
4. Hands up ____

Execution Phase

1. Take defender high (up lane) ____

2. Backdoor cut to basket ____
3. Hands up for lob pass ____

4. Catch ball with two hands ____
5. Ball protected in front of forehead ____
6. Elbows out ____
7. Jump stop ____
8. Land in balance in lane in front of basket ____

HOW TO READ YOUR LOW POST DEFENDER

Reading the defense means determining how your defender is playing you so you can react with the correct move. It involves seeing your opponent or feeling your defender's body against you. In the low post you read the position by seeing or feeling whether your defender is on the topside (toward the foul line) or the baseline side. In both cases you would drop step with the foot opposite the side of your defender. If you cannot locate your defender or are in doubt, use a front turn toward the baseline to face the basket and see your defender's position.

Before receiving the ball, you can anticipate your defender's position by recognizing where the pass will be coming from (that is, the corner, wing, or high post area) and by being aware of your defender's position in trying to prevent the pass.

Executing the Drop-Step Baseline Power Move

After catching the ball in the low post and reading your defender's position on the *topside*, make a ball fake to the middle by showing the ball above your shoulder. After the fake move the ball to a protected position in front of your forehead with your elbows out. Drop step to the baseline with your inside (closer-to-backboard) foot. As you make your drop step, keep your weight on your pivot foot to avoid dragging it. Try to get your shoulders parallel with the backboard and your defender on your back. Maintain a strong balanced stance with your back straight and the ball protected in front of your forehead, away from your defender.

Make a power move toward the basket, jumping off both feet. Shoot the ball with two hands, keeping your shoulders parallel to the board and without opening up on the shot. Aim the ball high above the box. Land in balance, ready to rebound a possible miss with two hands. Go up again with as many power moves as it takes to score (see Figure 6.2).

Figure 6.2   Keys to Success: Low Post Drop-Step Moves

Drop-Step Baseline Power Move

Preparation Phase

1. Jump stop as you catch ball ____
2. Balanced stance ____
3. Ball protected in front of forehead ____
4. Elbows out ____
5. Read defender topside ____
6. Ball fake middle ____

Execution Phase

1. Drop step baseline ____
2. Balanced stance ____
3. Ball protected in front of forehead ____
4. Elbows out ____
5. Shot fake ____

6. Make power move ____
7. Two-foot jump ____
8. Shoot with two hands ____

Follow-Through Phase

1. Land in balance ____
2. Hands up ____

3. Ready to rebound ____

Executing the Drop-Step Middle Hook

After catching the ball in the low post and reading your defender's position on the *baseline side*, make a ball fake to the baseline by showing the ball above your shoulder. After the fake drop step to the baseline with your outside (away-from-the-backboard) foot. As you make the drop step, move the ball to

hook shot position with your shooting hand under the ball and your balance hand behind and slightly on top of the ball: Hold the ball back, protecting it with your head and shoulders rather than leading with it. Pivot in toward the basket. Shoot a hook shot. Land in balance, ready to rebound a possible miss with two hands, and use a power move to score (see below).

Drop-Step Middle Hook

Preparation Phase

1. Jump stop as you catch ball ____
2. Balanced stance ____
3. Ball protected in front of forehead ____
4. Elbows out ____
5. Read defender baseline side ____
6. Ball fake baseline ____

Execution Phase

1. Drop step middle ____
2. Balanced stance ____
3. Hands in hook shot position ____
4. Hold ball back and protect with head and shoulders ____
5. Shoot hook shot ____
6. Two hands on ball until release ____

Follow-Through Phase

1. Land in balance ____
2. Hands up ____
3. Ready to rebound ____

EXECUTING THE LOW POST FRONT-TURN BASELINE MOVES

After catching the ball in the low post if you cannot see or feel your defender, make a front turn to the baseline to see your defender. On your front turn make an aggressive drive step

and shot fake. A drive step is a short (8- to 10-inch) jab step with one foot straight at the basket that should make your defender react with a retreat step. See the rim and your defender. Be a triple threat to shoot, pass, or drive. Hold the ball with your hands in shooting position. It is important to keep your balance and not rush. Depending on your defender's reaction, you can then execute either a front-turn baseline bank jump shot or a front-turn baseline crossover and hook.

Baseline Bank Jump Shot

If your defender retreats on your drive step, shoot a bank jump shot. Aim for the top near corner of the box on the backboard. Land in balance, ready to rebound a possible miss with two hands, and use a power move to score (see Figure 6.3).

Baseline Crossover and Hook

If your defender extends up on your shot fake, make a crossover step to the middle with the same foot you used for the drive step. As you cross over to the middle, aggressively move the ball across the front of your body to hook shot position. Hold the ball back, protecting it with your head and shoulders. Pivot in toward the basket and shoot a hook shot. Land in balance, ready to rebound a possible miss with two hands, and use a power move to score (see Figure 6.3).

Figure 6.3   Keys to Success: Low Post Front-Turn Baseline Moves

Front-Turn Baseline Bank Jump Shot

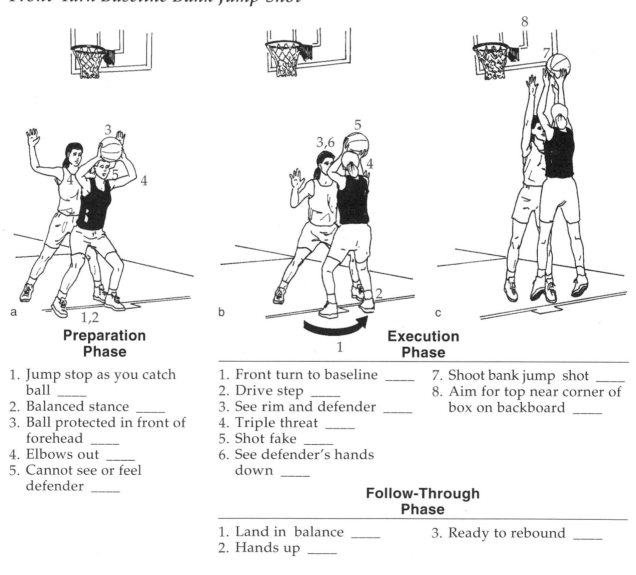

Preparation Phase

1. Jump stop as you catch ball ____
2. Balanced stance ____
3. Ball protected in front of forehead ____
4. Elbows out ____
5. Cannot see or feel defender ____

Execution Phase

1. Front turn to baseline ____
2. Drive step ____
3. See rim and defender ____
4. Triple threat ____
5. Shot fake ____
6. See defender's hands down ____
7. Shoot bank jump shot ____
8. Aim for top near corner of box on backboard ____

Follow-Through Phase

1. Land in balance ____
2. Hands up ____
3. Ready to rebound ____

Front-Turn Baseline Crossover and Hook

 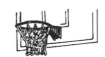 

a   1,2

b   1

c   7

d   10

**Preparation
Phase**

1. Jump stop as you catch ball ____
2. Balanced stance ____
3. Ball protected in front of forehead ____
4. Elbows out ____
5. Cannot see or feel defender ____

1. Front turn to baseline ____
2. Drive step ____
3. See rim and defender ____
4. Triple threat ____
5. Shot fake ____
6. See defender's hands up ____

**Execution
Phase**

7. Crossover step to middle ____
8. Hands in hook shot position ____
9. Hold ball back and protect with head and shoulders ____

10. Pivot in toward basket ____
11. Shoot hook shot ____
12. Two hands on ball until release ____

**Follow-Through
Phase**

1. Land in balance ____
2. Hands up ____

3. Ready to rebound ____

Detecting Errors in Low-Post Moves

The most common errors in low-post moves are listed here, along with suggestions to correct them.

ERROR   **CORRECTION**

ERROR	CORRECTION
1. You land with a one-two stop and can use only one foot as a pivot.	1. Land with a jump stop.

ERROR 🚫   **CORRECTION**

2. You dribble the ball before making your move.

2. Make your move without dribbling: Learn to save the dribble until after your crossover step, when you can fake a hook and then either dribble by your defender or reverse dribble for a power move.

3. You rush into the move before reading your defender's position.

3. After receiving a pass in the low post, stop for at least one count to take time to read your defender's position—then make your move.

4. Still in doubt about your defender's position, you front turn to the middle, which limits your moves to a jump shot to the middle or a crossover and hook from the baseline, which are both difficult.

4. When in doubt, always front turn to the baseline so you can use the bank jump shot or the crossover to the middle and hook.

GETTING OPEN TO RECEIVE A PASS ON THE PERIMETER

You may be a fine shooter and execute good offensive moves but if you cannot get open to receive the ball when you are being defended, all this ability with the ball is worthless. When you move to get open, try to see the ball, the basket, and your defender. If you don't see a ball being passed to you, the result will be a turnover and missed scoring opportunity.

Move to free yourself: You cannot stand still! Constantly change pace and direction. Creating space between players—often neglected—is important. Work for 12 to 15 feet of space, enough to keep one defender from guarding two offensive players. Try to move to an open area or to create an angle for an open passing lane between you and the passer. When the defender is denying you a passing lane on the perimeter, overplaying the passing lane between you and the passer, make a *backdoor cut* to the basket. If you still do not receive a pass after the backdoor cut, change direction and cut back to the outside. This is called a *V-cut*. Get open to receive the ball within your shooting range. Your *shooting range* is the distance within which you can consistently make an outside shot.

There are two methods for receiving the ball, depending on whether you are open or closely guarded. You read in Step 3 about catching the ball when you are open in position to shoot. Catching the ball when you are closely guarded in the scoring area requires a different technique.

CATCHING THE BALL WHEN CLOSELY GUARDED IN THE SCORING AREA

When you are closely guarded, come to *meet the pass*. By meeting the pass you can beat your defender to the ball.

Give the passer a good target. Your hands should be up above your waist for straight passes, above your head for lob passes, and above your knees (but below your waist) for bounce passes. Catch the ball with your hands in a relaxed position, giving with the ball as you catch it.

Land with a one-two stop. It is good to land first on your inside foot (the foot closer to the basket), establishing it as a pivot foot. You can then protect the ball with your body while you are in position to execute a reverse turn (drop step) with your opposite foot, should your defender overcommit going for the pass. After receiving the ball, use a front turn, face the basket, and see the rim. Focusing on the rim allows you to see the total picture, including whether your defender is playing you for the shot, drive, or pass. Hold the ball between your chest and waist with your hands in block-and-tuck position. Be a triple threat to shoot, drive, or pass.

EXECUTING THE TRIPLE-THREAT STANCE

When you receive the ball face the basket and your defender (also called *square up*). Being square to the basket positions you well as a triple threat to shoot, pass, or drive. See the rim and your defender. By focusing on the rim you can see more of the court and whether a teammate is open in position to score. You can also see your defender to read whether you are being played up close for a shot or back for a pass or drive.

Move the ball between shooting, passing, and driving positions, keeping it close to your chest and never lower than your waist. Your hands should remain in shooting position. You must first be a threat to shoot before the options of passing or driving become viable.

Make an aggressive drive step (also called a *jab step*). A drive step is a short (8-10 inches), quick step with your nonpivot foot straight toward your defender. Your weight should be on your pivot foot, with your knees flexed and your upper body erect. A drive step is used to fake a drive and force your defender to react with a retreat step (see Figure 6.4).

Figure 6.4   Keys to Success: *Triple-Threat Stance*

1. See rim and defender ____
2. Head over waist ____
3. Back straight ____
4. Block-and-tuck hand position ____
5. Ball moving close to chest ____
6. Knees flexed ____
7. Feet shoulder-width apart ____
8. Weight on pivot (back) foot ____
9. Short drive step with shooting foot ____

Detecting Errors in the Triple-Threat Stance

The most common errors in the triple-threat stance are listed here, along with suggestions to correct them.

ERROR	CORRECTION
1. You face your body toward the left or right, limiting your move with the ball to that direction.	1. Square up to the basket with your body facing the basket and defender in good position for a shot, pass, or drive to the right or left.
2. You hold the ball too far from your body, allowing your defender to grab it.	2. Keep the ball close to your chest and no lower than your waist as you move it between shooting, passing, and driving positions.
3. You lower the ball, limiting your offensive moves to a drive, or you raise the ball over your head, limiting your offensive moves to an overhead pass.	3. Keep the ball moving close to your chest so you are a triple threat to shoot, pass, or drive.

ERROR	CORRECTION
4. Your hands are on the sides of the ball and you must take time to adjust them to shoot, preventing you from shooting quickly.	4. Keep your hands in block-and-tuck shooting position on the ball so you can shoot quickly. By first being a threat to shoot, you will open the options to pass or drive. It is also easier to change from a shooting to a passing hand position than the opposite.

HOW TO READ YOUR DEFENDER WHEN FACING THE BASKET

Reading the defense when you are being guarded on the perimeter entails first determining how your defender reacts to your aggressive drive step and then reacting with the correct offensive move. From your triple-threat stance there are six basic one-on-one moves (see Classification of Moves), all starting with the drive step. Which move you choose depends on your defensive player's position in reaction to your drive step.

When your defender's hands are down, bring your drive step foot back to shooting position and shoot a jump shot. When your defender has a hand up to play your shot, drive the side the raised hand is on. The weakness in a defender's stance is the lead foot (the foot that is forward, or up). It is more difficult for your defender to stop a drive toward the lead foot because it necessitates a long drop step with that foot while reverse pivoting on the back foot. A drive toward the defender's back foot necessitates only a short retreat step. In a normal defensive stance, the hand your defender has up will be on the same side as the lead foot. Rather than looking down to check which foot is up, simply see which hand is up and drive to that side. Whichever hand is up is the side of your defender's lead foot and weakness. With your defender's hand up on the side of your drive step, use a straight drive. With your defender's hand up on the side away from your drive step, use a crossover drive.

Being a triple threat, making a drive step, and reading your defender's reaction and hand position are all extremely important. Do not rush: Keep your balance physically, mentally, and emotionally. Only by maintaining control and reading your defender can you successfully execute a one-on-one offensive move.

Drive-Step Jump Shot

If your defender's hands are down, quickly bring your drive-step foot back into a balanced shooting stance and make a jump shot (see Figure 6.5).

Straight Drive

If your defender's hand is up on the side of your drive step, take a longer step (with your drive-step foot) past your defender's lead foot. Take a long dribble with your outside (away-from-defender) hand and then push off your pivot foot, keeping your head up with eyes on the basket. The ball must leave your hand before you lift your pivot foot off the floor or it will be a traveling violation. Having your weight on your pivot foot during your drive step helps prevent traveling. Protect the ball with your inside hand and your body.

Drive in a straight line to the basket, close to your defender. Cut off your defender's retreat by closing the gap between your body and your defender's retreat step. After driving by your defender, see the basket and be alert for defensive help. You may decide to finish the play by going strong to the basket for a layup, exploding on your takeoff and protecting the ball with two hands (see Figure 6.5).

If a teammate's defender attempts to pick you up, pass to an open teammate who can score.

Crossover Drive

This one-on-one move is similar to the straight drive except that you cross the ball over in front of your chest and crossover step with your drive-step foot past your defender's lead foot. Then take a long dribble with your outside hand and continue as in the straight drive (see Figure 6.5).

Figure 6.5   Keys to Success: Drive-Step Moves

Drive-Step Jump Shot

Preparation Phase	**Execution Phase**		**Follow-Through Phase**
a	b	c	d

Preparation Phase

1. Triple-threat stance ____
2. See rim and defender ____
3. Short drive step ____
4. Read defender's hand down ____

Execution Phase

1. Bring drive step foot back ____
2. Shoot jump shot ____

Follow-Through Phase

1. Land in balance ____
2. Hand up until ball reaches basket ____
3. Ready to rebound or get back on defense ____

Drive-Step Straight Drive

 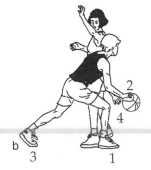  

a   b   c   d

Preparation Phase

1. Triple-threat stance ____
2. See rim and defender ____
3. Short drive step ____
4. Read defender's hand up on side of drive step ____

Execution Phase

1. Long step past defender's lead foot ____
2. Dribble ball past defender with outside hand ____
3. Push off pivot foot ____
4. Protect ball with inside hand ____
5. Close gap between your body and defender's retreat step ____
6. Pick ball up at shooting knee ____
7. Shooting hand on top of ball ____
8. Shoot layup or pass ____
9. Protect ball with two hands until release ____
10. Land in balance ____
11. Ready to rebound ____

Drive-Step Crossover Drive

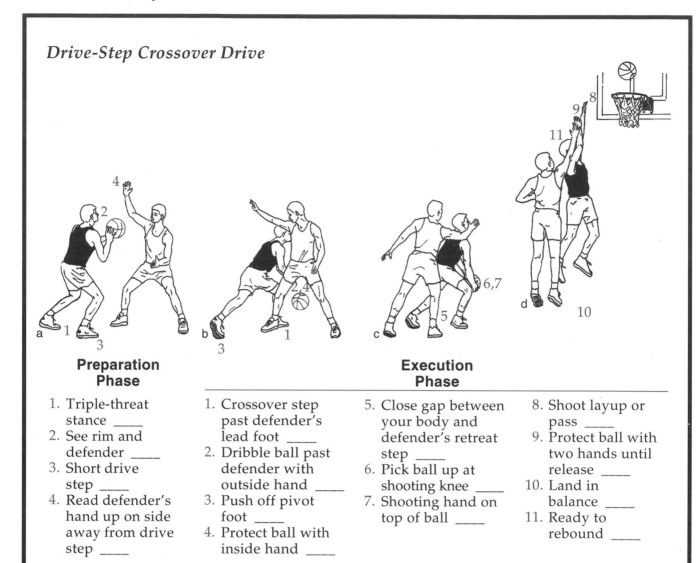

Preparation Phase

1. Triple-threat stance ____
2. See rim and defender ____
3. Short drive step ____
4. Read defender's hand up on side away from drive step ____

1. Crossover step past defender's lead foot ____
2. Dribble ball past defender with outside hand ____
3. Push off pivot foot ____
4. Protect ball with inside hand ____

Execution Phase

5. Close gap between your body and defender's retreat step ____
6. Pick ball up at shooting knee ____
7. Shooting hand on top of ball ____

8. Shoot layup or pass ____
9. Protect ball with two hands until release ____
10. Land in balance ____
11. Ready to rebound ____

HOW TO EXECUTE THE STRAIGHT-DRIVE ONE-DRIBBLE JUMP SHOT

From a triple-threat stance make an aggressive drive step. Stop and read your defender's hand position. If your defender's hand is up on the *same side* as your drive step, take a longer step (with your drive-step foot) past your defender's lead foot. Take one long dribble with your outside (away-from-defender) hand, and then push off your pivot foot. Aim your dribble for a spot past your defender's body, keeping your eyes on the basket. Protect the ball with your inside hand and body.

Move under your defender's arm and jump behind your defender's body. This move makes it difficult for your defender to block your shot without fouling you. If you go too wide, your defender will have time and space to block your shot. Pick the ball up in front of your shooting knee with your hands in block-and-tuck position and your shooting hand on top of the ball. Protect the ball with your head and shoulders and move it away from your defender's reach as you shoot a jump shot (see Figure 6.6).

Crossover-Drive One-Dribble Jump Shot

The crossover-drive one-dribble jump shot is similar to the straight drive one-dribble jump shot. If your defender's hand is up on the side *away* from your drive step, before the dribble cross the ball over in front of your chest. Crossover step with your drive-step foot past your defender's lead foot (see Figure 6.6).

Step-Back One-Dribble Jump Shot

If your defender makes a retreat step, take a quick step back away from your defender on the same foot you used for your drive step. Dribble back with your strong hand, jump behind the ball, and pick it up in front of your shooting knee with your shooting hand on top of the ball. Shoot a jump shot. It is important to pick the ball up at your knee and exaggerate your follow-through to counter any tendency to fade back on your shot (see Figure 6.6).

Figure 6.6   *Keys to Success:* **One-Dribble Jump Shots**

Straight-Drive Jump Shot

Preparation Phase

1. Triple-threat stance ____
2. See rim and defender ____
3. Short drive step ____
4. Read defender's hand up on side of drive step ____

Execution Phase

1. Long step past defender's lead foot ____
2. Dribble ball behind defender's body with outside hand ____
3. Push off pivot foot ____
4. Protect ball with inside hand ____

5. Move under defender's arm ____
6. Jump behind defender's body ____
7. Pick ball up at shooting knee ____
8. Shooting hand on top of ball ____

9. Protect ball with head and shoulders ____
10. Move ball away from defender ____
11. Expect to be fouled ____
12. Shoot jump shot ____

Crossover-Drive Jump Shot

Preparation Phase

1. Triple-threat stance ____
2. See rim and defender ____
3. Short drive step ____
4. Read defender's hand up on side away from drive step ____

Execution Phase

1. Crossover step past defender's lead foot ____
2. Dribble ball behind defender's body with outside hand ____
3. Push off pivot foot ____
4. Protect ball with inside hand ____
5. Move under defender's arm ____
6. Jump behind defender's body ____
7. Pick ball up at shooting knee ____
8. Shooting hand on top of ball ____
9. Protect ball with head and shoulders ____
10. Move ball away from defender ____
11. Expect to be fouled ____
12. Shoot jump shot ____

Step-Back Jump Shot

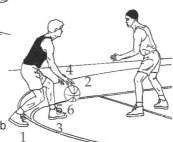

Preparation Phase	Execution Phase		Follow-Through Phase

Preparation Phase

1. Triple-threat stance ____
2. See rim and defender ____
3. Short drive step ____
4. Read defender's retreat on drive step ____

Execution Phase

1. Step back with drive-step foot ____
2. Dribble ball back with strong hand ____
3. Push off pivot foot ____
4. Protect ball with nondribbling hand ____
5. Pick ball up at shooting knee ____
6. Shooting hand on top of ball ____
7. Shoot jump shot ____
8. Exaggerate follow-through ____

Follow-Through Phase

1. Land in balance ____
2. Hand up until ball reaches basket ____
3. Ready to react for long rebound or get back on defense ____

Detecting Errors in Offensive Moves Facing the Basket

The most common errors in offensive moves facing the basket are listed here, along with suggestions to correct them.

ERROR 🚫

CORRECTION

ERROR	CORRECTION
1. You rush into your move before reading your defender's position.	1. After receiving a pass, take time to read your defender's position—then make your move.

ERROR   **CORRECTION**

2. You dribble the ball before making your move.	2. Make your move without dribbling: Learn to save your dribble.
3. Under pressure from your defender you lean back, losing your balance and aggressiveness.	3. Use an aggressive drive step to make your defender retreat.
4. You make your drive step too long or you lean, putting weight on your drive-step foot. This limits your ability to quickly move your lead foot in reaction to how your defender plays you.	4. Keep your weight on your pivot foot as you execute your drive step. This enables you to move your lead foot quickly to shoot, pass, or use a straight or crossover drive.
5. As you drive, you look down at your dribble.	5. Keep your head up as you dribble. The ball is round and will bounce straight: You will learn to feel for it while seeing it with peripheral vision. Focus on the rim and see the total picture so you have a better chance of making your shot or reacting to the defense with a pass to an open teammate.
6. On a drive to the basket you dribble too wide, allowing your defender more time to recover against your drive.	6. Dribble behind your defender to close the gap and cut off your defender's retreat step.
7. On a one-dribble jump shot you dribble too wide, allowing your defender time and space to block your shot.	7. Move under your defender's arm and jump past your defender's body, making it difficult for your defender to block your shot without fouling you.

Drills for Offensive Moves

1. Low-Post Moves

This drill covers the four low-post moves; that is, the drop-step baseline power move, drop-step middle hook, front-turn baseline bank jump shot, and front-turn baseline crossover and hook. When you practice each of them, begin by tossing and catching the ball in the low post. Starting under the basket, toss the ball so it will bounce at a low-post spot outside the lane and above the box on the lane line. Catch the ball with your back to the basket and make a jump stop, landing outside the lane and above the box. Catching the ball in the low post with your back to the basket, first look to your baseline side to determine the position of your defender.

a. Drop-Step Baseline Power Move. Assume your defender is not on your baseline side. Make a shot fake to the middle, and then protect the ball at your forehead. Make a drop step toward the baseline with your inside (closer-to-basket) foot, followed by another shot fake. Add a strong power move, jumping off both feet and keeping your shoulders parallel to the backboard as you shoot the ball with two hands. Aim the ball high above the box.

b. Drop-Step Middle Hook Shot. Assume your defender is on your baseline side. Make a shot fake to the baseline and then bring the ball to hook shot position with your shooting hand under the ball. Make a drop step toward the middle with your outside (farther-from-basket) foot, see the rim, and shoot a hook shot.

c. Front-Turn Baseline Bank Jump Shot. Assume you must use a front turn to determine the position of your defender. Make a front turn to the baseline, drive step, and see the rim. On your drive step show the ball, high faking a jump shot. Be a triple threat to shoot, pass, or drive. Aim for the top near corner of the backboard box and shoot a bank jump shot.

d. Front-Turn Baseline Crossover and Hook Shot. Make a front turn to the baseline and fake a shot, holding for a count of one before making your next move. Take a crossover step to the middle, aggressively moving the ball across the front of your body into hook shot position, with your shooting hand under the ball, and shoot a hook shot.

On each move land in balance, ready to rebound and go up again with as many power moves as necessary to score. Alternately toss the ball to the right, making each move on the right side of the basket, and to the left, making each move on the left side of the basket.

Success Goal = 5 consecutive shots on each move and from each side

Your Score =

a. (#) _____ consecutive drop-step baseline power moves made from right-side low post;
   (#) _____ from left-side low post

b. (#) _____ consecutive drop-step middle hook shots made from right-side low post;
   (#) _____ from left-side low post

c. (#) _____ consecutive front-turn baseline bank jump shots made from right-side low post;
   (#) _____ from left-side low post

d. (#) _____ consecutive front-turn baseline crossover and hook shots made from right-side low post;
   (#) _____ from left-side low post

2. Low Post Read-the-Defense

This drill gives you low-post practice in reading how your defender is playing you and reacting with the correct move. Select a partner to be a defensive player, defending you only until you read the defense and select the correct move—not while you make your move. After you catch the ball in the low post, your defender will vary the defensive positions—baseline side, topside, or off of you—to give you practice in making the correct decision. When you see or feel your defender on the topside (toward the foul line) or from the baseline side, drop step with the foot opposite the side of your defender and make the appropriate move. If you cannot locate your defender or are in doubt, use a front turn toward the baseline to face the basket and see your defender's position. After your front turn your partner's role will vary, playing you with a hand up or hands down. If your defender's hands are down, make a bank jump shot. If your defender's hand is up, use a crossover step to the middle, and shoot a hook shot. Continue the drill for 10 shots, awarding yourself 1 point for each correct read of the defense and 1 point for each shot you make.

Success Goal = 16 of 20 possible points

Your Score = (#) _____ points

3. *Low Post One-on-One in the Half Circle*

This competitive game develops your ability to read your defender and to use fakes, pivots, and different low-post moves to score or draw a foul. It also develops defense and rebounding. You will play offense against your partner who will play defense. Use the lower half of the free throw circle as a boundary. Your objective is to score with a low-post move. You may not dribble the ball but you may take one step outside of the lower half circle before releasing the ball on your shot.

The defender initiates play by getting in a defensive stance and then handing you the ball. You get 2 points each time you score. If you get fouled making the shot, you get a free throw. If you get fouled missing the shot, you get 2 free throws. If you miss the shot but get an offensive rebound, you may make a move and score from the spot where you rebounded the ball. Again, dribbling is not allowed. Continue the play until the offensive player scores or turns the ball over, or until the defender gets the ball on a steal or rebound and dribbles back past the free throw line. Switch offense and defense roles then with your partner. As a variation, start on offense with a ball and your back to the basket. The defender initiates play by touching the offensive player. Another variation is starting with your back to the basket in the low post on either side of the lane.

Success Goal = Score more points than your partner with 7 points winning the game

Your Score = (#) _____ your points; (#) _____ partner's points

4. *Chair Drill One-on-One Moves*

There are six one-on-one moves off a drive step to practice in this drill: drive-step jump shot, straight drive, crossover drive, straight-drive one-dribble jump shot, crossover-drive one-dribble jump shot, and the step-back one-dribble jump shot. Position a chair inside the free throw line to serve as an imaginary defender. To practice start at one of the elbows and toss the ball so it bounces at the free throw line and behind the chair. You are passing the ball to yourself (use a tossback if one is available). Catch the ball with a one-two stop. Your inside (closer-to-the-basket) foot should land first, making it your pivot foot. Make a front turn to the middle, drive step, and see the rim. Assume a triple-threat stance to shoot, pass, or drive.

   a. Drive-Step Jump Shot. After making the drive step, assume your defender's hands are down, and make a jump shot.

   b. Straight Drive. After making your drive step, assume your defender's outside hand is up. Make an aggressive shot fake and then a straight step by the chair, with the same foot you used for the drive step. Dribble beyond the chair with your outside hand, drive to the basket, and shoot a layup—making sure your pivot foot doesn't leave the floor before you release the ball on your shot. Use your inside hand for protection and keep your body close to the chair to cut off your imaginary defender's retreat step. After shooting a layup, land in balance ready to rebound and make as many power moves as necessary to score.

   c. Crossover Drive. After your drive step assume your defender's *inside* hand is up. Make an aggressive shot fake and then a crossover step by the chair, with the same foot you used for your drive step. On your crossover step aggressively move the ball across the front of your body. Dribble beyond the chair with your outside hand, drive to the basket, and shoot a layup. From this point continue as with the straight drive.

   d. Straight-Drive One-Dribble Jump Shot. After your drive step assume your defender's *outside* hand is up. Make an aggressive shot fake and then a straight step by the chair with the same foot you used for the drive step. Aim your dribble behind the chair. Dribble with your outside hand, jump behind the ball, and pick it up at your shooting knee with your shooting hand on top. Make a jump shot. Imagine that you are driving under your defender's arm, and keep your body close to the chair (imaginary defender) to prevent your shot being blocked. Use your head and shoulders for protection and try to draw a foul as you shoot for a possible 3-point play. After shooting land in balance, ready to rebound and make as many power moves as it takes to score.

e. Crossover-Drive One-Dribble Jump Shot. After the drive step assume your defender's *inside* hand is up. Make an aggressive shot fake and then a crossover step by the chair with the same foot you used for your drive step. On your crossover step aggressively move the ball across the front of your body, aiming your dribble for a spot behind the chair. Continue as you did in the straight-drive one-dribble jump shot.

f. Step-Back One-Dribble Jump Shot. After your drive step, assume this time that your defender makes a *retreat* step. Make a quick step back away from the chair with the same foot you used for your drive step. Dribble back with your strong hand and jump behind the ball. Shoot a jump shot. It is important to pick the ball up in front of your knee (with your shooting hand on top of the ball) and to exaggerate your follow-through to counter any tendency to fade back on your shot.

Alternately toss the ball to the right, making each move on the right side of the basket, and to the left, making each move on the left side of the basket.

Success Goal = 8 of 10 shots made off each jump-shot move and 10 of 10 layups made off each drive move

Your Score =

Shots made after tossing ball from	left elbow	right elbow
a. Jump shots	(#) _____	(#) _____
b. Straight-drive layups	(#) _____	(#) _____
c. Crossover-drive layups	(#) _____	(#) _____
d. Straight-drive one-dribble jump shots	(#) _____	(#) _____
e. Crossover-drive one-dribble jump shots	(#) _____	(#) _____
f. Step-back one-dribble jump shots	(#) _____	(#) _____

5. *One-on-One Read-the-Defense*

This drill gives you one-on-one practice in reading how your defender is playing you and reacting with the correct move. Select a partner to be a defensive player, defending you only until you read the defense and select the correct move—not while you make your move. After you catch the ball at the free throw line, your defender will vary the defensive positions—hands down or left or right hand up—to give you practice in making the correct decision. If you see your defender's hands down, shoot a jump shot. If you see your defender's hand up, drive to the side of that hand up with the appropriate straight drive or crossover drive. With your defender's hand up you also can use a straight or crossover one-dribble jump shot. If your defender retreats on your drive step, use the step-back one-dribble jump shot. Continue the drill until you have taken 10 shots. Award yourself 1 point for each correct read of the defense and 1 point for each shot made.

Success Goal = 16 of 20 possible points

Your Score = (#) _____ points

6. One-on-One in the Circle (One Dribble)

This competitive game develops ability to read your defender and to use fakes, pivots, and one-on-one moves to score or draw a foul. It also develops defense and rebounding.

You will play offense against a partner who will play defense. Use the full free throw circle as a boundary. Your objective is to score with a one-on-one move. You may use one dribble and may take one step outside of the circle before releasing the ball on your shot. The defender initiates play by getting in a defensive stance and then handing you the ball. You get 2 points each time you score. If you get fouled on a successful shot, you get a free throw. If you get fouled missing the shot, you get two free throws. If you miss the shot but get an offensive rebound, you may make a move and score from the spot where you rebounded the ball. Again, only one dribble is allowed. Continue the play until the offensive player scores or turns the ball over, or until the defender gets the ball on a steal or rebound and dribbles back past the free throw line. Switch offense and defense roles with your partner.

Success Goal = Score more points than your partner with 7 points winning the game

Your Score = (#) _____ your points; (#) _____ partner's points

7. Position One-on-One (Three Dribbles)

This competitive game also develops ability to read your defender and to use fakes, pivots, and one-on-one moves to score or draw a foul. It develops defense and rebounding. Proceed as with the previous drill, One-on-One in the Circle, but vary the game by starting at different positions, such as top, wing, and corner on each side of the court within your shooting range. Your objective again is to score with a one-on-one move but this time you may use *three* dribbles.

Success Goal = Score more points than your partner with 7 points winning the game

Your Score = (#) _____ your points; (#) _____ partner's points

8. One-on-One Pressure the Shooter

Work with a partner. You will play offense against your partner, who will play defense. Be in position to catch and shoot at the 3-point line (or within your shooting range). The defensive player starts under the basket by making a chest pass to your shooting hand. The defender then runs at you, attempting to pressure your shot without blocking it. You get a point each time you make a successful shot. After each attempt, switch offense and defense roles with your partner.

Success Goal = Score more points than your partner, with each of you taking 10 shots

Your Score = (#) _____ your points; (#) _____ partner's points

9. One-on-One Block the Shot

Work with a partner. You will play offense against your partner, who will play defense. Be in position to catch and shoot at the 3-point line (or within your shooting range). The defensive player starts under the basket by making a chest pass to your shooting hand. The defender then runs by you, attempting to block your shot. As the defender runs by you attempting to block your shot, make a shot fake, then take one dribble away from the shot blocker, and shoot a jump shot. You get a point each time you make a successful shot. After each attempt, switch offense and defense roles with your partner.

Success Goal = Score more points than your partner, with each of you taking 10 shots

Your Score = (#) _____ your points; (#) _____ partner's points

10. Dribble One-on-One

This is a variation of drills 6 and 7. The defender starts under the basket and makes a chest pass to you before quickly moving to meet you in a defensive position. Dribble at your defender, and use a footfire dribble as you meet. The footfire dribble is simply a rapid up-and-down moving of your feet that normally causes your defender to freeze for a second. It also allows you to gain balance, read your defender's position, and then make the appropriate one-on-one move. Scoring is the same as in drills 6 and 7.

Success Goal = Score more points than your partner with 7 points winning the game

Your Score = (#) _____ your points; (#) _____ partner's points

Offensive Moves Checks

The best players develop offensive moves and become triple threats—able to shoot, pass, or drive. You can help your team by using an offensive move to gain an advantage over your defender that forces defensive help from another defender and creates an opening for you to pass to your teammate for a score.

Have a trained observer—your coach, teacher, or a skilled player—evaluate your ability to get open, your triple-threat stance, and your low-post and one-on-one moves. The observer can use the checklists in Figures 6.1 to 6.6 to evaluate your performance and provide corrective feedback. Also, ask your coach to evaluate your decisions in reading your defender and reacting with the correct move.

Step 7   Two and Three Person Plays: Move Without the Ball

Basketball is a team game. Having the most talented players does not mean that your team will win. You must play as a team to win. Your team's success depends on your working together to allow all team members to fully utilize their offensive talents. On offense, the goal of your team is to score. This involves helping each other to create opportunities to get the best shot possible each time your team has possession of the ball. Only one of the team's five players can have the ball at a time, meaning that about 80 percent of the time you will be playing without the ball.

To help your team create scoring opportunities you must be able to move without the ball. Moving without the ball includes helping yourself or a teammate get open by setting or cutting off a screen and keeping your defender focused on your movements away from the ball, limiting defensive help on the ball.

Players tend not to move without the ball. Some players give more attention to their own scoring opportunities than to helping a teammate score. When you learn to move without the ball, you will not only make yourself a better player but also have more fun. The knowledge that you are helping your teammates brings its own satisfaction in addition to the acknowledgment you receive from an appreciative coach, teammates, and fans.

WHY MOVING WITHOUT THE BALL IS IMPORTANT

No matter how good your offensive skills with the ball, they will not help if you cannot get open to use them. First you must move to get open to receive the ball where you can be in position as a triple threat to shoot, drive, or pass. You also must move without the ball to provide opportunities for the shots you and your teammates want, such as an inside post-up, a one-on-one drive, or a jump shot that you can shoot in rhythm and range. Before shooting, you or your teammate must get open. Moving without the ball not only

includes getting yourself open, but setting and moving off screens to enable your teammate to get open.

Moving without the ball is also important when you are away from the ball. When your opponent is uncertain of your position, it is difficult for your defender to be alert to giving defensive help to a teammate guarding the player who has the ball.

Some specific opportunities for moving without the ball are to

- use various maneuvers to get open to receive the ball in position to be a triple threat to shoot, pass, or drive,
- set a screen on or off the ball, enabling a teammate to get open or forcing a switch that will get you open,
- cut off a screen to get yourself open or to force a switch that will get the screener open,
- keep moving, away from the ball, to make it difficult for your defender to see both you and the ball or to be in position to give defensive help to a teammate guarding the player with the ball,
- be alert to go after loose balls or to change from offense to defense when your team loses possession,
- move on a shot to get offensive rebound position or to get back on defense.

EXECUTING THE V-CUT

When your defender has a foot and hand in the passing lane to deny you from catching the ball, take your opponent toward the basket and then sharply change direction, cutting back to the outside. This is called a *V-cut*, and is the most commonly used way of getting open. You can use a V-cut from any position on the floor if an opponent is overplaying the passing lane between you and the passer.

The effectiveness of a V-cut depends on deception, timing, and changing direction sharply from cutting toward the basket to cutting back out. When you take a defender toward the basket, be deceptive before changing direction to cut back to the outside. Time your cut back out to coincide with the delivery of the pass.

As you change direction use a two-count move. First step with your inside foot and then your outside foot, without crossing your feet. On your first step use a three-quarter, rather than a full, step and flex your knee as you plant your foot firmly to stop your momentum. Turn on the ball of your inside foot and push off toward the outside. Shift your weight and take a long step with your outside foot, your toes pointing to the outside. Continue your move out, going to meet the ball as it is passed.

When you move to get open, see the ball, the basket, and your defender. Not seeing the ball being passed to you usually results in a turnover and missed scoring opportunity. After making your V-cut, get your lead hand up as a target for the pass. Beat your defender to the ball by going to meet the pass and catch it with two hands.

Land with a one-two stop. Land first on your inside (closer-to-basket) foot establishing it as your pivot foot. You can then protect the ball with your body and still be in position to execute a reverse turn (drop step) with your opposite foot, should your defender overcommit going for the pass. After you receive the pass, use a front turn to the middle, face the basket, see the rim, and be a triple threat to shoot, drive, or pass (see Figure 7.1).

EXECUTING THE BACKDOOR CUT

When your defender has a foot and hand in the passing lane to deny your catching the ball on the outside, change direction and cut behind your defender toward the basket. This is called a *backdoor cut*. You can use the backdoor cut from any position on the floor if an opponent is overplaying the passing lane between you and the passer.

With experience you will be able to use a backdoor cut automatically any time you are prevented from receiving a pass on the outside. Use this move also when you see your defender's head turned away from you and toward the ball. That momentary loss of vision can cause your defender to miss seeing you cut backdoor to the basket for a pass and possible layup.

The success of a backdoor cut comes from communication with the passer and sharply changing direction to the basket. The passer may throw the ball away when a backdoor cut is not made. Eliminate guesswork by using a designated key word to indicate to the passer that you are going backdoor. This key word signals that once you start you will continue your backdoor cut to the basket. A sharp, two syllable word works well because it coincides with your two-count footwork: Examples are *New York! L-A!* and *ice cream!* Set up the backdoor cut by taking your defender high (on the wing at least a step above the foul line extended and at the point a step above the free throw circle). Shout the key word to indicate your backdoor cut just before changing direction and cutting to the basket. Use a two-count move to change direction, stepping with your outside and then your inside foot (see the V-cut to review how).

The backdoor cut appears to be a relatively simple move but, in fact, it takes concentrated practice to execute sharply and effectively. Concentrate on a two-count move. Changing direction from right to left, you would concentrate on a two-count *right-left*, and going from left to right, you would concentrate on a two count *left-right*.

As with the V-cut, when you cut backdoor see the ball, the basket, and other defenders. You must also be alert for help-side defenders rotating to you and possibly trying to draw a charge on you after your cut. After making your backdoor cut, get your lead hand up as a target. After receiving the pass look to shoot, drive to the basket for a layup, or, if picked up by another defender, pass to the teammate who has been left open (see Figure 7.1).

Figure 7.1   Keys to Success: Getting Open

V-Cut

Execution Phase

1. Cut to basket ____
2. Concentrate on two-count move ____
3. Use deception and timing ____
4. Three-quarter step with inside foot ____
5. Knee flexed ____
6. Turn on ball of foot ____
7. Push off to outside ____
8. Shift weight ____
9. Long step with outside foot ____
10. Outside hand up as target ____
11. Continue cut outside ____
12. Meet the pass ____
13. Catch ball with two hands ____
14. Use one-two stop ____
15. Land on inside foot first ____
16. Front turn to middle ____
17. See the rim and defender ____
18. Triple-threat stance ____

Backdoor Cut

Execution Phase

1. Take defender high ____
2. Concentrate on two-count move ____
3. Shout key word for backdoor cut ____
4. Three-quarter step with outside foot ____
5. Knee flexed ____
6. Turn on ball of foot ____
7. Push off to inside ____
8. Shift weight ____
9. Long step with inside foot ____
10. Inside hand up as target ____
11. Continue cut to basket ____
12. Catch ball with two hands ____
13. Shoot layup or pass ____
14. Protect ball with two hands until release ____
15. Land in balance ____
16. Ready to rebound ____

Detecting Errors in the V-Cut and the Backdoor Cut

ERROR

The most common errors in the V-cut and the backdoor cut are listed here, along with suggestions to correct them.

CORRECTION

V-Cut

1. You are not deceptive because you slow up with short steps on your approach before making your change of direction.

2. You circle your change of direction, rather than making a sharp cut.

3. You do not give a target with your lead hand.

4. You do not see the ball, your defender, or where you are cutting.

1. Concentrate on a two-count move.

2. Use a two-count move, first making a three-quarter step and flexing your knee to pivot sharply and push off in the direction you want to go. Shift your weight and make a long second step.

3. After the change of direction get your lead hand up.

4. See the rim and ball; you should also be able to see your defender and where you are cutting.

Backdoor Cut

1. You do not have enough space on your backdoor cut to get open.

2. You are not deceptive because you slow up with short steps on your approach before making your backdoor cut.

3. You circle your change of direction, rather than making a sharp cut.

4. You stop on your backdoor cut and the pass is thrown away.

5. You do not give a target with your lead hand.

6. You do not see the ball, the basket, other defenders, or where you are cutting.

1. Take your defender high (on the wing at least a step above the foul line extended and at the point a step above the free throw circle).

2. Concentrate on a two-count move.

3. Use a two-count move, first making a three-quarter step and flexing your knee to pivot sharply and push off in the direction you want to go. Shift your weight and make a long second step.

4. Use a key word before your cut and continue cutting all the way to the basket.

5. After cutting backdoor, get your lead hand up.

6. See the rim and ball; you should also be able to see other defenders and where you are cutting.

EXECUTING THE GIVE-AND-GO

Part of the game since it first was played, the give-and-go is the most basic play in basketball. The name comes from the action: You give (pass) the ball to your teammate and go (cut) to the basket, looking to receive a return pass for a layup. The give-and-go exemplifies team play. By passing the ball and then moving without it you create your opportunity to score on a return pass. If you do not get open on the cut, your movement at least gives your teammate a better opportunity to initiate a one-on-one move because your defender will be in a less advantageous position to give defensive help.

It is important that after you initiate the give-and-go with a pass, you read your defender's position before making your cut to the basket. If your defender moves with you, continuing to guard you closely, you should simply make a hard cut to the basket. If your opponent drops off you, however, moving toward the ball on your pass (as most players learn to do), you should set up your defender with a fake before you cut. Fake by taking a step or two *away* from the ball, as though you are not involved in the play. As your defender moves with you, make a sharp change of direction and cut in front (*front cut*) to the basket. You can fake also by taking a step or two *toward* the ball, as though you are going to set a screen for or take a handoff from the player with the ball; then, as your defender moves with you, make a sharp change of direction and cut behind (*backdoor*) to the basket. As you gain experience in executing the give-and-go, you will learn to read your defender, use deception, and time your cut (see Figure 7.2).

Figure 7.2   Keys to Success: Give-and-Go

Step-Away and Front Cut

**Execution
Phase**

1. Pass to teammate ____
2. Step away from ball ____
3. Change direction and front cut to basket ____
4. Lead hand up ____
5. Catch ball with two hands ____

**Follow-Through
Phase**

1. Shoot layup ____

Step-to-Ball and Backdoor Cut

Execution Phase

1. Pass to teammate ____
2. Step toward ball ____
3. Change direction and backdoor cut to basket ____
4. Lead hand up ____
5. Catch ball with two hands ____

Follow-Through Phase

1. Shoot layup ____

Detecting Errors in the Give-and-Go

The most common errors in the give-and-go are listed here, along with suggestions to correct them.

ERROR

CORRECTION

ERROR	CORRECTION
1. You do not have enough space to get open.	1. At the point start the give-and-go at least a step above the free throw circle; on the wing start the give-and-go a step above the foul line extended.

ERROR	CORRECTION
2. After passing you do not read your defender's position and rush your cut.	2. Read your defender's position and if you are closely guarded, cut hard. If your defender moves back and toward the ball, fake away or toward the ball before you cut.
3. You do not give a target with your lead hand.	3. After making your cut, get your lead hand up.

SETTING A SCREEN AWAY FROM THE BALL

Setting a screen (also called a *pick*) is a maneuver to position yourself to block the path of your teammate's defender. Screens may be set for a player with or without the ball.

The pass-and-screen-away is basic to team play in basketball. It involves at least three players: screener, cutter, and passer. You set a screen for your teammate, who cuts off the screen to get open to receive a pass for a shot or drive. If your defender switches to your cutting teammate, you will be momentarily open and on the ball side of the defender whom you screened.

There are four steps in screening: setting the screen, seeing the screen, using the screen, and freeing the screen.

Setting the Screen

When setting a screen align the center of your body on your teammate's defender at an angle that can prevent your teammate's defender from going through it. Taking a few steps toward the basket before setting the screen enables you to get a better angle on your teammate's defender. To avoid an illegal moving block, use a wide, two-footed jump stop to establish a stationary position. You will be taking the blow of your teammate's defender moving into you, so you need good balance, with your feet wider than shoulder-width apart and your knees flexed. While your teammate uses your screen you are not allowed to move any body part into the defender: Keep

one arm in front of your crotch and the other in front of your chest for protection.

Seeing the Screen

Wait until the screen is set to prevent an illegal moving block. Be patient. Allow time for the screen to be set and to read how the defense is playing it. Most mistakes in using screens occur either because when using the screen you do not read the defense or you move too fast without setting up the defense.

Using the Screen

When you are cutting off a screen, approach it with control but then make an explosive move. Approach the screen under control. You can actually walk your defender into the screen while gaining a good angle for cutting off the screen: first move slowly in the direction your defender plays you before you cut hard off the screen in the opposite direction. As you cut off the screen, go shoulder to shoulder with the screener so your defender cannot get between you and the screen. It is important to cut far enough away from the screen so that one defender cannot guard both you and the screener and so you create spacing for a pass to the screener when there is a defensive switch.

Freeing the Screen

When you set a good screen, it will lead to two options: Either you or your teammate using the screen will be open. If your teammate cuts off your screen correctly, your defender's usual reaction is to give defensive help or switch. This momentarily allows you inside position on your defender who has given defensive help or—after a switch—on your new defender.

By using a roll you can keep your open position. A roll is executed by pivoting on your inside foot and opening your body in the direction of the ball, putting your defender on your back. If your teammate cuts to the outside, you will be free to roll in toward the basket and receive a pass for an inside shot. If your teammate cuts to the basket, you will be free to pop out and receive a pass for an outside shot.

You can also fake screen and cut (called *slipping the pick* or *early release*). This maneuver is effective if your defender decides to give help by stepping out hard to slow your teammate's cut off your screen. As you go to set the screen, if you see your defender leave you to step out toward the cutter, make a quick cut to the basket to receive a pass for an inside shot.

If both defenders are trying to take the cutter, move to an open area. After receiving the pass, you will have the defense outnumbered and be in position to drive or pass to a teammate for an open shot.

There are four basic options for cutting off a screen, depending on how it is defended: pop-out, curl, backdoor cut, and fade.

Pop-Out

When the screener's defender drops back to allow your defender to slide behind the screen, pop out to receive a chest or overhead pass for a *catch-and-shoot* jump shot in your rhythm and range. (See Figure 7.3.)

Curl (Front Cut)

If your defender *trails* your body over the top of the screen, curl (cut in front and completely around the screen) toward the basket to receive an overhead or bounce pass for an inside, baby hook shot. Signal this move by putting your arm around your screener's body as you curl. If the screener's defender helps slow your cut, the screener will then pop out for an open catch-and-shoot jump shot. (See Figure 7.3.)

Backdoor Cut

If your defender *tries to anticipate* your move over the top of the screen before you make your cut, step out above the screen with your outside foot and sharply change direction for a backdoor cut—behind the screen toward the basket—to receive a lob or bounce pass for a layup. Signal your backdoor cut before your jab step with a key two-syllable word, such as *eyeball!* At the same time give a passing target with your inside hand pointing toward the basket for a bounce pass or pointing up in the air for a lob pass. If the screener's defender gives help on your backdoor cut, the screener will then pop out and be open for a catch-and-shoot jump shot in rhythm and range. (See Figure 7.3.)

Fade

If your defender takes a shortcut to your anticipated cut by moving behind the screener's defender on the basket side of the screen, fade (flare) away from the screen. Signal this move by putting your hands on your screener's hip before you fade. Prepare to receive an overhead skip pass to the far side of the screen for a catch-and-shoot jump shot in your rhythm and range. If the screener's defender switches out to pressure your shot, the screener cuts in for post-up or rebound position.

As you and your teammates practice the screen-away, you will learn to read the defense and react with a pop-out, curl, backdoor cut, or fade to create an opening for a shot. Properly executed, the screen-away is a beautiful example of teamwork. By setting a screen for your teammate away from the ball, you create an opportunity for your teammate or you to score (see Figure 7.3).

Figure 7.3 Keys to Success: Options for Cutting Off a Screen Away From the Ball

Defender Slides Under Screen: Pop-Out

Preparation Phase

1. Screener sets screen ____
2. Jump stop ____
3. Wide base ____
4. Arms in ____
5. Cutter fakes in ____
6. Cutter waits for screen ____

Execution Phase

1. Defender slides under screen ____
2. Cutter reads defense ____
3. Cutter pops out ____
4. Screener rolls in toward basket ____

Follow-Through Phase

1. Ball is passed to open cutter in position to shoot jump shot ____

Defender Trails Body: Curl

Preparation
Phase

1. Screener sets screen ____
2. Jump stop ____
3. Wide base ____
4. Arms in ____
5. Cutter fakes in ____
6. Cutter waits for screen ____

a

Execution
Phase

1. Defender trails cutter's body around screen ____
2. Cutter reads defense ____
3. Cutter signals curl with arm around screener ____
4. Cutter curls in toward basket ____
5. Screener pops out ____

b

Follow-Through
Phase

1. Ball is passed to open cutter on curl for "baby" hook shot ____

c

Defender Steps Out Above Screen: Backdoor Cut

Preparation
Phase

1. Screener sets screen ____
2. Cutter waits for screen ____
3. Defender steps out ____
4. Cutter shouts key word for backdoor cut ____
5. Cutter fakes out ____

a

Execution
Phase

1. Defender steps out to deny pass ____
2. Cutter reads defense ____
3. Cutter cuts backdoor to basket ____
4. Screener pops out ____

b

Follow-Through
Phase

1. Backdoor cutter receives bounce pass or lob pass and shoots layup ____

c

Defender Takes Shortcut Behind Screen: Fade

Preparation
Phase

1. Screener sets screen ____
2. Cutter waits for screen ____
3. Defender takes shortcut ____
4. Cutter reads defense ____
5. Cutter signals fade with hands on screener's hips ____
6. Cutter shouts key word *fade!* ____

a

Execution
Phase

1. Defender shortcuts ____
2. Cutter fades away from ball ____
3. Screener pops out ____

b

Follow-Through
Phase

1. On fade, ball is passed to open cutter in position to shoot jump shot ____

c

Detecting Errors in Screening Away From the Ball

The most common errors in the screen away from the ball are listed here, along with suggestions to correct them.

ERROR

CORRECTION

1. You set an illegal moving block (your body or body part is moving when contact is made with the defender), and you are called for a foul.

1. Use a wide, two-footed jump stop before your teammate cuts to avoid an illegal moving block. Keep your arm and knee in as the defender fights to get through your screen.

2. You do not set a strong pick, and the defender is able to stay with the cutter.

2. Set your screen at an angle that makes the defender go under you. Use a wide base with your knees flexed to maintain balance. Keep one arm in front of your crotch and the other in front of your chest for protection as the defender fights to get through your pick.

3. You do not wait for the screen being set for you. You cut off the screen while the screener is still moving, causing a foul to be called on the screener.

3. Before using the screen you must wait until a legal screen is set and until you have read your defender's position.

4. As you cut off the screen, you do not create enough space to get open or to pass to your teammate.

4. Cut 12 to 15 feet past the screen to create operating space for you or the screener to receive a pass on a roll or pop-out.

5. You predetermine the cut when a screen is set for you, and do not read your defender's position. For example, you pop out when you should curl.

5. The success of your cut depends on reading the defense and reacting to how your defender plays the screen. Do not predetermine or rush your cut. If your defender drops back, you pop out. If your defender trails you, curl to the basket. If your defender steps out, anticipating your cut, use a backdoor cut. If your defender takes the shortcut route behind the screener and screener's defender, fade.

6. After you set the screen and a defensive switch occurs, you roll the wrong way, taking your eyes off the ball and not seeing a possible pass.

6. On a defensive switch, use a reverse pivot on your inside foot: Open your body to the ball as you roll so you will be able to see the pass.

7. As you cut, you do not give a target with your lead hand.

7. Make your cut and then get your lead hand up for a target.

EXECUTING THE PICK-AND-ROLL

The pick-and-roll is another basic play that has been a part of basketball since the game first was played. Its name, like the give-and-go's, comes from the action of the play. You set a pick (screen) for a teammate who dribbles by it for an outside shot or drive. If your defender switches to your teammate, you will momentarily be inside the defender whom you picked and free to roll toward the basket, looking to receive a return pass from the dribbler for a layup. When a pick is set for you, it is important to use at least two dribbles going by the pick to create space for a pass to the picker who rolls to the basket after a defensive switch.

There are other options to the basic pick-and-roll, depending on how it is defended, including the pick-and-pop, early release, and stretch-the-trap. On the basic pick-and-roll play, your pick is defended by a defensive switch: To combat that switch you roll to the basket for a pass and layup. (See Figure 7.4.)

Pick-and-Pop

The pick-and-pop, on the other hand, is used when your defender drops back to allow the defender that you screened to slide under your pick. Rather than rolling in, you can pop out to receive a pass for a jump shot. You can do this also when the defense switches, the defender you screen quickly spinning around your pick toward the basket. (See Figure 7.4.)

Early Release

Use the early release when your defender reacts to the pick-and-roll by stepping out hard to slow down your teammate as he dribbles off your screen. As you go to set the pick, if you see your defender leave you to step out toward the dribbler, you should release early and make a basket cut for a pass from your teammate. (See Figure 7.4.)

Stretch-the-Trap

When both defenders react to the pick-and-roll by trapping the player with the ball as you set the pick, a different adjustment is advantageous. It is called *stretch-the-trap*. When the trap occurs, your teammate should retreat dribble to stretch the defense, then pass to you as you move to an open area. After receiving the pass you will have the defense outnumbered, and be in position to drive or pass to a teammate for an open shot.

As you and your teammate become experienced in executing the pick-and-roll, you will learn to read how the pick is being defended and react with a roll, pop-out, or stretch dribble to create an opening for a shot. Properly executed, the pick-and-roll can create the opportunity for your teammate or you to score. It is another example of fine teamwork (see Figure 7.4).

Figure 7.4   Keys to Success: Pick-and-Roll Options

Pick-and-Roll

Preparation
Phase

1. Screener sets pick ____
2. Wait for pick ____
3. Defenders switch ____
4. Read defense ____

a

Execution
Phase

1. Drive off pick shoulder-to-shoulder ____
2. Take two dribbles past pick ____
3. Picker rolls to basket ____

b

Follow-Through
Phase

1. Bounce (or lob) pass to picker rolling to basket ____

c

Pick-and-Pop

Preparation
Phase

1. Screener sets pick ____
2. Wait for pick ____
3. Picker's defender drops back and your defender slides through ____
4. Read defense ____

Execution
Phase

1. Drive off pick shoulder-to-shoulder ____
2. Take two dribbles past pick ____
3. Picker pops out ____

Follow-Through
Phase

1. Pass back to picker popping out in position to shoot jump shot ____

Early Release

Preparation Phase

1. Screener sets pick ____
2. Wait for pick ____
3. Picker's defender steps out ____
4. Read defense ____

Execution Phase

1. Picker releases early for basket cut ____
2. Overhead lob pass to picker cutting for layup ____

Stretch-the-Trap

Preparation Phase

1. Screener sets pick ____
2. Wait for pick ____
3. Defenders trap ball ____
4. Read defense ____

Execution Phase

1. Retreat dribble to stretch trap ____
2. Take at least two dribbles back ____
3. Picker cuts to open area ____
4. Picker calls for ball ____
5. Overhead lob pass to picker ____

Detecting Errors in the Pick-and-Roll

The most common errors in the pick-and-roll are listed here, along with suggestions to correct them.

ERROR

CORRECTION

ERROR	CORRECTION
1. You are called for a foul because you move your body or body part into the path of the defender as your teammate dribbles off your pick.	1. Use a wide, two-footed jump stop before your teammate dribbles to avoid an illegal moving block. Keep your arm and knee in as the defender fights to get through your pick.
2. You do not set a strong pick, and the defender is able to stay with the dribbler.	2. Set your pick at an appropriate angle that will stop the defender from going through it. You want the defender to go under you. Use a wide base with your knees flexed to maintain balance. Keep one arm in front of your crotch and the other in front of your chest for protection against the defender.
3. You do not wait while the pick is being set for you. You dribble off the pick while your teammate is still moving, causing a foul on your teammate for setting an illegal moving block.	3. You must wait until a legal pick is set and until you have read your defender's position before you use the pick.
4. As you dribble off the pick, you do not have enough space to get open or pass to your teammate.	4. Make at least two dribbles past the pick to create operating space for you to shoot or pass to the picker on a roll or pop-out.
5. After you set the pick, you do not read your defender's position and rush a roll when you should pop out, or pop out when you should roll.	5. After setting a pick read your defender's position. On a defensive switch, roll to the basket. If your defender drops back, pop out. If your defender leaves you to step out, use an early release and basket cut. When your teammate retreat dribbles to stretch a trap, move to an open area and call for the ball.
6. After you set the pick and a defensive switch occurs, you roll the wrong way, taking your eyes off the dribbler and not seeing the return pass.	6. On a defensive switch use a reverse pivot on your inside foot and open your body to the ball as you roll to see a possible return pass.
7. As you roll or cut, you do not give a target with your lead hand.	7. After making your roll or cut, get your lead hand up for a target.

EXECUTING THE FLASH-AND-BACKDOOR CUT

A flash is a quick cut toward the ball. The flash-and-backdoor cut involves three players—a passer, an overplayed (being denied the ball) receiver, and a player who will flash. When a defender is denying your teammate from catching the ball and you are the next closest player to the would-be receiver, you should automatically flash to an open area between the passer and your overplayed teammate. Flashing to the ball relieves defensive pressure on your two teammates by giving the passer another outlet. A flash not only can prevent a possible turnover but also can create a scoring opportunity when you combine it with the overplayed receiver's well-timed backdoor cut.

As you flash signal the cut with the key word *flash!* On your flash go hard with two hands up to receive the pass. When you receive the ball, land with a one-two stop with your inside (closer-to-basket) foot landing first. Catch the ball and look for your overplayed teammate who should be setting up to make a backdoor cut toward the basket. Use a reverse pivot and make a bounce pass to your teammate cutting backdoor for a layup. If your teammate is covered on the backdoor cut, front turn into a triple-threat position for a possible shot, drive, or pass.

You should flash automatically whenever you see a teammate being overplayed. Usu-

ally you will flash high when your teammate is prevented from receiving a pass on the perimeter. You can also flash to the high post when a teammate is being fronted in the low post or you can flash to the low post when a teammate is being denied at the high post.

The success of the flash-and-backdoor cut is based on communication between teammates and on the timing of the overplayed receiver's backdoor cut. Using the key word signals to the passer that you are flashing and alerts your overplayed teammate to cut backdoor after you receive the pass. When overplayed, your teammate should set up the defense with a step away from the basket before the backdoor cut. The flash-and-backdoor cut requires alertness and timing to execute sharply and effectively (see Figure 7.5).

Figure 7.5   Keys to Success: *Flash-and-Backdoor Cut*

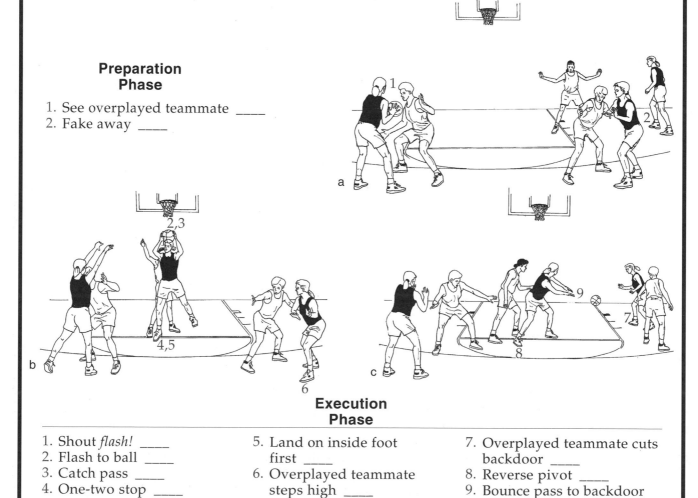

Preparation Phase

1. See overplayed teammate ____
2. Fake away ____

Execution Phase

1. Shout *flash!* ____
2. Flash to ball ____
3. Catch pass ____
4. One-two stop ____
5. Land on inside foot first ____
6. Overplayed teammate steps high ____
7. Overplayed teammate cuts backdoor ____
8. Reverse pivot ____
9. Bounce pass to backdoor cutter ____

Detecting Errors in the Flash-and-Backdoor Cut

The most common errors in the flash-and-backdoor cut are listed here, along with suggestions to correct them.

ERROR

CORRECTION

1. On your flash you do not get open.

2. On your flash your teammate is not alert to backdoor cut.

3. You catch the pass on your flash but have trouble seeing and passing to your teammate cutting backdoor.

4. The backdoor cut is made too soon.

5. If your teammate is not open on the backdoor cut, you are not a triple threat to shoot, pass, or drive.

1. Take your defender away from the ball and then cut hard to an open area between the passer and overplayed receiver.

2. Shout *flash!* as you make your flash to alert both the passer and the overplayed receiver.

3. Catch the ball with a one-two stop, reverse pivot away from your defender, and make a bounce pass to your teammate cutting backdoor.

4. The backdoor cut can be timed correctly by first stepping away from the basket just as the ball is caught by the flash cutter and then cutting backdoor.

5. When your teammate is not open on the backdoor cut, front turn to see the rim and be a triple threat.

EXECUTING THE DRIBBLE SCREEN AND WEAVE

A dribble screen occurs when you dribble toward your teammate to hand the ball off while you screen your teammate's defender. To execute the play you dribble to the inside of your teammate. Your teammate fakes in and then cuts to the outside and behind you to receive your handoff. To hand off the ball, pivot on your inside (closer-to-the-basket) foot, placing your body in the path of your teammate's defender. Be prepared for contact during the handoff. Maintain a strong balanced stance and use your body and two hands to protect the ball. After receiving your handoff, your teammate should be a triple threat to shoot, drive, or pass. After you make the handoff, read the defense and either roll to the basket, pop out, or move away from the ball to an open area.

The dribble screen is used to execute a *weave*, another basic basketball play. In a weave at least three players set dribble screens for each other. For example, you start the weave with a dribble screen and hand off to your teammate. After receiving a handoff, several options are available: You can shoot from behind the screen, drive to the basket, or continue the weave by dribbling toward another teammate for a dribble screen and handoff. The weave continues until you or a teammate takes advantage of an opening for a shot or drive to the basket.

One way to defend either the dribble screen or weave is getting in the path of the receiver to prevent the handoff. When you are the potential receiver and a defender gets in your path, take a step to the outside and make a backdoor cut to the basket for a possible pass and layup.

A second defense is to jump switch into the path of the receiver. A jump-switch is an aggressive early switch made to draw a charge or to change the direction of the player receiving the ball. To combat a jump-switch make a short, five- to ten-foot cut to an open area after your handoff and look for a quick return pass. When you anticipate a jump-switch, you also can fake the handoff and drive to the basket.

Another way to defend the weave is to have both defenders trap the player receiving the ball on the handoff. When the opponents trap, your teammate should retreat dribble to stretch the defense and then pass to you while you make a short, five- to ten-foot cut to an open area. After receiving the pass you will have the defense outnumbered and be in position to drive or pass to a teammate for an open shot.

With experience you and your teammates will learn to read how the weave is being defended so you can choose whether to react with a handoff, fake handoff, or backdoor cut to create an opening for a shot. The weave creates a variety of scoring opportunities and is yet another beautiful example of teamwork (see Figure 7.6).

Figure 7.6   Keys to Success: Options for Dribble Screen and Weave

Defender Slides Under Screen: Shoot, Drive, or Continue Weave

a

Execution Phase

1. Dribbler starts weave by dribbling to inside of teammate ____
2. Receiver steps away before cutting to outside of dribbler ____
3. Dribbler sets dribble screen to inside of receiver ____
4. Receiver cuts to outside for handoff ____
5. Dribbler's defender drops back and receiver's defender slides ____
6. Read defense ____
7. Dribbler hands ball off to receiver ____

Follow-Through Phase

1. Receiver shoots jump shot, drives to basket, or continues weave by dribbling toward another teammate ____
2. Screener cuts away from ball ____

b

Defender Denies Handoff: Cut Backdoor

Execution Phase

1. Dribbler starts weave by dribbling to inside of teammate ____
2. Receiver steps away before cutting to outside of dribbler ____
3. Dribbler sets dribble screen to inside of receiver ____

4. Receiver cuts to outside for handoff ____
5. Receiver's defender denies handoff ____
6. Read defense ____
7. Receiver shouts key word for backdoor cut ____

Follow-Through Phase

1. Receiver cuts backdoor ____

2. Dribbler makes overhead pass to backdoor cutter ____

Defenders Jump Switch: Fake Handoff and Drive

**Execution
Phase**

1. Dribbler starts weave by dribbling to inside of teammate ____
2. Receiver steps away before cutting to outside of dribbler ____
3. Dribbler sets dribble screen to inside of receiver ____

4. Receiver cuts to outside for handoff ____
5. Defenders jump switch ____
6. Read defense ____

**Follow-Through
Phase**

1. Dribbler fakes handoff, while continuing dribble ____

2. Dribbler drives between defenders to basket ____

Defenders Trap Receiver: Stretch Trap

a

**Execution
Phase**

1. Dribbler starts weave by dribbling to inside of teammate ____
2. Receiver steps away before cutting to outside of dribbler ____
3. Dribbler sets dribble screen to inside of receiver ____

4. Receiver cuts to outside for handoff ____
5. Defenders trap receiver ____
6. Read defense ____

b

7. Receiver retreat dribbles to stretch trap ____
8. Screener makes short cut to open area ____

9. Screener calls for ball ____
10. Overhead lob pass to screener ____

Detecting Errors in the Dribble Screen and Weave

The most common errors in the dribble screen and weave are listed here, along with suggestions to correct them.

ERROR 🚫

CORRECTION

1. As you dribble toward your teammate to set the dribble screen, you bump into each other.

2. You do not protect the ball on your handoff, and the receiver's defender steals the ball.

3. When you set the dribble screen, you get knocked off balance.

4. When a dribble screen is set for you, you do not read the defense. For example, your defender steps in the path of the handoff and you do not make a backdoor cut.

1. To prevent bumping into each other remember that the dribbler goes to the inside and the receiver cuts behind the dribbler and to the outside.

2. Protect the ball with your body and hand off with two hands.

3. Expect to be bumped and maintain your balance by widening your base and flexing your knees as you hand off.

4. Success on the weave depends on reading and reacting to how the defense plays it. Learn to read how the dribble screen is being defended and react with a handoff, a fake handoff, a backdoor cut, or a retreat dribble to create an opening for a shot.

Moving Without the Ball Drills

1. Give-and-Go (2-on-0)

Select a teammate to be your partner. Start with the ball at a box outside the lane and with your back to the basket. Your partner starts at the opposite box across the lane. Toss the ball diagonally across the lane to the opposite elbow. You are passing to yourself: Catch the ball with a one-two stop with your inside foot landing first. Pivot to the middle, see the rim, and make a drive step. Be a triple threat to shoot, pass, or drive. On your toss of the ball, your teammate runs to the opposite box, makes a sharp change of direction, and runs up the lane line to the elbow on the side opposite you.

Then make a chest pass to your teammate and cut to the basket (give-and-go). Your teammate makes a return bounce pass to you as you cut. Receive the pass and shoot a layup shot. Your teammate follows to rebound a possible miss and make as many power moves as necessary to score. Change positions and continue the drill, each player cutting and shooting 5 layups on each side.

Success Goal = 5 out of 5 layup shots made from each side

Your Score =

    a. (#) _____ layup shots made from right side out of (#) _____ attempts

    b. (#) _____ layup shots made from left side out of (#) _____ attempts

2. *Backdoor Cut (2-on-0)*

Set up as in the previous drill. On your toss of the ball, your teammate runs to the opposite box, makes a sharp change of direction, and runs up the lane line to the elbow on the side opposite you.

    On reaching the elbow, your teammate assumes that a defender is denying a pass at the elbow (a chair can represent a defender) and makes a backdoor cut to the basket, giving a verbal signal just before the backdoor cut. A two-syllable word, such as *eyeball!* or *onion!* is recommended to coincide with the sharp two-step change of direction needed to make a successful backdoor cut. Make a bounce pass to your teammate, who will receive the pass and shoot a layup. Follow in to rebound a possible miss and make a power move to score. Change positions and continue the drill, each player cutting and shooting 5 layups on each side. In total you and your partner should make 5 backdoor cuts and 5 layups each on each side, awarding yourselves 1 point for each correct backdoor cut or shot.

Success Goal = 16 of 20 possible points

Your Score = (#) _____ your points; (#) _____ partner's points

3. *Pick-and-Roll (2-on-0)*

Set up as in the previous drills. On your toss of the ball, your teammate runs to the opposite box, makes a sharp change of direction, and runs up the lane line to the elbow on the side opposite you.

    Make a chest pass to your teammate and set a screen on the inside (lane side) of your teammate's imaginary defender. Your teammate uses your screen, brushing your outside shoulder to prevent a defender from getting over the screen and staying with the dribbler.

    Your teammate dribbles at least two dribbles by your screen to create space for a pass as you roll to the basket. Execute the roll by opening to the ball with a reverse pivot on your inside (closer-to-basket) foot and seal out an imaginary defender. Your teammate makes a bounce or lob pass to you as you cut to the basket. You then shoot a layup. Your teammate follows to rebound a possible miss, making a power move to score. Change positions and continue the drill. Each player should execute 5 pick-and-rolls and 5 layups on each side. Award yourself 1 point for each correct, successful screen-and-roll or shot.

Success Goal = 16 of 20 possible points

Your Score = (#) _____ your points; (#) _____ partner's points

4. *Pick-and-Roll (2-on-1)*

Select a third player to join you, the three of you executing this drill the same way as the previous drill except for the additional player replacing the imaginary defender or chair. After you make a chest pass to your teammate, set a screen on the inside (lane side) of your teammate's defender. Change positions and continue the drill with each player executing 5 pick-and-rolls and shooting 5 layups on each side. Score as before.

Success Goal = 16 of 20 possible points

Your Score = (#) _____ your points; (#) _____ second player's points; (#) _____ third player's points

5. *Pick-and-Roll/Switching Defense (2-on-2)*

This drill gives you and your teammate practice at executing the pick-and-roll against a switching defense. Select two additional players to play defense on you and your teammate. Execute this drill in the same way as the previous one. After you make a chest pass to your teammate, set a screen on the inside (lane side) of your teammate's defender. The defenders should switch as your partner dribbles by your screen. You then roll to the basket. If the defender you screen defends your roll by quickly spinning around your pick toward the basket, rather than rolling in, you may pop out to receive a pass for a jump shot. Your team gets 2 points each time you score. If you or your teammate get fouled on a made shot, you get a free throw. If you get fouled on a missed shot, you get 2 free throws. If you miss the shot, you or your partner getting an offensive rebound, you may continue playing offense. Continue the play until the offensive team scores and turns the ball over, or until the defense gets the ball on a steal or rebound and dribbles back past the free throw line. The defense then goes to offense, and the offense goes to defense.

Success Goal = Score more points than your opponents with 7 points winning the game

Your Score = (#) _____ your points; (#) _____ opponents' points

6. *Pick-and-Pop/Sliding Defense (2-on-2)*

This drill adds practice at executing the pick-and-pop against a sliding defense. Except for the two defenders using a sliding defense, rather than switching as your teammate dribbles by your screen, this drill resembles the previous one. The screener's defender helps the defender *being* screened by *dropping back*, allowing the other defender to slide behind the screen and stay with the dribbler. After dropping back, the first defender recovers to a defensive position on the screener.

   When you set a pick and your defender drops back—allowing the screened defender to slide under your pick—rather than rolling in, pop out to receive a pass for a jump shot. Your teammate can either make a jump shot or pass to you for a jump shot, should your defender fail to recover after dropping back. Scoring is the same as the previous drill.

Success Goal = Score more points than your opponents with 7 points winning the game

Your Score = (#) _____ your points; (#) _____ opponents' points

7. Pick-and-Roll/Help-and-Recover Defense (2-on-2)

The only change in this drill, compared with the two previous drills, is that the two defenders use a help-and-recover defense as your teammate dribbles by your screen. The screener's defender helps the defender being screened by *stepping out* on the dribbler. This slows the dribbler's progress, allowing the second defender to stay with the dribbler. After stepping out the first defender recovers to a defensive position on the screener. Your teammate then can drive to the basket for a layup, shoot a jump shot, or pass back to you, should your defender fail to recover after giving help. Another option you have is an early release. This is used if your defender decides to defend the pick-and-roll by stepping out early to slow down your teammate before he dribbles off your pick. As you set the pick and see your defender leave early to step out toward the dribbler, you should release early and make a basket cut for a pass from your teammate. Scoring is the same as the previous drill.

Success Goal = Score more points than your opponents with 7 points winning the game

Your Score = (#) _____ your points; (#) _____ opponents' points

8. Pick-and-Roll/Trapping Defense (2-on-2)

This drill against a trapping defense is executed the same way as the three previous drills except that the two defenders use a trap against your pick: The screener's defender traps the dribbler as the pick is being set. If both defenders trap the dribbler during your screen, an adjustment called stretching-the-trap should be used. Your teammate should retreat dribble to stretch the defense and then pass to you, as you move to an open area. After receiving the pass you will have the defense outnumbered and be in position to drive to the basket. Scoring is the same as the previous drill.

Success Goal = Score more points than your opponents with 7 points winning the game

Your Score = (#) _____ your points; (#) _____ opponents' points

9. Pass and Cut (3-on-0)

Select two players to be your teammates. As player one you will start with the ball at the point position at the top of the free throw circle. Your teammates, players two and three, will start at the right and left wing positions (foul line extended), respectively. Pass to either of them and take one or two steps away from the ball toward the weak-side (away from the ball) wing. Then execute a sharp change of direction and cut toward the basket. As you cut to the basket, the weak-side wing replaces you at the point. The wing who received the pass may bounce pass to you, as you cut to the basket, or may pass to the player now occupying the point. If the ball is passed to the point, move to the open wing position (vacated when the player moved to the point). Continue the drill with the player at the point passing to either wing and cutting to the basket, having the wing fake a pass to the cutter before passing back to the point. Make at least 5 passes before passing the ball to a player cutting from the point to the basket for a layup. Continue the drill for a total of 30 passes and layups without error.

Success Goal = 30 consecutive passes and layups without error

Your Score = (#) _____ consecutive passes and layups without error

10. Pass and Screen Away (3-on-0)

The three of you begin as in the Pass-and-Cut Drill. In this drill when you pass to the player at either the right or left wing, fake a cut to the basket before setting a screen away from the ball on the inside of an imaginary defender on the weak-side wing (a chair can represent the defender). The weak-side wing has four options when using the screen: the front cut, backdoor cut, pop-out, or fade. If the weak-side wing uses your screen by cutting to the basket with a front cut or backdoor cut, you should pop back to the ball. If the weak-side wing pops out toward the ball to receive a possible pass for an outside jump shot, you should roll in to the basket by opening to the ball with a reverse pivot on your inside (closer-to-basket) foot and sealing out an imaginary defender. If the weak-side wing fades away from the ball, you can pop out or roll to the basket, depending on how you imagine the defense is being played.

The options of the wing who receives the pass are to make a bounce pass to the player cutting to the basket, pass to the player popping out, throw a skip pass (a pass that bypasses the next closest receiver) to the player fading, or pass or dribble the ball out to the point. A player receiving the pass on a cut to the basket should shoot a layup, rebounding any miss and scoring with a power move. After a pop-out or fade the receiver may take the outside shot or pass back to the point to restart the pass and screen away.

Change positions and continue the drill, each player executing 5 screen aways and reactions to how the screen is used. Award yourself 1 point for each correct screen away and for each correct reaction to the use of the screen.

Success Goal = 8 of 10 possible points

Your Score = (#) _____ your points;   (#) _____ second player's points;   (#) _____ third player's points

11. Flash Backdoor (3-on-0)

Begin as with the Pass-and-Cut and Pass-and-Screen-Away Drills. After passing to either the right or left wing, fake a screen away before cutting to the basket. The weak-side wing moves out to replace you at the point. Assume that an imaginary defender is denying a swing pass (toward the weak side) back to the point and flash to the ball-side elbow to receive a pass, shouting the signal *flash!* When you receive the pass at the elbow after your flash, the player at the point should make a backdoor cut to the basket. You reverse pivot on your inside foot and make a bounce pass to your teammate cutting backdoor to the basket. On receiving the pass the cutter should shoot a layup, rebounding any miss and scoring with a power move.

Change positions and continue the drill. Each player passes and cuts from the point, flashes from the weak-side and reverse pivots for a bounce pass to the backdoor cutter on each side. Award yourself 1 point for each flash and for each correct reverse pivot and bounce pass to the backdoor cutter.

Success Goal = 18 of 20 possible points

Your Score = (#) _____ your points; (#) _____ second player's points; (#) _____ third player's points

12. *Weave (3-on-0)*

Follow the setup of the three previous drills. Start the weave by dribbling toward one of the wings. Screen your teammate's defender while you hand the ball off to your teammate, dribbling to the inside while your teammate cuts to the outside and behind you to receive your handoff. Your teammate then should be a triple threat to shoot, drive, or pass. After you make the handoff, imagine how the defense is being played and either roll to the basket, pop out, or move away from the ball to an open area. If you receive a handoff, you have several options: You can shoot from behind the screen, drive to the basket, or continue the weave by dribbling toward another teammate for a dribble screen and handoff.

    The weave continues until a member of your team takes advantage of an opening for a shot or drive to the basket. Make at least 5 handoffs before passing to a player cutting to the basket for a layup. Continue the drill for a total of 30 correct handoffs and layups.

Success Goal = 30 correct consecutive handoffs and layups

Your Score = (#) _____ consecutive handoffs and layups without error

13. *Halfcourt Offense Versus Passive Defense (3-on-3)*

Select 5 other players for a halfcourt 3-on-3 game. Three of you will play offense and three will play passive (half-speed) defense. This drill gives you practice at executing offensive and defensive options in a 3-on-3 situation. Having the defense play half-speed helps the offensive players recognize which defense is being played, react with the correct offensive option, and develop confidence. The offensive options are to pass and cut (give-and-go), pass and screen away, pass and go to the ball for a pick-and-roll, flash backdoor, or weave. The defensive options are to switch, slide, help and recover, or trap.

    The game starts when the defensive team gives the offensive team the ball at halfcourt. The offensive team gets 1 point each time it scores. If the defense commits a foul, the offense gets the ball and starts again. If an offensive player misses a shot and a teammate gets an offensive rebound, continue playing. The defense gets a point if it gets the ball on a steal or rebound and makes an outlet pass past the free throw line or if it forces the offense into a violation. Five points win the game. The defense then goes to offense, and the offense goes to defense.

Success Goal = Score more points than your opponents with 5 points winning the game

Your Score = (#) _____ your points; (#) _____ opponents' points

14. Halfcourt (3-on-3)

When you are confident in executing 3-on-3 offense against a passive (half-speed) defense, you are ready to practice against an active (full-speed) defense. This drill gives you practice at executing offensive and defensive options in a 3-on-3 situation against active (full-speed) defense. Scoring is the same as the previous drill.

Success Goal = Score more points than your opponents with 5 points winning the game

Your Score = (#) _____ your points; (#) _____ opponents' points

15. Without Dribbling (3-on-3)

This drill gives you practice at executing 3-on-3 offensive options *without* dribbling, providing a greater challenge. You will have more opportunities to practice passing and cutting, especially using the backdoor cut and flash backdoor. Scoring is the same as the previous drill.

Success Goal = Score more points than your opponents with 5 points winning the game

Your Score = (#) _____ your points; (#) _____ opponents' points

Two and Three Person Plays: Checks

Basketball is a team game, and you must move without the ball to help your team. Moving without the ball includes helping yourself or a teammate get open by setting or cutting off a screen and keeping your defender focused on your movements away from the ball in order to limit defensive help on the ball.

Have a trained observer—your coach, teacher, or a skilled player—evaluate your ability to move without the ball and execute two and three person plays. The observer can use the checklists in Figures 7.1 to 7.6 to evaluate your performance and provide corrective feedback.

Step 8 Fast Break: Pass Ahead and Penetrate for Point Production

The fast break is exciting for both players and fans. The objective of the fast break is to advance the ball up the court for a high percentage shot, either by outnumbering the defense or by not allowing the defense an opportunity to get set. The fast break places a premium on physical condition, fundamentals, teamwork, and intelligent decisions.

WHY THE FAST BREAK IS IMPORTANT

Although successful execution of the fast break is important for several strategic reasons, for most players and fans it also adds fun and excitement to the game. The fast break creates the easiest way to score. A team that has to work hard for every shot against a set 5-on-5 halfcourt defense will have trouble beating a team that consistently gets fast-break baskets.

Creating an easy scoring opportunity by numerical advantage is the first objective of the fast break. The 2-on-1 and 3-on-2, the most common numerical advantages, often result in a layup. The 4-on-3 usually leads to an inside post-up shot. The 5-on-4 often allows for an easy swing of the ball away from the side of defensive pressure and for a possible open shot on the weak side.

A second objective is to attack before the opponents are set to play team defense or rebound. The fast break works well against zone defenses because the defenders do not have time to get set in their positions. A fast-breaking team's advantage over a halfcourt team is in combatting pressing defenses. A fast-breaking team is better prepared to inbound the ball quickly before the press is set. It is more experienced in passing on the move and it generally looks to score against the press rather than just getting it over halfcourt, which poses a greater threat to the pressing team. A fast-break attack also can create mismatches against player-to-player defenses.

Another important objective of playing basketball this way is motivating the fast-breaking team to play tough defense and to re-

bound. Good defense and rebounding are the best means for starting the fast break. A fast-breaking team also discourages its opponents from sending too many players to rebound its offensive board, for fear of not having players back to defend against the break. A fast-break style is very demanding and encourages a team to be in top physical condition.

There are different types of fast-break attacks. The main objectives remain the same: to attack the defense before the opponents are set to either play team defense or rebound and to create an easy scoring opportunity by numerical advantage.

The most common fast-break attack is the controlled three-lane fast break. In the controlled fast break, fundamental execution and making good decisions matter more than speed. The controlled fast break has three phases: starting the fast break, getting into position, and finishing the break with the correct scoring option.

STARTING THE FAST BREAK

First you must gain possession of the ball, for which good defense and rebounding are essential. Aggressive defense creates opportunities to get the ball from rebounds of missed shots, blocked shots, steals, interceptions, or violations by an opponent. Inbounding the ball quickly after an opponent scores from the field or on a free throw also provides an opportunity to start the fast break.

After gaining possession you should yell a key word, such as *ball!* Immediately look upcourt for the possibility of passing ahead to an open teammate for an uncontested break-away layup. When a quick pass ahead is not there, a quick outlet pass to your point guard (best ball handler and playmaker) is needed. The quicker you outlet the ball, the better—provided your pass is completed. When you are the rebounder, if there is too much congestion or you are trapped under your opponent's basket, use one or two strong power dribbles up the middle and then look to complete your outlet pass to the point guard. If your point guard is not open, pass to another teammate on the weak side of the court.

Your point guard will handle the ball in the middle of the fast break. The point guard should get open to receive an outlet pass in the area between the top of the circle and halfcourt on the side the ball was rebounded, calling for the ball by using a key word, such as *outlet!* If denied a pass in this area, the point guard should look to make a backdoor cut toward your basket. When the point guard is denied, a teammate (particularly a player on the weak-side wing) should be alert to flash back to the ball, then pass to the point guard on a backdoor cut toward the basket or on a front cut toward the ball. If the rebounder is in trouble and cannot make an outlet pass, the point guard should come back to that player to receive a short pass or handoff. As a point guard, use your voice to demand the ball and come to meet the pass. Catch the ball with a one-two stop, pivot to the middle, see the rim, and then look to quickly advance the ball up the court, either by a pass or a dribble (see Diagram 8.1).

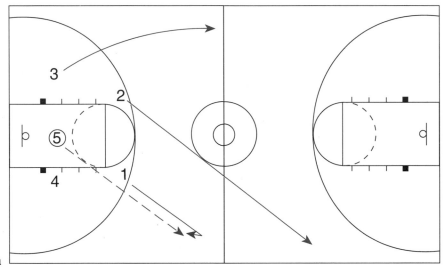

Rebounder (5) outlets to point guard (1)

Players 2 and 3 sprint ahead to fill outside lanes

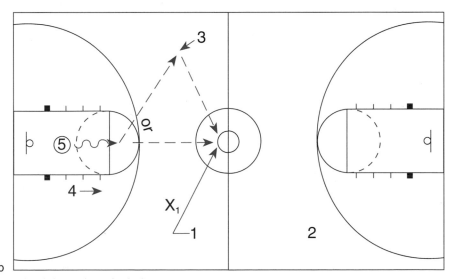

Point guard (1) cuts backdoor when denied

When in congested area or trapped, rebounder (5) power dribbles up middle and outlets to 1 or 3

Diagram 8.1   Possession phase: Starting the fast break.

Detecting Errors in Starting the Fast Break

The most common errors in starting the fast break are listed here, along with suggestions to correct them.

ERROR 🚫

CORRECTION

ERROR	CORRECTION
1. You anticipate someone on your team will gain possession and you run away from the ball to start the fast break before obtaining possession.	1. You must *first* gain possession of the ball—before starting your fast break.
2. After gaining possession of the ball, you do not see open players upcourt.	2. Once in possession of the ball, yell *ball!*, see the rim, and look to pass ahead to open receivers.
3. As a point guard, you do not get open to receive an outlet pass.	3. Get open to receive an outlet pass in the area between the top of the circle and halfcourt on the side the ball was rebounded, calling for the ball with the word *outlet!* If you are denied a pass in this area, look to make a backdoor cut toward your basket.
4. After rebounding you are trapped or you are in a congested area and unable to make the outlet pass.	4. As the rebounder unable to make the outlet pass, use one or two power dribbles up the middle and then look to pass. As the point guard who sees the rebounder is unable to make the outlet pass, come back to the rebounder to receive a short pass or handoff. Call out the word *ball!* to demand the ball.
5. As the point guard, you are denied receiving the outlet pass.	5. When you are denied, make a backdoor cut toward your basket. Signal your backdoor cut with a key word such as *eyeball!* If the rebounder is in trouble, come back to the ball for a short pass or handoff, calling out *ball!* to demand the ball.
6. You are the point guard, but your teammate does not pass you the ball.	6. As a point guard, use your voice to demand the ball and, if necessary, take it out of your teammate's hands.
7. As the point guard receiving an outlet pass, you dribble before looking upcourt.	7. Catch the ball with a one-two stop, pivot to middle, see the rim, and then look to quickly advance the ball up the court with a pass or dribble.

FILLING THE FAST-BREAK POSITIONS

After receiving the outlet pass, you should immediately look upcourt for the possibility of passing ahead to an open teammate for an uncontested breakaway layup or a 2-on-1 scoring opportunity. When you are the point guard and a quick pass ahead is not there, push the dribble upcourt into the middle of the floor. Signal your move by yelling *middle!* When you are *not* the point guard and a quick pass ahead is not there, look to pass the ball to the point guard in the middle of the floor.

To execute the controlled three-lane fast break, think of the court as divided by imaginary lines (into three lanes). The point guard (number 1) will handle the ball in the middle lane of the fast break, signaling this with the key word *middle!* The shooting guard (number 2) will be a wing and fill one of the out-side lanes, and the small forward (number 3) will also be a wing and fill the other outside lane.

If two players find themselves in the same lane, whoever gets there second must cut across to the lane on the other side of the court. The lanes should be called out: The player filling the right lane yells *right!* and the player filling the left lane yells *left!* The wings should stay wide, about 5 feet from the sideline, and run ahead of the ball. The remaining players—usually the power forward (number 4) and center (number 5)—will be trailers. The first trailer (usually your best *post-up* player) takes position several feet to the rear and left side of the middle player and yells *trailer left!* The second trailer (usually the best *passer* and *outside shooter* among your big players) follows the play upcourt, serving as a defensive safety (see Diagram 8.2)

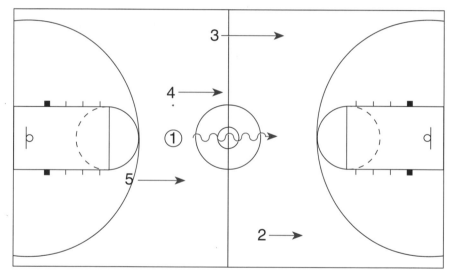

Point guard (1) dribbles middle

Wings (2 and 3) run ahead in outside lanes (5 feet from sideline)

Player 4 fills first trailer position (several feet to rear and side of middle player

Player 5 fills second trailer position (follows as defensive safety)

Diagram 8.2   Position phase: Filling lanes on the fast break.

Detecting Errors in Filling the Fast-Break Positions

The most common errors in filling the fast-break positions are listed here, along with suggestions to correct them.

ERROR 🚫

CORRECTION

ERROR	CORRECTION
1. A player other than the best ball handler dribbles middle, resulting in a possible turnover and missed scoring opportunity.	1. The point guard should demand the ball and if necessary take the ball out of a teammate's hands.
2. The fast break is too slow in developing.	2. The point guard on the fast break must look to pass ahead or pass to the trailer to encourage the wings and trailer to sprint to their positions.
3. Two or more players fill the same positions and may even bump into each other.	3. All players must communicate by yelling out their fast-break positions.
4. The wings run too close to the middle, allowing one defender to guard two or more players.	4. The wings should stay wide, about 5 feet from the sideline, and run ahead of the ball.

EXECUTING THE 2-ON-1 FAST BREAK

The 2-on-1 is a quick way to move the ball upcourt and should result in a scoring layup. When you gain possession of the ball, you should immediately look upcourt, read the offensive situation, and react to it. See whether the 2-on-1 fast break, a quick scoring option, is available.

When you and a teammate recognize a 2-on-1 fast-break situation, you should immediately alert each other by yelling, *2-on-1!* Move the ball upcourt, quickly passing back and forth to each other while maintaining lane-wide position (12-feet width of the free throw lane). Being wider than that results in longer passes that are more easily intercepted and in a slower break. Being any narrower than that, however, allows the defender to guard both offensive players more easily.

When you have the ball as you reach the scoring area (just above the top of the circle), you must decide whether to pass or drive. Good decisions come from reading the defense. When the defender attacks you and is on your driving line, pass to an open team-

mate cutting to the basket. Use a quick inside-hand bounce pass with a smaller player and a sure two-handed lob with a taller teammate or someone with great leaping ability. Both the bounce and lob passes have less chance of being intercepted than a chest pass. When the defender is off the driving line, drive to the basket. The usual defensive adjustment is to stop the ball high, a step above the foul line. On a pass to the cutter a larger defender will react by trying to block the shot behind the shooter's head. A smaller player, however, will attempt to draw a charge or steal the ball. As you drive to the basket, you should react to the defense and take the ball to the basket with a strong, two-handed layup. Your teammate should follow in prepared to rebound a possible miss and score with a power move.

Within the scoring area penetrate past the foul line to score only if the defense gives you an open driving line to the basket. Penetrating past the foul line and then attempting to pass creates congestion and allows one defender to guard two players. This can result in an interception or charging foul.

When executed properly, the 2-on-1 fast break is a fine example of teamwork and one of the most exciting plays in basketball (see Diagram 8.3).

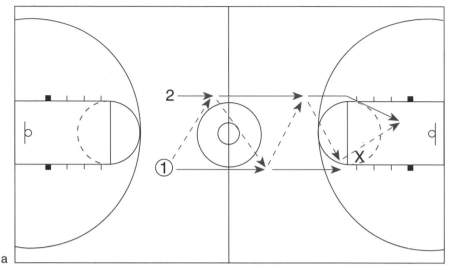

a

Player 1 sees defender on driving line and passes to cutting teammate

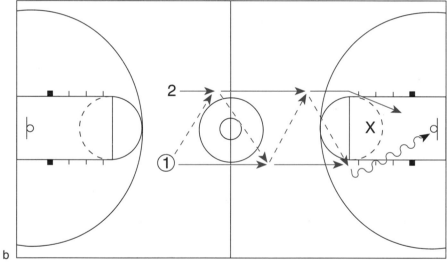

b

Player 1 sees defender off driving line and drives to basket

Diagram 8.3   Scoring phase: 2-on-1 fast break.

Detecting Errors in the 2-on-1 Fast Break

The most common errors in the 2-on-1 fast break are listed here, along with suggestions to correct them.

ERROR 🚫

1. You are too slow moving the ball upcourt.

2. When you reach the scoring area (just above the top of the circle), you do not read the defense and make a poor decision on whether to pass or drive.

3. In the scoring area you penetrate past the foul line before passing, which creates congestion and allows one defender to guard two players or results in an interception or charging foul.

CORRECTION

1. Maintain lane-wide position while passing and cutting for quicker movement upcourt.

2. Read the defense when you reach the scoring area. If your defender is on your driving line, pass to the cutter. If your defender is off the driving line, drive to the basket.

3. Only penetrate past the foul line to score if the defense gives you an open driving line to the basket.

EXECUTING THE 3-ON-2 FAST BREAK

The 3-on-2 is a classic fast-break situation. The point guard should have the ball and read the situation when the fast-breaking team enters the scoring area (normally a step outside the 3-point line). Correct decisions are needed on whether to penetrate to the basket or pass to the wing. The point guard should penetrate past the foul line and drive for a score only if the defense gives an open driving line to the basket. Otherwise, it is always better to stop above the foul line. Too much penetration causes congestion and may result in a charging foul.

The two defenders normally will be in tandem, with the top defender meeting the player with the ball slightly ahead of the foul line. When the wings reach the foul line extended, they should cut at a 45-degree angle toward the basket. When attacked by the top defender, the point guard should pass to the open wing player and cut to the ball-side elbow. In turn, the wing player should catch the pass in position to shoot and react to the defense. If the back defender does not come out, the wing should be in position for a catch-and-shoot bank jump shot, a short drive for a pull-up bank jump shot in rhythm and range, or a drive to the basket.

The normal defensive adjustment is for the back player to yell *ball!* and cover the pass to the wing, while the top player yells *you have help!* and drops back to give help on a drive or block out on a shot. When this occurs reverse the ball to the point guard, who may shoot or pass to the weak-side wing for a jump shot. The offense should not only get an open shot but also establish offensive rebounding position (see Diagram 8.4).

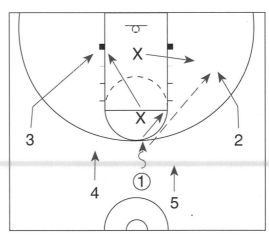

At foul line extended, wings (2 and 3) make sharp 45-degree cut to basket

Point guard (1) bounce passes to open wing (2) and then cuts to ball-side elbow

Player 4 trails play, then spots up at weak-side elbow

Player 5 trails as defensive safety

Diagram 8.4   Scoring phase: 3-on-2 fast break.

Detecting Errors in the 3-on-2 Fast Break

The most common errors in the 3-on-2 fast break are listed here, along with suggestions to correct them.

ERROR **CORRECTION**

ERROR	CORRECTION
1. The point guard does not have the ball when the fast-breaking team enters the scoring area, which lessens passing possibilities and scoring options.	1. The point guard should demand the ball and, if necessary, take the ball from a teammate's hands.
2. The point guard penetrates past the foul line before passing, which creates congestion and either allows one defender to guard two players or results in a charging foul.	2. The point guard should only penetrate past the foul line to score if the defense gives an open driving line to the basket. Otherwise, it is always better to stop above the foul line.
3. The wings cut to the corners, making for a difficult corner shot rather than an easier bank jump shot.	3. The wings should cut at a 45-degree angle to be in position for a catch-and-shoot bank jump shot, a short drive for a pull-up bank jump shot in rhythm and range, or a drive to the basket.
4. After passing to the wing, the point guard does not cut to the ball-side elbow.	4. Follow the pass to the ball-side elbow, positioning yourself to receive a return pass for a jump shot or a pass to the weak-side wing.

EXECUTING THE 4-ON-3 FAST BREAK

The 4-on-3 fast break uses the first trailer. When the defense gets three players back, the wing player should dribble to the corner and look to pass to the first trailer cutting to the ball-side box. The wing player should keep the dribble alive until able to pass to the trailer or reverse the ball to the middle. The first trailer should first cut to the weak-side elbow and then make a diagonal cut to a post-up position above the ball-side box, looking to receive a pass from the wing. After beating the defense to the box, the trailer should seal a retreating defender on the topside and look for a pass from the baseline side. The wing then should pass to the trailer with a sidearm bounce pass from the baseline side (see Diagram 8.5).

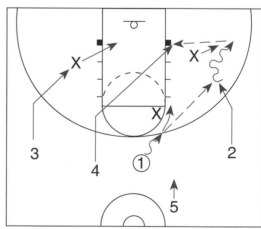

Point guard (1) bounce passes to open wing (2) and then cuts to ball-side elbow

Wing 2 dribbles to corner, then makes sidearm bounce pass to trailer

Wing 3 prepares to rebound

First trailer (4) makes diagonal cut to low post at ball-side block

Second trailer (5) follows as defensive safety

Diagram 8.5 Scoring phase: 4-on-3 fast break.

Detecting Errors in the 4-on-3 Fast Break

The most common errors in the 4-on-3 fast break are listed here, along with suggestions to correct them.

ERROR

CORRECTION

1. The wing has trouble passing the ball to the first trailer because they are too close to each other.

1. The wing player should dribble to the corner to create enough spacing to pass the ball to the first trailer, who posts up above the ball-side box.

2. The wing stops dribbling, is unable to pass to the trailer or back to the point guard, and is vulnerable to being trapped in the corner.

2. The wing player should keep the dribble alive until passing to the trailer or reversing the ball back to the point guard.

EXECUTING THE FAST-BREAK SWING

In the fast-break swing the second trailer receives a pass and swings the ball from the ball side to the weak side. When the defense gets four or five players back, and the wing player cannot pass to the first trailer in the post, each of the other players should spot up within shooting range to swing (reverse) the ball to the weak side. The point guard should spot up above the ball-side elbow, while the second trailer spots up above the weak-side elbow. Meanwhile, the weak-side wing should maintain spacing at the imaginary foul line extended. After receiving a swing pass, each perimeter player's options are to (in order) (a) pass inside to the post-up player moving across the lane, (b) swing the ball to the weak side, and (c) shoot the outside shot. During the swing of the ball the post-up player should move on each pass across the lane to the weak-side box.

The second trailer has an important role during the swing. If the defense denies him the first swing pass, the point guard should either cut through to the weak-side corner or pull out to the ball-side sideline. As this happens the second trailer must immediately flash to the ball-side elbow to receive a pass from the wing. Receiving the pass the second trailer's options are to (in order) (a) pass to the weak-side wing, (b) pass inside, and (c) shoot.

When a swing of the ball to the weak side does not produce an open inside or outside shot, the team can get into a passing game offense or the point guard can demand the ball and run a set play (see Diagram 8.6).

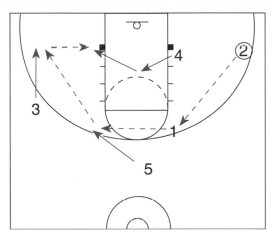

Post-up player (4) moves from block to block as ball is passed (swings) to players spotting up on perimeter

If defense denies first swing pass, point guard (1) cuts through or pulls and second trailer (5) flashes to ballside

Diagram 8.6   Scoring phase: Fast break swing.

Detecting Errors in the Fast-Break Swing

ERROR

The most common errors in the fast-break swing are listed here, along with suggestions to correct them.

CORRECTION

ERROR	CORRECTION
1. On a swing of the ball, the perimeter players first look to shoot, rather than looking inside first and weak side second.	1. The swing players' options are to first look to pass inside, then look weak side to continue the swing of the ball, and last look to shoot.
2. After swinging the ball to the weak side, the point guard does not direct the team.	2. After swinging the ball one time from ball side to weak side, the point guard should direct the team to get into the passing game or should demand the ball and direct a set play.

Fast Break Drills

1. Three-Player Parallel Lane Passing

Select two players as teammates. Get in three lanes evenly spaced along the baseline. One player starts with the ball in the middle lane, tosses it high on the backboard, and rebounds with two hands yelling *ball!* On the rebound the wing on the right runs to an outlet position past the foul line extended, yelling *outlet!* The rebounder makes a two-handed overhead outlet pass to the right wing beyond the foul line extended. The rebounder sprints up the middle yelling *middle!* and receives a return chest pass. The left wing sprints up the court yelling *left!* The player in the middle makes a chest pass to the left wing who has sprinted ahead. Continue the drill up the court, each player passing and sprinting in parallel lanes while calling out lanes.

When the ball is received above the free throw line in the scoring area, the middle player makes a bounce pass to the weak-side wing for a bank jump shot. At the foul line extended each wing should cut at a sharp 45-degree angle to the basket. The wing who receives the pass shoots a bank jump shot from 15 to 18 feet. The other wing should follow in, prepared to rebound a possible miss and score with a power move. After a score switch lanes—in a middle to right to left order—and continue the drill back down the court.

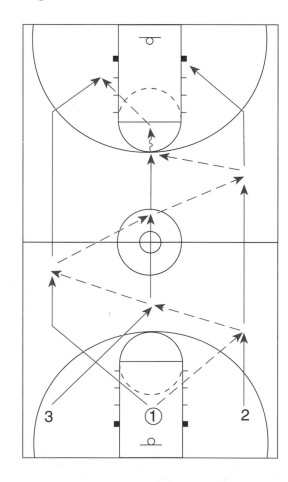

Success Goal = 2 out of 3 bank jump shots made from each side

Your Score =

a. (#) _____ bank jump shots made out of (#) _____ attempts from right side

b. (#) _____ bank jump shots made out of (#) _____ attempts from left side

2. Three-Player Weave (Pass and Go Behind)

Select two players as your teammates and proceed as in the three-player parallel lane passing drill. After making a two-handed overhead outlet pass to the player in the right lane, the rebounder follows the pass (sprinting behind the player passed to), filling the right lane, and yelling *right!* The player in the left lane then sprints to the middle lane yelling *middle!* The player in the right lane makes a chest pass to the player now in the middle, follows the pass (sprinting behind the player passed to), filling the left lane, and yelling *left!* Continue the drill up the court with each player passing and going behind the player who received the pass, making a weave pattern and filling and calling out a lane. When the ball is received above the free throw line in the scoring area the middle player makes a bounce pass to the weak-side wing for a bank jump shot. At the foul line extended each wing should cut at a sharp 45-degree angle to the basket, continuing as with the first drill.

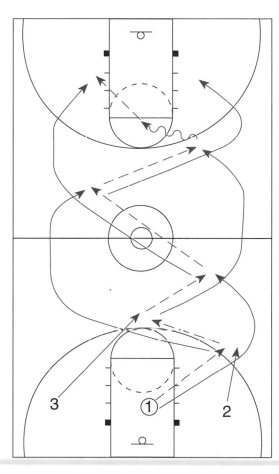

Success Goal = 2 out of 3 bank jump shots made from each side

Your Score =

a. (#) _____ bank jump shots made out of (#) _____ attempts from right side

b. (#) _____ bank jump shots made out of (#) _____ attempts from left side

3. 2-on-1

Three players are necessary for this drill: two on offense and one on defense. The two offensive players start at the boxes outside the lane on their defensive end, and the defensive player starts just inside the foul line with a ball. The defender starts the drill by passing to one of the offensive players and then sprinting back to the free throw line in the scoring area.

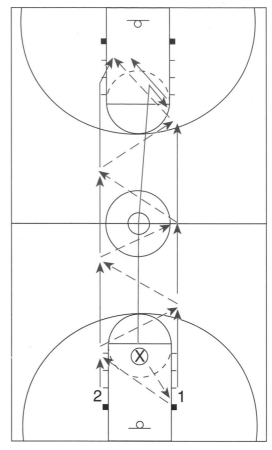

Both offensive players yell out *2-on-1!* and move the ball upcourt, quickly passing back and forth while maintaining lane-wide position (12-feet width of the free throw lane). If you have the ball as you reach the scoring area (just above the top of the circle), read the defense and decide whether to pass or drive. If the defender attacks you on your driving line, pass to your teammate cutting to the basket. Use a quick, inside-hand bounce pass with a smaller player or a two-handed lob with a taller player or one with great leaping ability.

When the defender is off the driving line, drive to the basket, taking the ball to the basket with a strong, two-handed layup. The offense should not only get an open shot but also establish offensive rebounding position.

When you play on defense, stop the ball high, a step above the foul line. React on a pass to the cutter by trying to block the shot behind the shooter's head, draw a charge, or steal the ball.

Change positions and continue the drill. On offense award yourself 1 point each time you or your teammate score. On defense award yourself 1 point each time you stop the two offensive players from scoring.

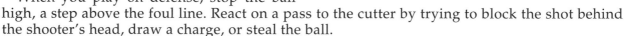

Success Goal = Score more points than the other players, with 5 points winning the game

Your Score =

  a. (#) _____ your points

  b. (#) _____ second player's points

  c. (#) _____ third player's points

4. 3-on-2

Five players are necessary for this drill: three on offense and two on defense. The defensive players start at halfcourt and sprint to defensive positions in tandem just inside the free throw line in the scoring area. The offensive players are positioned evenly spaced along the baseline in three lanes. One player, starting with the ball in the middle lane, tosses it high on the backboard and rebounds it with two hands yelling *ball!* On the rebound the right wing runs to an outlet position past the foul line extended and yells *outlet!* The rebounder makes a two-handed overhead outlet pass to the right wing beyond the foul line extended, sprints up the middle yelling *middle!* and receives a return chest pass. The left wing sprints up the court yelling *left!* The middle player makes a chest pass to the left wing who has sprinted ahead. Continue the drill up the court with each player passing and sprinting in parallel position and calling out their lanes. When the ball is received above the free throw line in the scoring area, the middle player reads the position of the defensive players.

The defensive players should be in tandem, with one on top and one behind. The top defensive player defends the player with the ball, yelling *I've got the ball!* The bottom defender near the basket yells *I've got the hole!* On a pass to the wing, the bottom defender takes the ball and the top defender retreats to defend the basket or block out the weak-side wing and rebound a possible missed shot.

At the foul line extended, each wing should cut at a sharp 45-degree angle to the basket. The offensive player in the middle makes a bounce pass to one of the wings for a bank jump shot from 15 to 18 feet or makes a driving layup. The other wing follows in, prepared to rebound a possible miss and to score with a power move. The middle player stays back for a swing of the ball, in case the wing decides not to shoot, or for defensive balance on a shot. After a score switch lanes—in a middle to right to left order—and continue the drill back down the court.

Change positions and continue the drill. On offense you get 1 point each time you or your teammates score. On defense, you get 1 point each time you stop the three offensive players from scoring.

Success Goal = Score more points than the other players, with 5 points winning the game

Your Score =

a. (#) _____ your points

b. (#) _____ second player's points

c. (#) _____ third player's points

d. (#) _____ fourth player's points

e. (#) _____ fifth player's points

5. *Continuous 3-on-2, 2-on-1*

Select at least 5 and no more than 15 players for this drill. Two defensive players start in tandem just inside the free throw line in the scoring area. Three offensive players are evenly spaced along the baseline in three lanes. Start with the ball in the middle lane as in the previous drill. After a rebound and two-handed outlet pass, the three offensive players move up the court to the scoring area where they attempt to score against the two defenders. When either the offense scores or the defense obtains possession by an interception or rebound, the original two defenders start a 2-on-1 fast break in the other direction, with the shooter retreating back on defense to defend in a 2-on-1 situation. The other two original offensive players remain back as the defense for the next 3-on-2 fast break finishing at that end. Now when the offense scores or the defensive player obtains possession by an interception or rebound, a three-lane fast break begins in the other direction, with the two offensive players joined by the defender or with three new players if they are available. The drill becomes a 3-on-2 and 2-on-1 continuous fast-break drill. On offense award yourself 1 point each time you or your teammates score. On defense award yourself 1 point each time you stop the three offensive players from scoring.

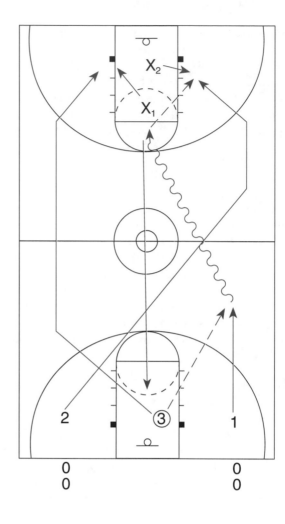

Success Goal = Score more points than the other players, with 5 points winning the game

Your Score =

    a. (#) _____ your points

    b. (#) _____ second player's points

    c. (#) _____ third player's points

    d. (#) _____ fourth player's points

    e. (#) _____ fifth player's points

6. 3-on-2 with Defensive Trailer

Select at least 9 but no more than 15 players, grouping them into three or more teams with three players on a team. Team 1 starts on offense, its three players evenly spaced along the baseline in three lanes, with the middle player having a ball. Team 2 will be out of bounds at halfcourt, ready to start on defense while the remaining teams wait their turn. The middle player on Team 1 starts the drill by tossing the ball high on the backboard and rebounding it with two hands. As the ball is rebounded, two players from Team 2 run and touch a foot in the center circle before sprinting back to tandem defensive positions just inside the free throw line in the scoring area. The three offensive players move up the court to the scoring area where they attempt to score. After one of the offensive players crosses halfcourt, the remaining defensive player from Team 2 is allowed to run and touch the center circle and sprint back as a defensive trailer. After the offense (Team 1) scores or the defense obtains possession by an interception or rebound, the original offensive team gets off the court and becomes the last team waiting out of bounds at halfcourt.

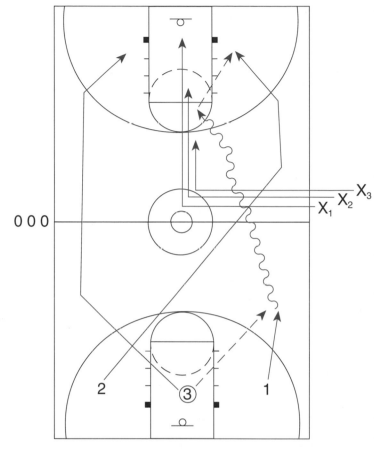

Team 2, the original defensive team, now starts a three-lane fast break in the other direction. Two players from Team 3 run and touch a foot in the center circle and sprint back on defense, with the third player running and touching a foot in the center circle after a player from the offensive team crosses halfcourt. The drill becomes a continuous 3-on-2 with a defensive trailer fast break. A variation is to allow any team that scores to press up to halfcourt. Award your team 1 point for each score.

Success Goal = Score more points than the other teams, with 7 points winning the game

Your Score =

   a. (#) _____ your points

   b. (#) _____ second team's points

   c. (#) _____ third team's points

   d. (#) _____ fourth team's points

   e. (#) _____ fifth team's points

7. 4-on-3 with Defensive Trailer

Select 12 to 16 players, grouping them into three or more teams with 4 players on a team. The drill is the same as the previous one except that (a) four players are on offense and (b) three players from each defensive team run and touch a foot in the center circle before sprinting back to defensive positions as the offensive players move up the court. Again, as one of the offensive players crosses halfcourt, the remaining defensive player runs and touches a foot in the center circle and sprints back as a defensive trailer. The drill becomes a continuous 4-on-3 with a defensive trailer fast break. Award your team 1 point for each score.

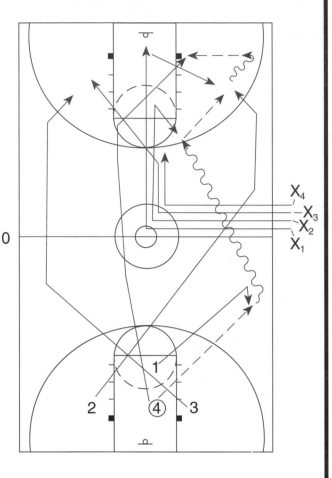

Success Goal = Score more points than the other teams, with 7 points winning the game

Your Score =

   a. (#) _____ your team's points

   b. (#) _____ second team's points

   c. (#) _____ third team's points

   d. (#) _____ fourth team's points

8. 5-on-0 Fast Break Options

Select 5 to 15 players, grouping them into one or more teams of 5 each. Each team will run the fast break using a different scoring option down the court each time. The drill starts with the fast-breaking team in defensive positions at the defensive end. Either the center or power forward tosses the ball on the backboard, rebounds it, and makes an outlet pass to the point guard. The scoring options include the following:

- Pass to the strong-side wing for a bank jump shot.
- Pass to the weak-side wing for a bank jump shot.
- Pass to the strong-side wing who then passes to the first trailer at the strong-side box for a low-post move.
- Pass to the strong-side wing who then passes back to the point guard at the strong-side elbow for a jump shot.
- Pass to the strong-side wing. Then the point guard either cuts through to the weak-side corner or pulls out to the ball-side sideline. The strong-side wing then passes to the second trailer, who is flashing to the ball-side elbow for a jump shot.
- Pass to the strong-side wing, and have the point guard either cut through to the weak-side corner or pull out to the ball-side sideline. The strong-side wing then passes to the second trailer, who is flashing to the ball-side elbow, and who then passes inside to the first trailer for a low-post move.
- Pass to the strong-side wing. The point guard either cuts through to the weak-side corner or pulls out to the ball-side sideline. The strong-side wing then passes to the second trailer, who is

flashing to the ball-side elbow, and who then passes to the weak-side wing for a jump shot.

- Pass to the strong-side wing who then swings the ball to the weak side by passing to the point guard at the ball-side elbow, who passes to the second trailer at the weak-side elbow, who passes to the weak-side wing. The weak-side wing takes a jump shot or passes inside to the first trailer, who moves high across the lane on each pass from the strong-side box to the weak-side box.

Award your team 1 point for correct execution of each fast-break scoring option and 1 point for each shot made at the end of the scoring option.

Success Goal = 12 of 16 possible points

Your Score =

    a. (#) _____ your team's points   c. (#) _____ third team's points

    b. (#) _____ second team's points

9. 5-on-1 Swing

Select 5 to 15 players, grouping them into one or more teams of 5 each. Select a player from one of the teams to play defense on the first trailer. Each offensive team will run a fast break swing option, looking to get the ball inside to the first trailer. The offensive team will swing the ball, with each perimeter player looking to pass inside to the first trailer who attempts to get open—by moving high across the lane on each pass from the strong-side box to the weak-side box. On receiving a pass the first trailer attempts to score with a low-post move. Award your team 1 point for each shot made by the first trailer.

Success Goal = Score more points than the other teams, with 5 points winning the game

Your Score =

    a. (#) _____ your team's points   c. (#) _____ third team's points

    b. (#) _____ second team's points

10. 5-on-1 Deny the Point Guard

This drill is the same as the previous one except that a defender is placed on the point guard, or middle player, instead of the first trailer. Only the point guard is allowed to score. Again using 5 to 15 players grouped into teams of five, select a player from one of the teams to play defense on the point guard. This gives the point guard practice in moving without the ball, such as cutting through to the weak-side corner or pulling out to the ball-side sideline, while being denied from receiving a return pass at the ball-side elbow. It also gives the other offensive players practice when the point guard is denied the ball, such as flashing to the ball. Your team gets 1 point for each shot made by the point guard.

Success Goal = Score more points than the other teams, with 5 points winning the game

Your Score =

    a. (#) _____ your team's points

    b. (#) _____ second team's points   c. (#) _____ third team's points

11. 5-on-2 Fast Break

This drill is the same as the previous two drills except that now two defenders are used. Therefore, select two players from one of the teams to play defense. These defenders can be placed on the point guard and the first trailer, on the two wings, or on any other two players. Only the defended players may score. Award your team 1 point for each shot made by one of the defended players.

Success Goal = Score more points than the other teams, with 5 points winning the game

Your Score =

    a. (#) _____ your team's points   c. (#) _____ third team's points

    b. (#) _____ second team's points

12. 5-on-(2 + 1 + 2) Fast Break

This drill is used to give a fast-breaking team practice in reading and reacting to various defensive options. Select 10 players, grouping 5 as the offensive team and 5 as the defensive team. The offensive team will run a fast break and the defensive team will choose defensive options to defend against it. Divide the full court into three equal areas: Area I (initial area), Area II (secondary area), and Area III (scoring area). The defensive team will be spread into a 2 + 1 + 2 alignment with two defenders in Area I, one defender in Area II, and two defenders in Area III. The drill starts with a coach, teacher, or extra player intentionally missing a shot. Five members of the fast-breaking team start in defensive positions, block out their two opponents, and rebound the ball. The defenders in Area I have several options:

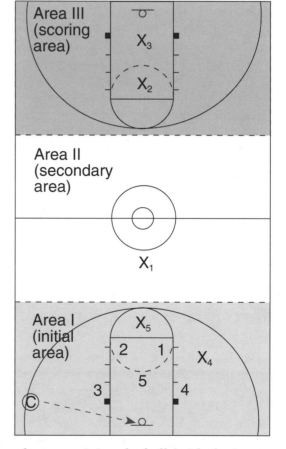

- Going for the rebound
- Trapping the rebounder
- Stealing the ball from the rebounder
- Dropping back to deny a passing lane to the favorite or other potential outlet receiver
- Intercepting the outlet pass

Once the fast-breaking team advances the ball into Area II, the secondary area, the single defender in Area II has several options:

- Overplay the outlet receiver and deny the outlet pass
- Allow the outlet pass and pop up on the offensive player receiving the ball (with the intent to draw a charge)
- Pressure the dribbler to delay the fast break
- Allow the dribbler to go by
- Try to steal the ball by flicking the ball from behind

Once the fast-breaking team advances the ball into Area III, the scoring area, the two defenders in Area III have several options:

- Trap the player with the ball
- Play a tandem defense inside the free throw lane

- Pressure the shooter
- Rebound a possible missed shot

The offensive team gets 1 point each time it scores. If the defense commits a foul, the offense gets the ball and starts again. If an offensive player misses a shot and a teammate gets an offensive rebound, continue playing. The defense gets a point if it gets the ball on a steal or rebound or if it forces the offense into a violation. Five points win the game. The defense then goes to offense, and the offense goes to defense.

Success Goal = Win more games than your opponents, with 5 points winning each game

Your Score =

a. (#) _____ games won by your team

b. (#) _____ games won by opponents

13. 5-on-5 Fast Break

This drill gives the offensive team practice in running a fast break and the defensive team practice in defending against the fast break. Select 10 players for this drill, grouping them into two teams of 5 each. One team plays offense and the other plays defense.

To defend against the fast break, the defensive team should have the player nearest to the rebounder pressure the outlet pass. Also have a defender deny a passing lane to the favorite or other potential outlet receiver. The other defenders should quickly retreat to the scoring area by sprinting back on the ball side of the floor while calling out their individual assignments in order—with the first player back taking the most dangerous offensive player (usually the one near the basket). The second player back should take the second most dangerous player (usually the player with the ball). The third player back takes the third most dangerous player (the opposing team's best shooter). You may instead decide to have your defensive center always take the offensive center. Once you have two defensive players back, you can have a defensive guard attack the offensive player receiving the ball, with the intent to pressure the dribbler to delay the fast break.

Success Goal = Win more games than your opponents, with 5 points winning each game

Your Score =

a. (#) _____ games won by your team

b. (#) _____ games won by opponents

Fast Break Checks

The fast break places a premium on physical condition, fundamentals, teamwork, and intelligent decisions. Creating an easy scoring opportunity by numerical advantage is the first objective of the fast break. The 2-on-1 and 3-on-2 often result in a layup. The 4-on-3 usually leads to an inside post-up shot, and the 5-on-4 often allows for an easy swing and open shot on the weak side. A second objective is to attack before the opponents are set to play team defense or rebound, and a third objective is motivating the fast-breaking team to play tough defense and rebound. The controlled three-lane fast break is the most common fast-break attack. In the controlled fast break, fundamental execution and making good decisions matter more than speed. The controlled fast break has three phases: starting the fast break, getting into position, and finishing the break with the correct scoring option.

Have a trained observer—your coach, teacher, or a skilled player—subjectively evaluate your skills and decision making at different fast break positions.

Step 9 Team Offense: Execute the Passing Game

The passing game, or motion offense, is one of the most popular team offenses in basketball. Used early in the history of the game, it is again being used to some extent by a majority of teams. In the passing game players are guided more by principles than a strict set of specific assigned responsibilities. At its best basketball is a team game played by five players moving the ball, moving without the ball, and making quick, intelligent decisions, especially in regard to shot selection. These are the objectives of the passing game offense.

WHY THE PASSING GAME IS IMPORTANT

Every player should learn to execute the passing game, because it teaches team play to developing players and is an offense used by many teams. The passing game depends on the sound execution of fundamentals, including moving the ball and moving without the ball. It depends also on intelligent decisions and unselfish team play.

EXECUTING THE PASSING GAME

The passing game can be started from a variety of offensive formations, or sets, including the 3-2, 2-3, 1-3-1, 2-1-2, and 1-4. The 3-2 open, or spread, set is the most basic formation for learning to play team offense. It involves three perimeter players and two baseline players. The point position is above the top of the circle. The wing positions are at the imaginary foul line extended on each side. The baseline positions are at the midpoint between the corner and the basket on each side. The open set encourages versatility, rather than forcing a player into a restricted role as a center, power forward, small forward, shooting guard, or point guard. It allows each player the opportunity to handle the ball, cut, screen, and move outside and inside. The 3-2 set provides initial structure and spacing that allow players to execute basic two- and three-person plays and plays involving all five players, such as a five-player weave or five-player give-and-go offense (see Diagram 9.1)

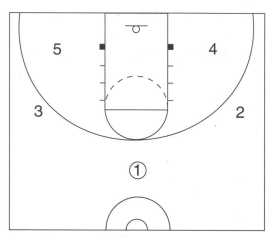

Player 1 at point position (top of circle)

Players 2 and 3 at wing positions (foul line extended)

Players 4 and 5 at baseline positions (midpoint between corner and basket)

Diagram 9.1   3-2 open, or spread, formation.

BASIC PRINCIPLES

When executing the passing game, keep in mind these basic principles of good teamwork.

1. Talk. Communication is a key to all aspects of team offense. The passing game is not a set play offense, and players are not assigned a specific set of responsibilities. Therefore, continuing communication between players becomes especially important when executing the passing game.

2. See the rim. By seeing the rim, you see the entire court. When you have the ball, see the rim and look for teammates cutting to the basket, posting up, and cutting off of screens. When you do *not* have the ball, see the rim and the player with the ball.

3. Maintain spacing and court balance. Start in an open formation, with players spread 15 to 20 feet apart. Space yourselves high at the top, wide on the wing, and at the midpoint between the basket and corner on the baseline.

4. Backdoor cut when overplayed. When you are overplayed by your defender who denies you from receiving a pass, make a backdoor cut all the way to the basket. When backdoor cuts are frequently used, the passing game becomes a great offense for beating pressure defenses.

5. Flash between the passer and overplayed receiver. When a defender denies your teammate from catching the ball and you are the next player away from the receiver, you should automatically flash to an open area between the passer and the overplayed receiver. Flashing to the ball helps relieve defensive pressure on your teammates by giving the passer another outlet. A flash not only can prevent a possible turnover but also can create a scoring opportunity if the overplayed receiver combines it with a well-timed backdoor cut.

6. Keep the middle open. When you cut to the basket and do not receive a pass, you should continue on through and fill an open spot on the side of the court with fewer players. This will keep the middle open and the floor balanced. Do not stay in the post area for more than one count.

7. Move to a vacated spot quickly. When you are the next player away from a cutting player, you should quickly move to the vacated spot. It is especially important to replace a player who has cut from the point or top position. To replace the player at the point, cut high above the 3-point line, creating a better passing angle to receive a swing pass from a wing and a better angle to reverse the ball to the weak side. This will also force the defense to cover more of the court, thus providing more space for cutting, driving, and posting up.

8. Options for wing position. When you are on the wing, your options are to catch and shoot within your rhythm and range or to continue your cut out wide. When you catch the ball outside of your range, look to pass inside to a cutter or player posting up. On the wing hold the ball for a count or two to allow cutters and post-up players time to get open. If you are unable to pass from there to an open teammate cutting or posting up, look to penetrate and pass (draw-and-kick) or try to balance the court by quickly dribbling to the point. Look to pass to a baseline player only if that teammate (a) is open for a catch-and-shoot jump shot within rhythm and range or (b) can make an easy pass to a player cutting inside or posting up. You can move the ball more quickly if you swing it from wing to point to wing and keep it off the baseline.

9. Options for point position. When you are at the point position, your options, in or-

der, are to (a) reverse the ball quickly to the weak side, (b) look inside for a pass to a post-up player, (c) penetrate and pass (draw-and-kick), or (d) fake a pass to the weak side and make a quick snapback pass to the wing on the side from which you received the pass.

10. Options for baseline position. When you are at a baseline position, look to set up your defender for a cut off a downscreen or set a back pick for a wing player. On the baseline you should especially be alert to flash to the ball when a wing is denied from receiving a pass. Look to receive a pass on the baseline only when you are in an open catch-and-shoot position (within your rhythm and range) or can make an easy pass to a player cutting inside or posting up. The ball can be moved quicker if it is kept off the baseline.

11. Options for post-up player. When you receive the ball in the low post, read the defense and look to score before passing out to a perimeter player. When you do not receive a pass in the low post, look to set a back pick for a perimeter player. After setting it, pop out to receive a pass on the perimeter for a possible jump shot within your rhythm and range.

12. Rebounding and defensive balance. On a shot inside players should rebound, while the point guard and another outside player should get back for defensive balance. When you take an outside shot (outside of the lane area), you should get back for defensive balance. Any time the player at the point drives to the basket, players in the wing positions should get back for defensive balance.

STARTING THE PASSING GAME OFFENSE

A member of your team, usually the point guard, signals the start of the passing game with a simple verbal call, such as *passing game!* or *motion!* or with a hand signal, such as circling one finger up. The best way to start is to pass the ball to the wing, and then work together, using basic passing game actions. After receiving a pass on the wing, you should be a triple threat to pass, shoot, or drive to the basket. On a drive, look to score or to penetrate and pass (draw-and-kick) inside or outside to an open teammate.

When the ball is at the point, the closest wing player should initiate movement by cutting through to create an open area for a baseline player who will cut to the wing for a pass from the point. When you are at the point and cannot pass to the wing, initiate movement by dribbling at the wing and using a dribble screen or weave action (see Diagram 9.2).

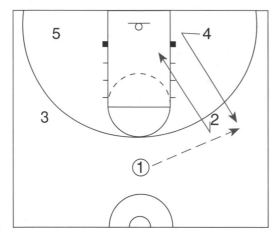

a

Wing player 2 cuts through to create opening for player 4

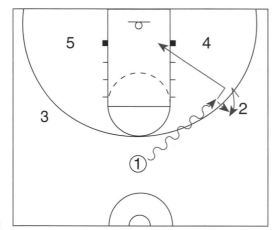

b

Player at point (1) sets dribble screen for wing 2 and then cuts to basket

---

Diagram 9.2   Start of passing game: Wing cut and dribble screen.

EXECUTING BASIC PASSING GAME ACTIONS

Some of the basic actions used in the passing game are the backdoor cut, flash, give-and-go, dribble screen or weave, downscreen, back pick, elbow curl, cross-screen, pick-and-roll, and draw-and-kick.

Backdoor Cut

A backdoor cut should be used automatically any time you are overplayed by a defender and prevented from receiving a

pass. It should also be used when your defender's head is turned away from you, causing a momentary loss of visual contact. Use a designated key word such as *eyeball!* to signal the passer that you are going backdoor. The designated word indicates that you will continue your backdoor cut to the basket once you start it. Set up your defender when you are on the wing by taking a step above the foul line extended or when you are at the point by taking a step above the free throw circle. After receiving the pass, look to shoot, drive to the basket for a layup, or penetrate and pass (draw-and-kick) (see Diagram 9.3).

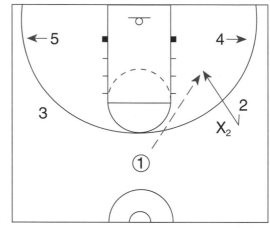

a

Offensive player 2, denied pass at wing, cuts backdoor

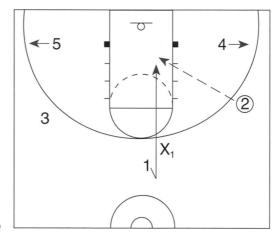

b

Offensive player 1, denied pass at top, cuts backdoor

Diagram 9.3   Backdoor cut: Two examples.

Flash

Any time you see a teammate being denied from receiving a pass and you are the next player away, you should automatically flash to an open area between the passer and overplayed receiver. Flashing to the ball relieves defensive pressure on your teammates by giving the passer another outlet. A flash not only can prevent a possible turnover but, combined with a well-timed backdoor cut by the overplayed receiver, it also can create a scoring opportunity. Signal your flash cut with the key word *flash!* As you receive the pass, look to pass to your overplayed teammate cutting backdoor to the basket. If your teammate is covered on the backdoor cut, front turn into a triple-threat position for a possible shot, drive to the basket, or pass.

Flash high when your teammate is prevented from receiving a pass on the perimeter. You can also flash to the high post when your teammate is being fronted in the low post, and you can flash to the low post if your teammate is being denied at the high post (see Diagram 9.4).

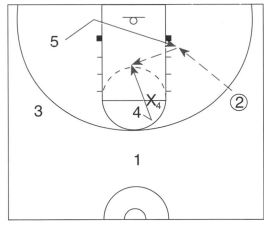

c

Player 5 sees high post 4 being denied, flashes to low post, receives pass from 2, and passes to 4 cutting backdoor

---

Diagram 9.4   Flash: Three examples.

Give-and-Go

The give-and-go is the most basic play in basketball. Give (pass) the ball to your teammate and go (cut) to the basket, looking to receive a return pass for a layup. Read and set up your defender with a well-timed fake before your cut. Fake by taking a step or two away from the ball (as if you were not involved in the play). Then, as your defender moves with you, change direction sharply and use a front cut to the basket. Another fake is taking a step or two toward the ball (as if you were going to set a screen for or take a handoff from the player with the ball). As your defender moves with you, change direction sharply and make a backdoor cut behind (refer back to Figure 7.2). Diagram 9.5 shows a five-player give-and-go offensive pattern.

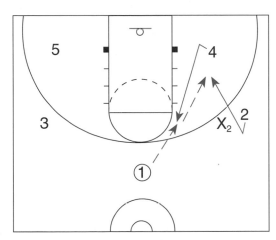

a

Player 4 sees wing 2 being denied, flashes high, receives pass from 1, and passes to 2 cutting backdoor

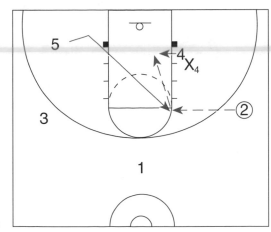

b

Player 5 sees low post 4 being denied, flashes high, receives pass from 2, and passes to 4 cutting to basket

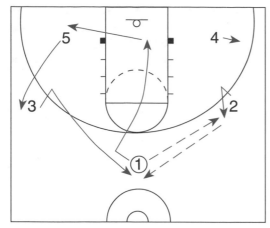

a

Start of give-and-go:

Point player (1) passes to wing 2 and cuts to basket

Weak-side wing (3) quickly replaces point and receives
   pass from 2

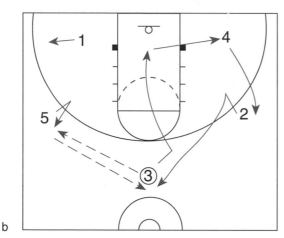

b

Continuity:

Player 3 passes to opposite wing 5 and cuts to basket

Weak-side wing (2) quickly replaces point and receives
   pass from 5

Diagram 9.5   5-player give-and-go pattern.

Dribble Screen or Weave

A dribble screen is set by dribbling toward a
teammate and screening the defender while
you hand the ball off to your teammate (refer
back to Figure 7.6). On a dribble screen the
defensive reaction usually will be for the
screener's defender to give defensive help or

to switch. Before receiving the handoff, you
should read the defensive positioning. When
your defender attempts to prevent the
handoff by getting in your path, make a
backdoor cut to the basket. After you receive
a handoff on a dribble screen read the defense: If the defenders do not switch and *your*
defender is slow getting over the screen, you
should turn the corner and drive to the basket. If your defender slides behind the screen,
you should look to take the outside shot. If
your *teammate's* defender switches to you as
you receive the handoff for an outside shot,
go at least two dribbles by the screen and
pass back to the screener, either rolling to the
basket or popping out.

One way to defend the dribble screen is
having the dribble screener's defender jump
switch into the path of the receiver, with the
intent of drawing a charge or changing the
direction of the player receiving the ball. To
combat the jump switch after your handoff
make a short, 5- to 10-foot cut to an open
area and look for a quick return pass. If you
anticipate a jump switch, you can fake the
handoff and drive to the basket.

Another defense for the dribble screen is
having both defenders trap the player receiving the ball on the handoff. If the defenders
trap you, retreat dribble to stretch the defense and then pass to your teammate, making a short, 5- to 10-foot cut to an open area.
The defense will then be outnumbered and
the player with the ball will be able to drive
or pass to an open teammate for a shot.

The dribble screen is used to execute a
weave, which is a basic play in basketball. A
weave involves at least three players who set
dribble screens for each other. It starts with a
dribble screen and handoff to your teammate.
After receiving the handoff, you can shoot
from behind the screen, drive to the basket,
or continue the weave by dribbling toward
another teammate again for a dribble screen
and handoff. The weave continues until you
or a teammate can take advantage of an opening for a shot or drive to the basket (see Diagram 9.6).

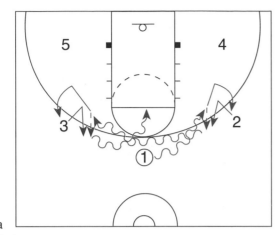

a
3-player weave

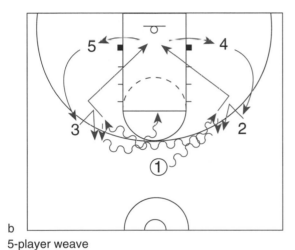

b
5-player weave

Diagram 9.6 Dribble screen: 3-player weave and 5-player weave.

Downscreen

A screen set by a player screening down for a teammate is called a downscreen. By setting a downscreen for your teammate, you create a scoring opportunity. By cutting off your downscreen, your teammate can get open to receive a pass for a shot or drive. If your defender switches to your cutting teammate, you will be on the ball side of the defender whom you screened—momentarily open. Taking a few steps toward the basket before setting your screen enables you to get a better angle on the defender. You want the defender to go under your pick. As you set your downscreen, communicate with your teammate by using a designated key word, such as *down!*

Use the four basic options for cutting off a screen, depending on how it is defended:

pop-out, curl, backdoor cut, and fade (see Figure 7.3). Be patient: Wait until the screen is set (to prevent an illegal moving block) and read how the defense is playing it. Before using the screen slowly set up your move off it. You can set a good angle for cutting off the screen if you first move slowly in the direction your defender plays you and then cut hard off the screen in the opposite direction. Cut far enough away from the screen so that one defender cannot guard both you and the screener. This creates space for a pass to the screener if there is a defensive switch.

When you cut off a screen correctly, the reaction usually is the screener's defender giving defensive help or switching. If you cut to the outside, the screener will be free to roll in toward the basket and receive a pass for an inside shot. If you cut to the basket, the screener becomes free to pop out and receive a pass for an outside shot (see Diagram 9.7).

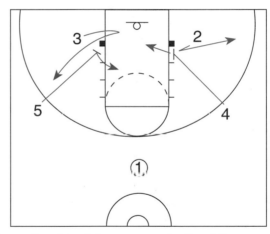

Players 5 and 4 set downscreens for 3 and 2

Cutter 3 pops out and screener 5 rolls

Cutter 2 fades and screener 4 cuts to basket

Diagram 9.7 Downscreen: Pop and fade options.

Back Pick (Upscreen)

When you screen for your teammate by setting a pick behind your teammate's defender, it is called a back pick or upscreen. By setting a back pick for a teammate you create the opportunity for either the teammate or you to score. By cutting off your back pick, your teammate can get open to receive a pass for a layup or drive. If your defender switches to your cutting teammate, you will be on the ball side of your teammate's defender, free to pop out to the ball to receive a pass for a jump shot. Take a few steps toward the basket to get a better angle on the defender you will back pick, communicating to your teammate by shouting your designated key word, such as *up!*

Make certain that you set a legal screen. With a back pick you are not allowed a position closer than a normal step from a stationary opponent if that opponent is unaware of your screen. You also may not take a position so close that a moving opponent cannot avoid contact without changing direction or stopping. Your opponent's speed determines what your screening position may be: This position will vary and might be one to two normal steps away.

As with the downscreen, wait until the back pick is set before cutting off it to prevent an illegal screen and to read the defense. Slowly set up your move off it for a good angle before you cut hard off it in the opposite direction. If you cut to the basket with a front cut or backdoor cut, the screener will be free to pop out and receive a pass for an outside shot. If you fake a cut to the basket and pop out or if you fake to receive a pass for an outside shot, the screener should cut to the basket. The four basic options for cutting off a back pick, depending on how it is defended, are the front cut, backdoor cut, pop-out, and fade (see Diagram 9.8).

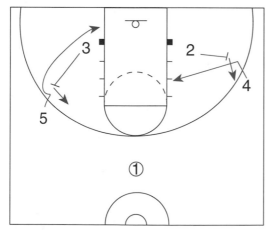

Players 2 and 3 set back picks for 4 and 5

Cutter 5 goes backdoor and screener 3 pops out

Cutter 4 front cuts and screener 2 pops out

Diagram 9.8   Back pick (upscreen).

Elbow Curl

When you screen down for a teammate positioned at the elbow, your teammate should look to curl off your downscreen. On an elbow curl your defender usually will give defensive help or switch. This momentarily frees you to pop out and receive a pass for a jump shot. The elbow curl is best used when a smaller player sets a downscreen at the elbow for a bigger player: The bigger player can curl to the basket and the smaller player can pop out for a catch-and-shoot jump shot. To set the screen for an elbow curl, again take a few steps toward the basket to get a better angle on the defender. Signal to your teammate to curl off your downscreen by shouting the key word *curl!* (see Diagram 9.9).

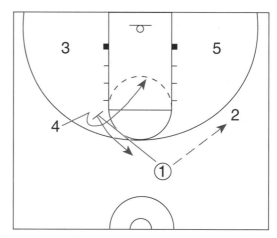

Player 1 sets elbow screen for 4

Cutter 4 curls and screener 1 pops out

Diagram 9.9   Elbow curl.

Cross-Screen

A cross-screen is set by starting on one block and screening across the lane for a teammate at the opposite block. On a cross-screen the screener's defender usually reacts by giving defensive help or switching.

When you cut off a cross-screen, you should read the defensive positioning, and either cut over or cut under the screen. When you set a cross-screen and your teammate cuts low to the block—by cutting over or under the cross-screen—you should pop out high to the elbow area and receive a pass for an outside shot. If your teammate flashes high to the elbow to receive a pass for an outside shot, you should roll back to the ball-side block (see Diagram 9.10).

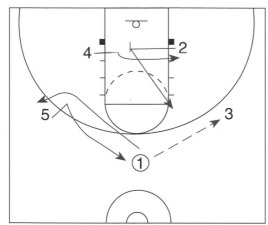

a

Player 2 sets cross-screen for 4

Cutter 4 cuts low to block and screener 2 rolls high

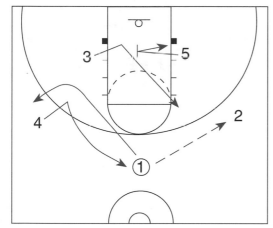

b

Player 5 sets cross-screen for 3

Cutter 3 cuts high and screener 5 rolls low to block

Diagram 9.10   Cross-screen.

Pick-and-Roll

The pick-and-roll, another basic basketball play, gets its name from the action: You set a pick (screen) for your teammate who dribbles by it for an outside shot or drive. If your defender switches to your teammate, you will be momentarily inside the defender whom you screened and free to roll toward the basket, looking to receive a return pass from the dribbler for a layup. Four options with the pick-and-roll, depending on how it is defended, are pick-and-roll, pick-and-pop, early release, and stretch-the-trap (refer to Figure 7.4). Diagram 9.11 shows the basic option when defenders switch.

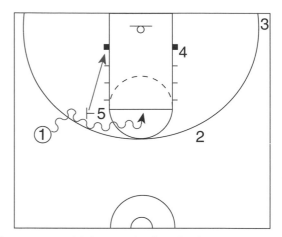

Player 5 sets pick for 1 and rolls to basket

Diagram 9.11   Pick-and-roll.

Draw-and-Kick (Penetrate and Pass)

When you penetrate by your defender, and your teammate's defender leaves to give defensive help on you, an open passing lane to your teammate is created. This action of penetrating and passing is called draw-and-kick. You should always be alert for an opportunity to drive by your defender to score or to create an open shot for your teammate whose defender is drawn to you. Also look for an opening, or gap, between two defenders to penetrate with one or two dribbles and draw the defenders to you.

Effective use of the draw-and-kick depends on judging well when and where to penetrate. But it also depends on players without the ball moving to open spots. Because the passing game depends primarily on moving the ball, over-dribbling becomes counterproductive. The draw-and-kick is best used from the wing after a swing of the ball from ball side to weak side. When penetrating your options include a drive to the basket, shooting an in-between runner (pull-up jump shot), penetrating and passing inside (draw-and-kick in), and penetrating and passing outside (draw-and-kick out) (see Diagram 9.12).

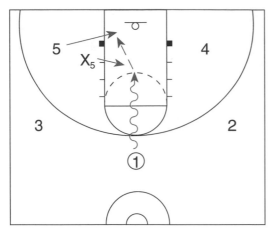

a

Draw-and-kick in:

Player 1 penetrates (draws defender off player 5) and
passes (kicks in) to player 5 cutting to basket

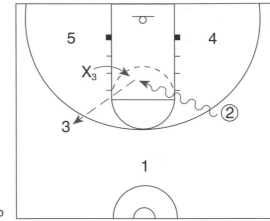

b

Draw-and-kick out:

Player 2 penetrates (draws defender off player 3) and
passes (kicks out) to player 3 spotting up outside

Diagram 9.12   Draw-and-kick: In and out.

Detecting Errors in the Passing Game

The most common errors in the passing game
are listed here, along with suggestions to correct them.

ERROR

CORRECTION

1. Players on your team tend to crowd together either near the ball or too close to
the basket.

1. Maintain spacing and balance in an open
formation, spread 15 to 20 feet apart. Keep
the middle open. When you cut to the basket and do not receive a pass, continue
through and fill a spot on the side with
fewer players.

2. Pressure defense prevents you and your
teammates from getting open to receive a
pass.

2. When your defender overplays you and
denies you from receiving a pass, make a
backdoor cut to the basket. When you see
a defender denying your teammate from
receiving a pass, you should automatically
flash.

3. You and your teammates overuse the
dribble without a plan. You do not move
the ball and players enough to break down
the defense.

3. The passing game is most effective when
there is both ball and player movement.
Too much dribbling is counterproductive.
Reverse the ball to the weak-side wing before using the draw-and-kick.

4. You and your teammates have difficulty
seeing each other when you get open on a
cut, off a screen, or posting up.

4. Players with the ball should see the rim
and, thus, the entire court. When you see
the rim, you can see when your teammates
are open.

ERROR	CORRECTION
5. You and your teammates get confused about what each other is doing.	5. Talk! The passing game is not a set play offense, with each player having a specific assignment or set of responsibilities. Communication is especially important in it, so use designated key words for basic passing game actions.
6. Your team has difficulty moving the ball from the ball side to the weak side, and your swing passes are easily intercepted.	6. When you are replacing the point from the weak side, cut high above the circle to receive a pass and swing the ball. A shallow cut allows your defender to have a good angle to deny and intercept a pass. If you cut high and your defender continues to go with you, cut backdoor.
7. Fouls are called on you and your teammates for setting illegal screens.	7. Be patient. For setting a screen, use a jump stop to prevent moving when your teammate uses your screen. When a screen is being set for you, wait until it is set before using it. You can be late to cut or dribble off a screen but you should never be early. Waiting for the screen to be set prevents an illegal moving screen and gives you time to read the defense.

ZONE OFFENSE

In zone defenses, defenders are assigned to a designated area of the court rather than an individual offensive opponent. When you attack zone defenses you should understand the type of zone you are playing against. Different zones employ different strategies, from sagging inside to pressuring outside shots, overplaying passing lanes, or trapping the ball. Zone defenses are named according to the alignment of players from the top toward the basket and include the 2-1-2, 2-3, 1-2-2, 3-2, and 1-3-1 zones.

There are several common set offenses that are used against zones. One method of attacking a zone is to use an offset alignment. You attack a zone that has an even front (two players) with an odd front (one player), and vice versa. This allows you to get into the gaps or seams (areas between defensive players) of the zone where the defenders may be indecisive or late in covering. Other set attacks against the zone include sending a cutter or cutters through to open areas on the weak side and inside, and overloading a zone area.

PRINCIPLES FOR ATTACKING ZONES

Basic principles for attacking zones are more important than a set zone offense.

1. Fast break. Beat the zone upcourt and attack it before the defenders get to their zone positions.

2. Use good spacing. Spread the zone. Three-point shooters should spot up behind the 3-point line.

3. Move the ball. The ball can move faster than the zone can shift. Pass the ball from the ball side to the weak side. Move the ball inside, then out.

4. Reverse the ball. Pass the ball to make the defense move in one direction, then quickly reverse the ball back (snapback) to the opposite side.

5. Be a triple threat. Square up to the basket and be a threat to score. Make use of shot fakes and pass fakes.

6. Split the zone. Outside players should move into the gaps or seams of the zone (between defenders) and within shooting range.

7. Draw and kick. Penetrate between defenders to draw your teammate's defender to you and create an open passing lane to your teammate.

8. Send cutter(s) through. Send a cutter or cutters through to the weak side or to the inside behind the defense. It is very difficult for the defense to have visual contact with both the ball and an offensive player cutting through and from behind.

9. Show patience, poise, and good shot selection. When you are patient the defense can become fatigued and make mistakes.

10. Attack the offensive boards. Although better rebounders can be positioned in the inside zone areas, they have a more difficult time matching up to block out aggressive offensive rebounders.

Team Offense Drills

1. 5-on-0 Give-and-Go (No Dribble)

Select four players as your teammates. Your team will set up in a 3-2 open, or spread, formation with three perimeter players and two baseline players. This is the most basic formation and is good for learning to play team offense. Run a give-and-go (pass-and-cut) offense against an imaginary defense. The offense may not dribble the ball except on a drive to the basket.

A team member, usually the point guard, signals the start of the offense with a simple verbal call, such as *pass-and-cut!* or *give-and-go!* When the ball is at the point the closest wing player should initiate movement by cutting through to create an open area. Then a baseline player can cut to the wing for a pass from the point. Pass the ball to your teammate and cut to the basket, looking to receive a return pass for a layup.

Use your imagination, deception, and timing before cutting. Set up a fake either by taking a step or two away from the ball or by taking a step or two toward the ball before sharply changing direction and cutting to the basket. After receiving a pass on the wing, be a triple threat. As you cut to the basket the weak-side wing replaces you at the point and the weak-side corner replaces the weak-side wing.

The wing's options after receiving the pass are to make a bounce pass to you as you cut to the basket, pass to the player now occupying the point, or cut to the basket. If the ball is passed to the point, the cutter moves to the open corner position that has been vacated.

Continue the drill with the player at the point passing to either wing, cutting to the basket, and having the wing fake a pass to the cutter before passing back to the point. Make at least 5 passes before passing to a cutter or driving to the basket. On a drive from the wing look to score or use the draw-and-kick. Also use your imagination! At times, assume defensive pressure and use the backdoor cut and flash backdoor options. Continue the drill for a total of 30 passes and layups without error.

Success Goal = 30 consecutive passes and layups without error

Your Score = (#) _____ consecutive passes and layups without error

2. 5-on-2 Give-and-Go (No Dribble)

This drill is the same as the previous one but uses two defenders. Select at least ten players divided into two teams of five players. One team will be on offense and one on defense. Select two players from the defensive team to play defense on two selected players from the offensive team. Only the defended players are allowed to score. This drill gives the two offensive players practice in moving without the ball, such as cutting backdoor, and all players practice the flash backdoor.

A backdoor cut should be used automatically any time a defender overplays and prevents you from receiving a pass. Use a designated key word, such as *eyeball!* to indicate to the passer that you are going backdoor. A flash-and-backdoor cut also is effective against a defender denying your teammate from catching the ball when you are the next closest player. Flash to an open area between the passer and overplayed receiver. As you flash signal your cut with the key word *flash!* Catch the ball and look for your overplayed teammate, who should make a backdoor cut toward the basket.

The offense may not dribble the ball. If the ball bounces to the floor on a missed or deflected pass, it is not counted as a dribble. Award your team 1 point for each shot made by a defended player.

Success Goal = Score more points than the other team, with 5 points winning

Your Score = (#) _____ your team's points; (#) _____ second team's points

3. 5-on-5 Give-and-Go (No Dribble)

This drill is the same as the previous drill but uses all five defenders. Select at least ten players divided into two teams of five players each on offense and defense.

The offense may not dribble the ball. If the ball bounces to the floor on a missed or deflected pass, it is not counted as a dribble. This drill gives the offense practice in moving without the ball, using the give-and-go, backdoor cut, and flash backdoor. When the defensive team is instructed to pressure the ball and deny all passes, it also becomes an extremely challenging team defensive drill.

The offensive team gets 1 point each time it scores. If the defense commits a foul, the offense gets the ball and starts again. If an offensive player misses a shot and a teammate gets an offensive rebound, continue playing. The defense gets 1 point if it gets the ball on a steal or rebound or if it forces the offense into a violation. Five points win the game, the teams then switching roles.

Success Goal = Win more games than your opponents, with 5 points winning each game

Your Score = (#) _____ games your team won; (#) _____ games opponents won

4. 5-on-0 Weave

Select four players as your teammates and set up in a 3-2 open, or spread, formation with three perimeter players and two baseline players. Run a weave offense against an imaginary defense.

A member of your team, usually the point guard, signals the start of the weave with a simple verbal call, such as *weave!* or *figure!* The point guard initiates the weave by dribbling to the inside of one of the wings. The wing should create an opening by faking away and then cutting to the outside of the dribbler for a handoff. The point guard hands off and cuts to the basket, looking to receive a return pass for a layup.

Use imagination, deception, and timing before you cut. As you cut to the basket, the weak-side wing replaces you at the point and the weak-side corner replaces the weak-side wing. After receiving a handoff, the wing should be a triple threat and can bounce pass to the cutter, shoot, drive, or continue the weave by dribbling to the inside of the player now occupying the point. If the weave is continued, the cutter moves to the vacated, open corner position. Continue the weave, making at least 5 handoffs before passing to a player cutting or driving to the basket. On a drive or receiving a pass after a cut, look to score or draw-and-kick. Use your imagination to mix in various offensive options off the weave. You might assume your defender attempts to get in your path to prevent the handoff and make a backdoor cut before the handoff. After your handoff, you might assume the defense is jump switching or trapping and make a short, 5- to 10-foot cut to an open area, look for a quick return pass, and drive to the basket. Continue the drill for a total of 30 handoffs and layups without error.

Success Goal = 30 consecutive handoffs and layups without error

Your Score = (#) _____ consecutive handoffs and layups without error

5. 5-on-5 Weave

This drill is the same as the previous drill but uses a defensive team. Select at least ten players grouped into two teams of five players each on offense and defense.

This drill gives the offense practice in executing the weave against various defensive strategies. Practice different defensive options against the weave, such as opening up and sliding, pressuring the ball and denying all passes, jump switching, and trapping.

The offensive team gets 1 point each time it scores. If the defense commits a foul, the offense gets the ball and starts again. If an offensive player misses a shot and a teammate gets an offensive rebound, continue playing. The defense gets 1 point if it gets the ball on a steal or rebound or if it forces the offense into a violation. Five points win the game, the teams then switching roles.

Success Goal = Win more games than your opponents, with 5 points winning each game

Your Score = (#) _____ games your team won; (#) _____ games opponents won

6. 5-on-0 Passing Game

Select four players as your teammates for this drill. Set up in a 3-2 open, or spread, formation with three perimeter players and two baseline players and run a passing game offense against an imaginary defense.

A member of your team, usually the point guard, signals the start with a simple verbal call, such as *passing game!* or *motion!* or a hand signal, such as circling one finger up. Pass the ball to the wing and have the other players work together using basic passing game actions. After receiving a pass on the wing you should be a triple threat. On a drive, look to score or draw-and-kick. When the ball is at the point, the closest wing player should initiate movement, cutting through to create an open area for a baseline player to cut to the wing for a pass from the point. When you are at the point and cannot pass to the wing, you can initiate movement by dribbling at the wing and using a dribble screen or weave action.

Use your imagination to mix in various offensive options, such as the backdoor cut, flash backdoor, give-and-go, weave, downscreen, back pick, cross-screen, elbow curl, pick-and-roll, and draw-and-kick. Work on the basic options for cutting off a screen: pop-out, curl, backdoor cut, and fade. Practice communicating by using designated key words, such as *flash! down! up! cross! pick!* and *weave!* Continue for a total of 30 passes and layups without error.

Success Goal = 30 consecutive passes and layups without error

Your Score = (#) _____ consecutive passes and layups without error

7. 5-on-2 Passing Game

This drill is the same as the previous one but uses two defenders. After grouping two teams of five players each into offense and defense, select two players from the defensive team to play defense on two selected offensive players. Only the defended players may score.

This drill focuses on the two offensive players as they practice executing the various passing game options (see Drill 6) and the basic options for cutting off a screen (see Drill 6). Again practice communicating to your teammate with designated key words. The two defenders can practice pressuring the ball, strong-side denial, weak-side help, and combating screens with a slide, jump switch, or trap.

Award your team 1 point for each successful shot a defended player makes.

Success Goal = Score more points than the other team, with 5 points winning

Your Score = (#) _____ your team's points; (#) _____ second team's points

8. 5-on-5 Passing Game

Here all five defensive players are used. Group as before into two teams of five players each on offense and defense.

The offensive team practices various passing game options, basic options for cutting off a screen, and communicating with designated key words (see Drill 6). The defense practices pressuring the ball, strong-side denial, weak-side help, and combating screens with a slide, jump switch, or trap.

The offensive team gets 1 point each time it scores. If the defense commits a foul, the offense gets the ball and starts again. If an offensive player misses a shot, and a teammate gets an offensive rebound, continue playing. The defense gets 1 point if it gets the ball on a steal or rebound or if it forces the offense into a violation. Five points win the game, the teams then switching roles.

Success Goal = Win more games than your opponents, with 5 points winning each game

Your Score = (#) _____ games your team won; (#) _____ games opponents won

Team Offense Checks

Basketball at its best is a team game, and the passing game, or motion offense, is one of the most basic offenses for teaching team play to developing players. The passing game depends on the sound execution of fundamentals including moving the ball and moving without the ball, making intelligent decisions, and unselfish team play, especially in regard to shot selection. Players are guided by principles rather than a strict set of specific assigned responsibilities.

Have a trained observer—your coach, teacher, or a skilled player—subjectively evaluate your ability to execute the basic actions and decision making when playing the passing game.

Step 10   Team Defense: Win the Championship

You win with defense. More than requiring skill, defense requires desire and intelligence. Coaches seek players who use their heads. You have to be smart to play winning defense. The most important quality coaches look for is heart—giving maximum effort every second you are on the court. It takes a lot of heart to be a great defensive player. Defense is mostly desire, but the desire to play defense is limited by your physical condition. As fatigue sets in, you lose your ability to execute skills accompanied by a more harmful loss in the desire to compete.

Playing tough defense seldom brings the public acclaim of successful offense, yet you can gain immeasurable self-satisfaction. Most coaches recognize the value of tough defense and defensive stoppers. You can make your team by being a great defender. Mastering offensive skills takes time. Defensive skills take less time to develop, but they do require hard work. You can become a tough defensive player if you have the desire to work hard at conditioning and if you play with heart and intelligence in games.

Striving on defense not only helps you become a better player, but helps you contribute to your team's success. Your enthusiastic desire, intelligence, and maximum effort on defense can be contagious: It can foster a greater team defensive effort and team spirit. By committing to exert maximum effort to stop your opponent, and to help your teammates stop their opponents, you can inspire your teammates to make the same commitment.

WHY TEAM DEFENSE IS IMPORTANT

A team's success depends on defense. Good defense inhibits your opponents by limiting uncontested open shots. Good team defense not only reduces scoring opportunities for your opponent but opens them to your team. An aggressive pressure defense leads to steals, interceptions, and missed shots that enable your team to create scoring opportunities.

More often than not, steals and interceptions lead to high percentage shots at the end of fast breaks.

Fans and the media glamorize offensive play, but coaches know that defense wins games and championships. Teams with less than average offensive talent can be successful by playing hard, intelligent team defense. Defense is more consistent than offense because it is based mostly on desire and effort, while offense is based on a high degree of skill. You may have an off game in shooting: However, you control your desire and, therefore, you need never have an off game defensively.

WHAT IT TAKES TO WIN WITH DEFENSE

The factors that determine defensive success may be classified as emotional, mental, and physical.

Emotional

Desire. Wanting to play great defense is most important. Offense is mostly fun. Defense, while hard work, can also be fun as you stop what your opponent wants to do. Desire in defense is giving maximum effort and concentration on each play. Playing defense with intensity involves great efforts at running at full speed in transition from offense to defense, maintaining a defensive stance with your hands up at all times, drawing the charge, diving for loose balls, blocking out for defensive rebounds, and communicating to your teammates by using key defensive words.

Discipline. Desire is a start, but you must discipline yourself to stick with your goal of becoming a great defensive player. The hard work of developing superior physical condition, practicing defensive skills, and playing tough defense in games requires continuous self-discipline. Defense cannot be part-time. Defense must be played hard all of the time. This takes discipline, and tough defenders have learned to appreciate and gain satisfaction from discipline.

Aggressiveness. Defense is a battle. In playing offense you have the advantage of knowing what your next move will be. In playing defense the tendency is to react to the offensive player's moves. This is a negative view. Take the positive approach of being aggressive on defense, thereby forcing the offensive player to react. Being an aggressive defender means that your attitude is to dominate your opponent in all ways. You do not allow the moves your opponent wants to make. You take the initiative. Aggressive defense forces your opponent to react to what you do. Examples of aggressive defense are pressuring the dribbler, fighting over the top of screens, pressuring the shooter, denying passes and going for interceptions, taking the charge, diving for loose balls, and rebounding missed shots.

Mental Toughness. The physical demands of aggressive defense can exhaust even the most highly conditioned athlete. The progressive discomfort of defensive movements plus the physical hurts of fighting over screens, drawing the charge, diving for loose balls, and battling for rebounds can take a toll. Being a mentally tough defender means overcoming this physical discomfort and pain. You bounce up from the floor each time you are knocked down. You do not need excessive encouragement from your coach: On the contrary, your mental toughness inspires others, including coaches, teammates, and fans.

Mental

Knowledge of Your Opponent. Successful defense requires analyzing your opponent and your opponent's team offense. Prepare by studying scouting reports, watching videos, and observing your opponent during the game's early stages. Judge your opponent's quickness and strength. Ask yourself questions. What are the opponent's offensive tendencies? Does your opponent want to shoot or drive? What are your opponent's offensive moves and which direction is favored on each? If your opponent is great with the ball, should you overplay or does your opponent move well also without the ball? Maybe the place to be alert is in preventing your opponent from scoring on rebounds and loose balls near the basket.

From a team standpoint, would your opposition rather beat you on fast breaks or with a set offense? Which plays will the opposing team run against your team, and which plays will they run when they need a key basket? Who are their outside shooters, drivers, and post-up players?

Study both your individual opponent and the team. Know what your opponent does best—and work to take it away.

Anticipation. Anticipation is knowing tendencies and adjusting to each situation to gain an advantage. Playing offense gives you the advantage of knowing your next move, but in playing defense you must react to the offensive player's move—that is, you react unless you use anticipation. By knowing your opponent's tendencies you can adjust accordingly and anticipate the next move. You should *not guess* on defense but you should make a *calculated* move based on intelligent study of your individual opponent and opponent's team.

Concentration. To concentrate is to focus completely on the assignment and not be distracted. Potential distractions are the opponent's trash talk, the action of fans, an official's call, and your own negative thoughts. When you recognize that you are being distracted or are thinking negatively, interrupt the distraction by saying a key word to yourself, such as *stop!* Then replace the distraction with a positive statement to yourself. Concentrate on your defensive assignment, rather than allowing yourself to be distracted.

Alertness. Alertness involves being in a state of readiness at all times, able to react instantly. On the ball, be ready to defend your opponent's shot, drive, or pass, and remain alert to being screened. Off the ball, see the ball and your opponent. Be alert to stop a cut, defend a screen, go for an interception, dive for a loose ball, or rebound a missed shot.

Judgment. Judgment is the ability to size up the game situation and decide on the appropriate action. Numerous situations on defense call for good judgment. One example is deciding whether to pressure the ball on the perimeter or to drop back to prevent a pass inside. Another example is deciding whether to go for an interception or to play it safe. The decision will involve comparing your ability with your opponent's, the tempo of the game, the score, and the time remaining. Using good defensive judgment is particularly important near the end of close games.

Physical

Physical Condition. Physical condition is a prerequisite to good defense. Over the course of a game your desire to compete will be proportional to your level of physical condition. The physical condition needed to play defense develops through specific physical conditioning programs and even more through expending great effort both in practice and games. Dominating an opponent requires strength, muscular endurance, and circulatory-respiratory endurance. Work to improve your total body strength so you can particularly withstand the body contact in defending a low-post player. You must also improve the muscular endurance of your legs. It is not just how quickly you can move but whether you can move quickly *throughout* the game.

Quickness and Balance. Quickness refers to speed of movement in performing a skill, not simply running speed. Moving your feet quickly is the most important physical skill for a defensive player and you must develop the ability. Being able to change direction laterally is very important.

Although many people consider it difficult to make great improvements in quickness, three factors can help. First, you can improve speed through hard work on defensive footwork drills and by jumping rope. Second, you can be mentally quick, using intelligence to anticipate your opponent's offensive moves and, thus, get more quickly to the right place at the right time. Knowing and anticipating your opponent can compensate for less physical quickness. Third, being balanced and under control is critical: Quickness without balance can be useless. Because defensive quickness involves the ability to start, stop, and change direction, you must also have control. Quickness under control, or quickness with balance, is what you need in playing defense.

PLAYING DEFENSE ON THE BALL

The most vital aspect of playing great defense is pressuring the dribbler. Pressuring the offensive point guard and best ball handler throughout the game prevents your opponent from focusing on running an offense.

Where on the court you will pick up the dribbler (fullcourt, halfcourt, top of the circle, etc.) will be determined by team strategy. When you are guarding an opponent with the ball, the position you maintain should be between your opponent and the basket. Strive to give ground grudgingly. Whenever possible force your opponent to pick up (stop) the dribble. Then you can apply more pressure against a shot or a pass, with both your hands up. Four basic situations will determine how your team's defensive strategy establishes the position you take: turning the dribbler, forcing the dribbler sideline, funneling the dribbler middle, and forcing the dribbler to use the weak hand.

Turning the Dribbler (Forcing the Reverse Dribble)

The basic idea in turning the dribbler is to dominate your opponent by applying maximum pressure on the ball. Work to establish defensive position a half body ahead in the direction the dribbler wants to go. This position is called *chest on the ball*. The objective is preventing another dribble in the same direction and forcing the dribbler into a reverse dribble. With good anticipation you may even draw a charge.

If the dribbler tries a front change-of-direction, you should be able to steal the ball with a quick flick upward of your near hand. On the dribbler's reverse dribble quickly change direction and again move for chest-on-the-ball position, at least a half body ahead of the direction the dribbler wants to go. Continue forcing the dribbler to reverse turn.

Forcing the Dribbler Sideline

Forced sideline, the dribbler can pass in only one direction, and the sideline can serve as a defensive aid. Work for position a half body to the inside of the court, with your inside (closer-to-middle) foot forward and your outside foot back. Force the dribbler to the sideline. Then do not allow a reverse dribble back to the middle of the court. By dribbling to the middle, the dribbler has more options to pass to either side or to attempt a high percentage shot.

Funneling the Dribbler Middle

By taking a defensive position a half body to the outside of the court, you can funnel the dribbler to the middle. This strategy will move the dribbler toward your defensive teammate off the ball. In turn, your teammate may use one of several teaming tactics, including a switch, fake switch (hedge), trap, or steal.

If your team has a shot blocker, you may benefit by funneling the dribbler in the direction of the shot blocker. The danger in funneling the dribbler middle is allowing that player to penetrate by you into the lane for a high percentage shot or pass to either side.

Forcing the Dribbler to Use the Weak Hand

Few dribblers can drive with the weak hand as effectively as with the strong hand. By overplaying the dribbler's strong hand you force the opponent to dribble with the weak hand. Overplay the dribbler by taking a position a half body to the dribbler's strong-hand side, with your forward foot outside and back foot aligned with the middle of the dribbler's body.

PLAYING DEFENSE OFF THE BALL

Positioning off the ball is an important part of team defense. To better understand team defensive positioning think of how the court is divided from basket to basket into a strong side (also called ball side) and weak side (also called help side). The strong side refers to the ball side of the court, and the weak side refers to the side of the court away from the ball.

Playing good defense involves defending your opponent, the ball, and the basket. To accomplish this you will move continually from one defensive responsibility to another. The phrase *help and recover* refers to being in good defensive position off the ball to help stop a penetrating pass or dribble by the player with the ball and then recovering to your own opponent.

When you are off the ball, you should take a position off your opponent and toward the ball, able to see both the ball and your opponent. This is called the *ball–you–player principle*. You want to form an imaginary triangle between you, the ball, and your opponent.

The closer your opponent is to the ball, the closer you should be to your opponent. The farther the ball is from your opponent, the farther away you can play from your opponent and still give help to your teammate guarding the ball.

Strong-Side Wing Denial Defensive Position

When you are off the ball on the strong side, you should work to deny a penetrating pass to a receiver on the wing inside the foul line extended. To deny a pass to the ball-side wing, first take a ball–you–player position. Overplay your opponent by using a closed stance, your lead foot and hand up in the passing lane. See the ball and your opponent by keeping your head up and looking over the shoulder of your lead arm. Be ready to knock away a pass by having the palm of your lead hand facing out with your thumb down. Your back arm should be flexed and close to your body. Having your back hand touching your opponent can help you monitor movement. Be ready to move, keeping a wide base and flexed knees. React to your opponent's movements by using short, quick steps: As you move, keep your feet close to the floor and at least shoulder-width apart. Do not cross your feet or hop. Keep your head steady and over your waist, with your back straight to keep from leaning off balance. Be alert to knock away an outside pass to your opponent.

On a backdoor pass open to the ball on the pass and knock the pass away. Open to the ball by pivoting on your inside foot while dropping your lead foot back and toward the ball. (See Figure 10.1.)

Weak-Side Help Defensive Position

When you are on the weak side, sag off your opponent and form an imaginary flat triangle between you, your opponent, and the ball. Be in an open stance to see both the ball and your opponent without turning your head. Point one hand at the ball and one hand at your opponent. Be able to help on a drive or pass inside by the player with the ball. Communicate that you are in position to help, yelling to your teammate on the ball *You've got help!* (see Figure 10.1).

Figure 10.1   Keys to Success: Defensive Positioning

**Execution
Phase**

Strong-Side Denial   **Weak-Side Help**

____ 1. See the ball and opponent ____

2. Touching distance from opponent ____   2. Sag off opponent ____
3. Closed stance ____   3. Open stance ____

____ 4. Ball–you–player ____

5. Hand and foot up in passing lane ____   5. Inside hand pointed at opponent ____
6. Outside hand knocks ball away ____   6. Outside hand pointed at ball ____

____ 7. Wide base ____
____ 8. Knees flexed ____
____ 9. Short quick steps ____
____ 10. Feet move shoulder-width apart (never cross feet) ____

11. Open to ball and knock ball away on backdoor pass ____   11. Ready to help teammate on backdoor pass ____

Detecting Errors in Defensive Positioning

The most common errors in defensive positioning are listed here, along with suggestions to correct them.

ERROR 🚫

CORRECTION

Strong-Side Denial

1. Defending on the strong side you are not in position to deny an entry pass to a receiver on the wing.

2. You are unable to deny the pass after the wing fakes a step to the basket and cuts back for the ball.

3. You are unable to deflect a pass to a receiver cutting backdoor.

1. Take a ball–you–player position. Overplay your opponent by using a closed stance with your lead foot and hand up in the passing lane. See both the ball and opponent, staying alert to knock the pass away.

2. Learn to ignore the wing's first step to the basket and understand that you will have defensive help from weak-side defenders on a backdoor pass.

3. On a backdoor pass open to the ball as the pass is thrown, and knock the pass away.

Weak-Side Help

1. Defending on the weak side you are too close to your opponent and not in position to give help on a drive or pass inside.

1. On the weak side, sag off your opponent and form an imaginary flat triangle between you, your opponent, and the ball. Be in an open stance to see both ball and opponent. Communicate that you are in position to help by yelling to your teammate on the ball *You've got help!*

Defending Ball-Side Guard With Ball at Wing

When you defend the ball-side guard while the wing has the ball, you can choose from two options, depending on your team's defensive strategy. One option is to prevent ball reversal to the ball-side guard by overplaying the guard with a closed stance, your lead foot and hand up in the passing lane. The other option is getting into a help-and-recover position to help on a drive middle by the wing and to discourage a pass to the high post. Keep an open stance at least one step off an imaginary line between your opponent and the basket in a ball–you–player position: You want to form an imaginary flat triangle between you, your opponent, and the ball. Get your inside hand in the passing lane between the ball and the high post, and point your other hand at your opponent. Communicate that you are in position to help, yelling to your teammate on the ball *You've got help!* Be alert to prevent the ball-side guard from receiving a pass on a possible front cut or backdoor cut to the basket (see Diagram 10.1).

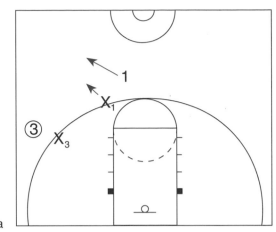

a

Denial defensive position:

Defensive player X₁ takes closed stance position to prevent ball reversal from wing (3) to ball-side guard (1)

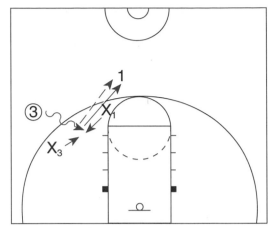

b

Help-and-recover defensive position:

Defensive player X₁ takes open stance sagging off ball-side guard (1) to give help to teammate X₃ on drive middle by wing (3) and then recover on pass to ball-side guard (1)

Diagram 10.1   Two defensive options for defending ball-side guard with ball at wing.

Defending Weak-Side Guard When Other Guard Has Ball

Be in an open stance at least one step off an imaginary line between your opponent and the basket, in a ball–you–player position, and in position to see both the ball and your opponent without turning your head. Point one hand at the ball and one hand at your opponent. Get in a help-and-recover position and communicate that you are in position to help, yelling to your teammate on the ball *You've got help!* (see Diagram 10.2).

Defending Weak-Side Wing When Guard Has Ball

Sag off your opponent in a ball–you–player position. Be in an open stance, at least one foot in the lane and able to see both the ball and your opponent without turning your head. Point one hand at the ball and one hand at your opponent. Communicate that you are in position to help, yelling to your teammate on the ball *You've got help!* (see Diagram 10.3).

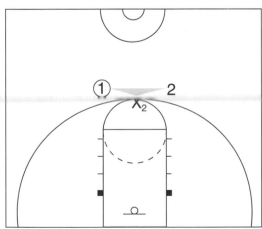

Defensive player X₂ takes open stance sagging off weak-side guard (2) to prevent front cut by 2, give help on drive middle by 1, and recover on pass to 2

Diagram 10.2   Defending weak-side guard when other guard has ball.

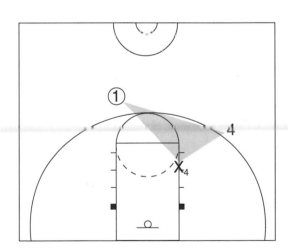

Defensive player X₄ takes open stance sagging off weak-side wing (4) to prevent flash cut by 4, give help on drive middle or pass inside by 1, and recover on pass to 4

Diagram 10.3   Defending weak-side wing when guard has ball.

Defending Weak-Side Guard With Ball at Wing

Sag off your opponent in a ball–you–player position. Be in an open stance, one step to the weak side of the basket and able to see both the ball and your opponent without turning your head. Point one hand at the ball and one hand at your opponent. Communicate that you are in position to help, yelling to your teammate on the ball *You've got help!* Be alert to prevent the weak-side guard from receiving a pass on a possible cut to the basket (see Diagram 10.4).

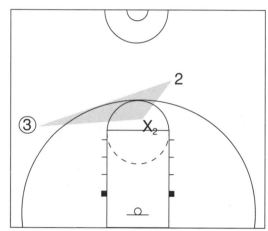

Defensive player X₂ takes open stance sagging further off weak-side guard (2) to prevent cut to basket by 2, give help on drive middle by 3, and recover on pass to 2

Diagram 10.4   Defending weak-side guard with ball at the wing.

Defending Weak-Side Wing With Ball at Wing

Sag off your opponent in a ball–you–player position and follow the previous instructions. Be alert to prevent the weak-side wing from receiving a pass on a possible flash cut to the ball-side elbow or a cut to the low post (see Diagram 10.5).

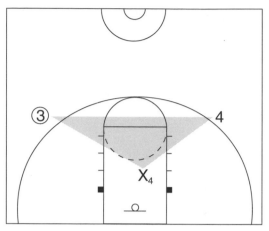

Defensive player X₄ takes open stance sagging further off weak-side wing (4) to prevent flash to ball-side elbow or cut to low post by 4, give help on drive baseline or backdoor cut by 3, and recover on pass to 4

Diagram 10.5   Defending weak-side wing with ball at the wing.

PLAYING DEFENSE IN THE LOW POST

You should always attempt to deny your opponent from receiving a pass in good low-post position. Use a closed stance with your body in three-quarter defensive position between the ball and your opponent. When the ball is *above* the imaginary foul line extended, deny your low-post opponent from the topside. When the ball is *below* the imaginary foul line extended, deny your low-post opponent from the baseline side.

When a wing above the foul line extended passes the ball to a player in the corner below the foul line extended or in the reverse direction, from the corner to the wing, move quickly from one side of the low post to the other. A denial defensive position can be maintained by stepping in front of the low-post player as you change sides. Use quick footwork. First step through on your inside (closer-to-opponent) foot, then step through with your outside foot (see Diagram 10.6).

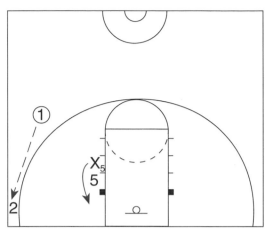

As the ball is passed from wing player 1 to corner player 2, X_5 quickly changes from *topside* to *baseline* side, stepping in front of low-post player 5

Diagram 10.6   Low post defensive positioning: Changing sides.

Detecting Errors in Defending the Low Post

The most common errors in defending the low post are listed here, along with suggestions to correct them.

ERROR

CORRECTION

1. You are not on the correct side to defend the low post.

1. When the ball is *above* the imaginary foul line extended, deny your low-post opponent from the *topside*. When the ball is *below* the imaginary foul line extended, deny your low-post opponent from the *baseline* side.

2. When the ball is passed from wing to corner or vice versa, you are unable to deny a pass to the low post.

2. As the ball is passed, change sides but maintain a denial position by stepping in front of the low-post player with a quick two-step move.

DEFENDING THE CUTTER

When the opponent you are closely guarding on the perimeter passes the ball, you must move off your opponent in the direction of the pass. This is called *jump to the ball*. Jumping to the ball positions you to defend a give-and-go cut by your opponent and to give help on the ball.

It is important that you move on the pass to establish ball–you–player position. If you wait for your opponent to cut before you move, you will get beat. The pass-and-cut is the most basic offensive play in basketball: It is as old as the game itself.

For playing defense off the ball you should be in position to see both the ball and your opponent. To defend a cutter, position your-self off the cutter and toward the ball: Do not allow the cutter to move between you and the ball. Be in a strong, balanced stance, ready to withstand any contact that may occur as you prevent the cutter from going between you and the ball.

When the cutter approaches the lane area, be in position to bump the cutter. Use a *bump-and-release* technique. Bump the cutter with the inside part of your body and release to a position between the cutter and the ball. If your opponent makes a backdoor cut to the basket, maintain a closed stance as you move with your opponent on the cut and then open to the ball as the pass is thrown. Use your lead hand to knock away a pass (see Diagram 10.7).

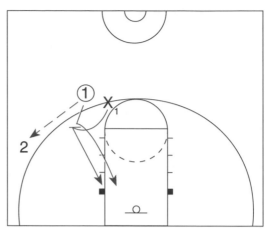

As offensive player 1 passes to player 2, X₁ quickly *jumps to the ball* and uses the *bump and release* technique, staying between the ball and player 1 on 1's cut

Diagram 10.7   Defending the cutter.

Detecting Errors in Defending the Cutter

The most common errors in defending the cutter are listed here, along with suggestions to correct them.

ERROR 🚫

CORRECTION

ERROR	CORRECTION
1. On the pass you wait for your opponent to cut before you move.	1. It is important that you move in the direction of the pass (jump to the ball) on the pass to establish ball–you–opponent position.
2. On a cut you allow the cutter to cut between you and the ball.	2. Change to a closed stance and get your lead foot and hand into the passing lane. Force the cutter to go behind you.
3. You do not deny the pass on a cut to the basket.	3. Maintain a closed stance as you move with your opponent on the cut—then open to the ball as the pass is thrown.

DEFENDING THE FLASH CUT

A flash cut is a quick move by your opponent from the weak side toward the ball. Most offenses use a flash cut from the weak side into the high-post area. As a defender on the weak side, you should be in an open stance and in position to see both ball and opponent. When your opponent flashes to the high-post area, be alert to move and stop the flash. Change to a closed stance with your lead foot and hand in the passing lane. Be in a strong, balanced stance and ready to withstand any contact that may take place as you stop the flash cut. Use your lead hand to knock away a pass.

If your opponent flashes high and then makes a backdoor cut to the basket, you must first get in a closed stance to deny the flash high. On the backdoor cut to the basket, maintain a closed stance as you move with your opponent on the cut. Then open to the ball as the pass is thrown (see Diagram 10.8).

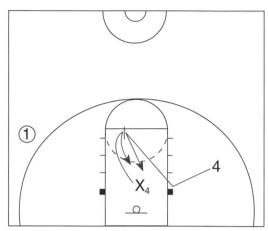

Defensive player X₄ changes to a closed stance to deny offensive player 4's flash high, then moves with player 4 on 4's backdoor cut

Diagram 10.8   Defending the flash cut.

Detecting Errors in Defending the Flash Cut

The most common errors in defending the flash cut are listed here, along with suggestions to correct them.

ERROR

CORRECTION

ERROR	CORRECTION
1. You are not alert for a flash cut.	1. Take a good weak-side position with an open stance and your eyes on the ball and your opponent to be alert to move and stop the flash.
2. On a flash you are unable to deflect a pass.	2. Change to a closed stance, and get your lead foot and hand into the passing lane. Use your lead hand to knock away a pass.
3. You get bumped off balance as you attempt to stop your opponent's flash cut.	3. Be in a strong, balanced stance and ready to withstand any contact that may take place as you stop the flash cut.
4. Your opponent flashes high and then beats you on a backdoor cut to the basket.	4. First get in a closed stance to deny the flash high. Maintain a closed stance as you move with your opponent on a backdoor cut, and then open to the ball as the pass is thrown.

DEFENDING AGAINST A SCREEN

To defend screens you and your teammate must be able to communicate and help each other. The defender on the opponent who is setting the screen must alert the defender being screened by calling out the direction of the screen with the words *Screen right!* or *Screen left!* The defender on the screener should also communicate how the screen will be defended.

There are four players directly involved in the screen—two on offense (screener and cutter) and their two defenders. To aid our understanding of defending a screen, the cutter is always referred to as the *first* player. If the defender on the cutter goes over the screen, this is said to be going over or simply going *second*. If the defender on the cutter goes under the screen, this is said to be going under or *third*. If the defender on the cutter goes under both the screener and the screener's defender, this is said to be going *fourth*.

Four basic methods to defend a screen are to fight over the top, slide through, switch, and squeeze (see Diagram 10.9).

Fight Over the Top

When your opponent sets a screen on a teammate guarding inside a good shooter's range, you should help your teammate fight over the top of the screen (go second). After calling out the screen, yell *Get over!* You must also step out into the path of the cutter to fake a switch, or *hedge*. This hedging action will delay the cut or force the cutter to veer wide and allow your teammate time to fight over the top of the screen. When you are the defensive player being screened, work to get over the screen by first getting a foot over the screen and then the remainder of your body.

Slide Through

When your opponent sets a screen on a teammate guarding a quick driver or when outside your opponent's shooting range, you should help your teammate slide through the screen between you and the screener (go third). Call out the screen, and yell *slide!* or *through!* Drop back (open) to allow room for your teammate to move under the screen and stay with the cutter.

Switch

When you and your teammate are of equal size and defensive ability you should switch opponents. If your size and defensive ability differ, switching should be your last option, as it allows the offense to take advantage of the mismatch. If you switch you must first call out the screen by yelling *switch!* As you switch you must aggressively get position to deny a pass to the cutter (switch and deny): The screener will roll to the basket or pop out for an outside shot. When you are the player being screened and you hear *switch!* work to get defensive position on the ball side of the screener.

Squeeze

Occasionally, when the cutter is a good driver or likes to curl or cut inside and the screener is a good shooter and likes to pop out to shoot after screening, you should squeeze on the screener. This helps your teammate take a shortcut route under both you and the screener (go fourth). Call out the screen and yell *squeeze!* Stay close to the screener allowing room for your teammate to go under both of you to get to the cutter.

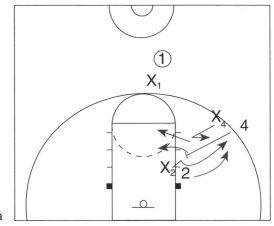

a

Fight over the top:

Player 4 sets screen for 2

Defender X_4 hedges into 2's path allowing teammate X_2 time to trail or fight over the top of the screen (go second)

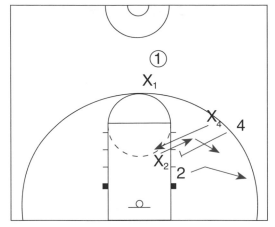

b

Slide:

Player 4 sets screen for 2

Defender X_4 drops back (opens) allowing room for teammate X_2 to move under or slide through the screen (go third)

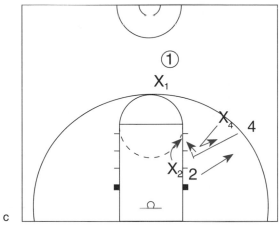

c

Switch:

Player 4 sets screen for 2

Defender X_4 switches and denies a pass to 2

Defender X_2 works to get defensive position on the ball side of screener 4, who is rolling to the basket

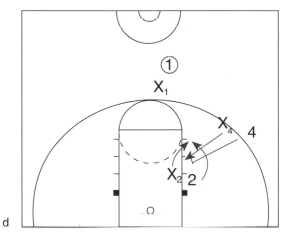

d

Squoozo:

Player 4 sets screen for 2

Defender X_4 squeezes on screener allowing room for teammate X_2 to take a shortcut move under both screener 4 and defender X_4 (go fourth)

Diagram 10.9   Defending against a screen: Four methods.

Detecting Errors in Defending Against a Screen

The most common errors in defending against a screen are listed here, along with suggestions to correct them.

ERROR

CORRECTION

ERROR	CORRECTION
1. Your teammate is not alert to being screened by your opponent.	1. As your opponent moves to set a screen on your teammate, call out the screen and its direction.
2. Your teammate attempts to fight over the top, but gets beat on a quick cut.	2. Step out into the path of the cutter with a fake switch (hedge) to delay the cut or force the cutter to veer wide, allowing your teammate time to fight over the top of the screen. When you are the defensive player being screened, work to get over the screen by getting a foot over the screen and then the remainder of your body.
3. Your teammate attempts to go under but bumps into you.	3. Call out the screen and yell *slide!* or *squeeze!* Drop back (open) to allow room for your teammate to move between you and the screener, or squeeze so your teammate can go under both of you.
4. On a defensive switch the screener gets open on a roll to the basket or a pop-out for an outside shot.	4. If you as the player being screened hear *switch!* you must work to get defensive position on the ball side of the screener.

EXECUTING DEFENSIVE ROTATIONS

Defensive rotation means that when a team member leaves an assigned opponent to defend another player, teammates must rotate defensive positions to cover the player left open. Rotations may involve all five defenders: All defensive players must play as a team and communicate well. Communication is helped by using such key words or phrases as *switch! I've got the ball! I've got the post! I'm back!* and *I'm up!*

Here are two situations that require defensive rotation: Your team traps the ball, either away from the basket or in the low post; and one of your teammates gets beat, such as on a penetrating drive or a cut to an open area.

When your team traps the ball, the defenders off the ball should rotate toward the ball to cover the immediate open receivers. As they rotate the defender farthest from the ball should split the distance and guard the two offensive players farthest from the ball.

When one of your teammates gets beat by a drive or backdoor cut, your teammates should rotate defensive positions closer to the ball. The nearest defender—either on the low post or the weak-side wing—rotates to the player with the ball, the defender on the weak-side guard drops back to cover the basket, and the defenders on the high post and ball-side guard drop into the lane (see Diagram 10.10).

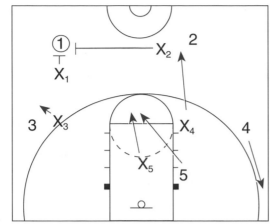

a

Rotating up on a guard-to-guard trap:

Defender X₂ leaves player 2 to trap player 1

Weak-side defender X₄ rotates up to deny pass to weak-side guard 2

Farthest defender (X₅) covers two farthest offensive players, 4 and 5

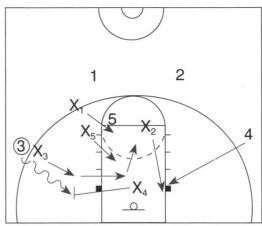

b

Rotating back to cover baseline drive:

Wing 3 beats defender X₃ on baseline drive

X₄ rotates to help and switches to player 3

X₂ rotates down to cover for teammate X₄

X₃ can trap with X₄ or rotate to weak side looking to pick up first player 4 then player 2

X₁ and X₅ drop back into lane

Diagram 10.10   Defensive rotation: Two examples.

Detecting Errors in Defensive Rotation

The most common errors in defensive rotation are listed here, along with suggestions to correct them.

ERROR

CORRECTION

1. When you leave an assigned opponent to defend another player, your teammates, unaware of what you are doing, fail to rotate defensive positions to cover the player you left open.

2. You leave an assigned opponent near the basket to defend another player, but your teammates do not have time to rotate defensive positions to cover the player you left open, resulting in a pass to your opponent for an easy basket.

1. It is imperative that you communicate to your teammates what you are doing. Reacting to any defensive situation, particularly one involving a defensive rotation, requires that all defensive players work as a team and communicate by using key words or phrases.

2. Use judgment and a defensive fake before leaving an opponent near the basket to pick up an open player. This will allow your teammates time to rotate to the player you are leaving.

ZONE DEFENSE

When you play zone defense you are assigned to a designated area of the court, or zone, rather than to an individual offensive opponent. Your zone position changes with each move of the ball. Zones may be adjusted from sagging inside to pressuring outside shots, overplaying passing lanes, and trapping the ball. Zone defenses are named according to the alignment of players from the top toward the basket and include the 2-1-2, 2-3, 1-2-2, 3-2, and 1-3-1 zones.

Each zone defense has strengths and weaknesses. The 2-1-2 and 2-3 zones are strong inside and in the corners, but are susceptible on the top and wings (see Diagram 10.11). The 1-2-2 and 3-2 zones are strong against outside shooting, but are vulnerable inside and in the corners. The 1-3-1 protects the high post and wing areas, but it can leave openings at the blocks and corners and is also susceptible to good offensive rebounding.

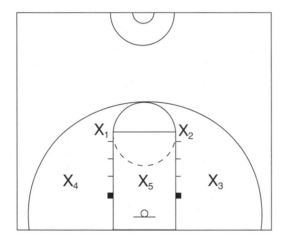

Diagram 10.11   The 2-3 zone defense.

Strengths and Weaknesses of Zone Defense

Reasons to use a zone defense include the following:

1. Protects the inside against a team with good drivers and post-up players, and poor outside shooters.
2. More effective against screening and cutting.
3. Defenders may be positioned in areas according to size and defensive skill. Taller players can be assigned to inside areas for shot blocking and rebounding, while smaller, quicker players can be assigned to outside areas for pressuring the ball and covering passing lanes.
4. Players are in a better position to start the fast break.
5. Easier to learn and may overcome weaknesses in individual defensive fundamentals.
6. Protects players who are in foul trouble.
7. Changing to a zone may disrupt an opponent's rhythm.

Weaknesses of a zone defense include the following:

1. Susceptible against good outside shooting—especially 3-point shooting—that can also stretch your zone, creating openings inside.
2. A fast break can beat the zone down court before it sets up since it takes time to get players in their assigned zones.
3. Quick passing moves the ball quicker than zone defenders can shift.
4. Weak against penetration (draw and kick).
5. The opposing team may stall more easily against a zone, causing you to change to individual defense if you are behind late in a game.
6. Individual defensive skills are not developed.

Match-up Zone

Any of the zone defenses may be adjusted to a *match-up* zone. This enables you to match up with an individual opponent in your zone area. If no one is in your area, drop back toward the basket and middle looking for someone flashing into your area from behind. The match-up zone is particularly effective against an offense that does not use much movement.

Combination Defenses

Combination defenses are defenses that have one or two players assigned to selected individual opponents—an outstanding shooter or ballhandler—and the other players deployed in zone areas. Three types of combination defenses are the box-and-one, the diamond-and-one, and the triangle-and-two.

The Box-and-One. One player is assigned to deny the ball to the opponent's best scorer, shooter, or ballhandler, while the four other players set up in a 2-2 zone, or box formation.

The Diamond-and-One. This defense is similar to the box-and-one as one player is assigned to deny the ball to the opponent's best scorer, shooter, or ballhandler. However, the other four players are set up in a 1-2-1 zone, or diamond alignment.

The Triangle-and-Two. Two players are assigned to individually defend two selected opponents while three defenders set up in a 1-2 zone, or triangle inside the free throw line.

Team Defensive Drills

1. Wing Denial

A good defender is able to pressure and deny a penetrating pass to the ball-side wing. This drill gives you practice in denying a pass inside the foul line extended. Select two offensive players to join you. You will start on defense. Offensive player 1 starts with the ball at the point position at the top of the circle. Offensive player 2 plays ball-side wing starting at the foul line extended. You take a denial defensive position on player 2.

To deny a pass to the ball-side wing first take a ball–you–player position. Overplay your opponent by using a closed stance with your lead foot and hand up in the passing lane. See the ball and your opponent by keeping your head up and looking over the shoulder of your lead arm. Be ready to knock away a pass by having the palm of your lead hand facing out with your thumb down. Player 2, the ball-side wing, attempts to get open, moving within the area bounded by one step above the foul line extended, lane line, baseline, and sideline. React to the opponent's movements, using short, quick steps at least shoulder-width apart, staying alert to knock away an outside pass to your opponent. On a backdoor pass open to the ball and knock the pass away by pivoting on your inside foot while dropping your lead foot back and toward the ball.

When the offensive wing receives the ball, the drill becomes a 1-on-1 drill until the wing scores or you obtain possession by a rebound, steal, or interception. Continue the drill for 30 seconds before changing positions. Each of you should play wing denial defense 5 times, getting no more than 30 seconds each time. Award 1 point for each deflection of a pass to the wing and 1 point for stopping the wing from scoring.

Success Goal = Score more points than your opponents

Your Score =

   a. (#) _____ your points

   b. (#) _____ points for player 1

   c. (#) _____ points for player 2

2. Low-Post Denial

You should always attempt to deny your opponent from receiving a pass in good low-post position, and this drill gives you practice. Select three players to join you: You will start on defense and the others will be on offense.

Offensive player 1 starts with the ball above the foul line extended on the ball side. Offensive player 2 takes a position below the foul line extended in the corner. Offensive player 3 takes a position in the low post above the box outside the lane. You take a position denying a pass to player 3 in the low post. Use a closed stance with your body in three-quarter defensive position between the ball and your opponent. Players 1 and 2 attempt to pass the ball inside to the low post, while you attempt to deny a pass to the low post. Players 1 and 2 should pass the ball to each other while player 3 should get good low-post position by sealing you off.

When the ball is above the imaginary foul line extended, deny the low post from the topside. When the ball is below the imaginary foul line extended, deny the low post from the baseline side. As player 1 above the foul line extended passes the ball to player 2 in the corner below the foul line extended, or as player 2 passes to player 1, move quickly from one side of the low post to the other. Maintain your denial defensive position by stepping in front of the low-post player as you change sides.

Quick footwork is needed. Step through first with your inside foot and then with your outside foot. When player 3 receives the ball in the low post, the drill becomes a 1-on-1 drill until either the low post scores or you obtain possession by a rebound, steal, or interception.

Continue the drill for 30 seconds before changing positions. Allow each player to play low-post denial defense 3 times, with 30 seconds maximum each time—then change sides. Award 1 point for each deflection of a pass to the low post and 1 point for stopping the low post from scoring.

Success Goal = Score more points than your opponents

Your Score =

    a. (#) _____ your points   c. (#) _____ points for player 2

    b. (#) _____ points for player 1   d. (#) _____ points for player 3

3. Weak-Side Help and Recover

This is a drill in opening up on the weak side, helping on a penetrating drive by the ball-side wing, and then when the ball is passed out recovering to the player you are guarding. Select two offensive players to join you. You start on defense, and offensive player 1 starts with the ball at the foul line extended, and offensive player 2 starts as a weak-side wing at the foul line extended. You will take a weak-side defensive position on player 2, the weak-side wing.

From the weak side sag off your opponent in a ball–you–player position, forming an imaginary flat triangle between you, your opponent, and the ball. Be in an open stance, one step to the weak side of the basket: Position yourself to see both the ball and your opponent without turning your head. Point one hand at the ball and one hand at your opponent. Communicate that you are in position to help, yelling to your imaginary teammate on the ball *You've got help!*

Player 1 drives by an imaginary ball-side defensive wing on the baseline side toward the basket. Give help to this imaginary ball-side defensive wing by moving to the ball side of the basket to stop the drive or draw a charge. As you move player 1 passes out to player 2, the weak-side wing, who is flashing to the weak-side elbow. On the pass recover quickly but under control to player 2. When player 2 receives the ball at the weak-side elbow, player 1 steps off the court, and the drill becomes a 1-on-1 contest between you and player 2.

Continue until the wing scores or you obtain possession by a rebound, steal, or interception. Change positions and continue the drill. Allow each player to play weak-side help-and-recover defense 3 times before changing sides. Award 1 point for each reaction to stop a drive by the ball-side wing and 1 point for stopping the weak-side wing from scoring.

Success Goal = Score more points than your opponents

Your Score =

   a. (#) _____ your points   c. (#) _____ points for player 2

   b. (#) _____ points for player 1

4. Deny the Flash and Deny the Backdoor Cut

This drill gives you practice in denying both a flash cut and a backdoor cut. Select two players to join you on offense as you start on defense. Offensive player 1 starts with two balls at the foul line extended. Offensive player 2 is a weak-side wing, starting at the weak-side foul line extended. Take a weak-side defensive position on player 2, in an open stance, pointing one hand at the ball and the other at your opponent. Communicate that you are in position to help, yelling to your imaginary teammate on the ball *You've got help!*

Player 2 starts the drill by cutting toward the basket for a few steps and then flashing to the ball-side elbow. React to stop the flash by changing to a closed stance, beating the weak-side wing to the ball-side elbow, with your lead foot and hand up in the passing lane to deny a pass. Be strong and ready to withstand any contact that may take place as you stop player 2's flash. Use your lead hand to knock away a pass.

Player 1 will attempt to pass the first ball to player 2 at the ball-side elbow. React to a pass on the flash cut by deflecting the ball. Once you deny the flash, player 2 cuts backdoor to the basket. Player 1 then attempts to pass the second ball to player 2 cutting backdoor. React to a pass on the backdoor cut by opening up as the pass is thrown and then deflecting the ball. Change positions and continue the drill, with each player denying the flash cut and the backdoor cut 3 times before changing sides.

Success Goal – 10 out of 12 possible deflections

Your Score = (#) _____ deflections

5. Six Point

This drill adds practice to the previous drills in stopping the drive, blocking out, rebounding, making an outlet pass, and converting from defense to offense. You will practice six points of defense: deny the wing; deny the low post; weak-side help position; deny the flash; stop the drive; and block out, rebound, outlet, and convert to offense.

Select two offensive players to join you. Start by playing defense on player 2 who again is a ball-side wing and starts at the foul line extended. Offensive player 1 starts with the ball at point position at the top of the circle and gives commands.

The drill begins with player 1 calling out *deny!* On this command, player 2 works to get open on the wing and you work to deny the pass. Player 1 then yells *low post!* and dribbles from above to below the foul line extended, while player 2 moves to get open in the low post on the ball side. Deny a pass to the low post by moving from the topside to baseline side of the low post as the ball is dribbled from above to below the foul line extended. Player 1 then yells *away!* On this command, player 2 moves away from the ball to the weak-side wing. Move only to a weak-side help-and-recover position one step to the weak side of the basket. Be in an open stance, pointing one hand at the ball and one hand at your opponent, and use your key phrase to communicate to the imaginary teammate on the ball that you are in position to help. Player 1 then calls out *flash!* and player 2 cuts toward the basket a few steps before flashing to the ball-side elbow. React to stop the flash by closing your stance and beating player 2 to the ball-side elbow with your lead foot and hand up in the passing lane to deny a pass. Player 1 next yells *out!* and player 2 moves out to the top of the circle to receive a pass. Allow the pass to player 2, but then stop the 1-on-1 drive to the basket. On a missed shot, rebound and make an outlet pass to player 1 on the wing. On a shot, block out and go for the rebound. On a made shot, take the ball out of the net, run out of bounds, and make the outlet pass. Then run to the foul line for a return pass. Change positions and continue the drill, allowing each player to play defense before changing sides. Award 1 point for each correct defensive reaction to each of the six defensive moves.

Success Goal = 10 out of 12 possible points

Your Score = (#) _____ your points

6. Shell Drill—Defensive Position

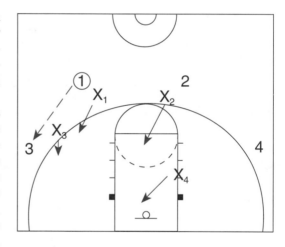

This drill gives you practice in defensive position on the ball as well as defensive help-and-recover positioning for defending the ball-side and weak-side guard and forward. Select eight players, grouping them into four players each on offense and defense.

The four offensive players start with two guards at the top of the circle and two forwards at the wing positions. Each defender takes the correct defensive position. One of the offensive players is selected as the point guard or leader who will give commands. On the command *in!* the guard passes the ball to the ball-side wing. On the command *out!* the ball is passed back out from the wing to the ball-side guard. On the command *over!* the ball is passed from guard to guard. Pass the ball around the perimeter (shell) in this drill for six passes: in, out, over, in, out, over. Check the defensive positioning after each pass.

Each defender moves on each pass, adjusting defensive positioning. If the opponent you are guarding passes the ball, you must move off in the direction of the pass. The call for this move is *jump to the ball!* By jumping to the ball, you get in position to defend a cut by your opponent and to give help on the ball.

Allow each defensive player to play for 6 passes at each of the 4 defensive positions. The defense then goes to offense, and the offense goes to defense. Award 1 point for each correct change of defensive position on each pass.

Success Goal = 24 out of 24 possible points

Your Score = (#) _____ your points

7. Shell Drill—Help and Recover

This drill is the same as the previous shell drill except that each offensive player with the ball is allowed only one penetrating dribble, giving practice in defensive help and recover. It is also a good offensive drill in establishing a triple-threat position and being able to penetrate and pass (draw-and-kick). Eight players form teams of four players each, offense and defense.

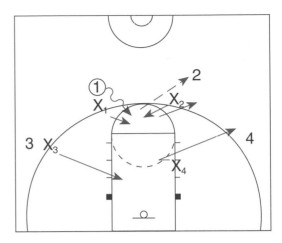

Start with the four offensive players as two guards at the top of the circle and two forwards at the wing positions. Any offensive player with the ball is allowed *one* penetrating dribble. The defender nearest the ball moves to help stop penetration. Once the penetrating dribble is stopped, the penetrator passes the ball out to whichever player the helping defender left. After giving help to stop penetration, the defender recovers to his original opponent. The offensive player receiving the pass should be a triple threat to shoot, pass, or drive.

The offensive team gets 1 point each time it scores. If the defense commits a foul, the offense gets the ball and starts again. If an offensive player misses a shot and a teammate gets an offensive rebound, continue playing. The defense gets a point when it gets the ball on a steal or rebound or when it forces the offense into a violation. Five points win the game. The teams then switch roles.

Success Goal = Win more games than your opponents, with 5 points winning each game

Your Score =

   a.   (#) _____ games your team won   b.   (#) _____ games opponents won

8. Shell Drill—Defend the Cutter

This drill is the same as the other shell drills except that you will allow cuts to the basket and unlimited dribbling. Cutting will only be allowed from one position, designated from among the ball-side guard, weak-side guard, or weak-side wing. After cutting to the basket, the cutting player moves to an open weak-side position. Each of the offensive players may rotate to the designated position for cutting, so you will have practice in defending a cut by the ball-side guard, weak-side guard, or weak-side wing.

To defend a cutter be in position off the cutter and toward the ball: Do not allow the cutter to move between you and the ball. Be ready to withstand any contact that may occur as you prevent the cutter from going between you and the ball. If the cutter approaches the lane area, bump the cutter using the bump-and-release technique keeping between the cutter and the ball. If your opponent makes a backdoor cut to the basket, maintain a closed stance as you move on the ball side of the cutter, opening to the ball as the pass is thrown. Use your lead hand to knock away a pass.

This drill provides offensive practice in making a front cut, backdoor cut, or flash cut. Start with two teams of four players each on offense and defense. The four offensive players again are two guards at the top of the circle and two forwards at the wing positions. Scoring is the same as for the previous drill.

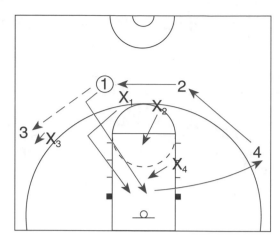

Success Goal = Win more games than your opponents, with 5 points winning each game

Your Score =

   a. (#) _____ games your team won

   b. (#) _____ games opponents won

9. Shell Drill—Defensive Rotation

You start this drill with a baseline drive or backdoor cut by an offensive wing, giving you defensive practice in rotating positions. After allowing one of your defensive wings to get beat by a drive or backdoor cut, the drill becomes live. The offense attempts to score, and the defense tries to prevent a score by attacking the player with the ball and rotating defensive positions. The defender on the weak-side wing yells *switch!* before attacking the player with the ball. The defender on the weak-side guard drops back to cover the weak-side wing, and the defender on the ball-side guard drops back into the lane and covers the weak-side guard. The wing who gets beat retreats to the basket, looking to recover to the originally guarded

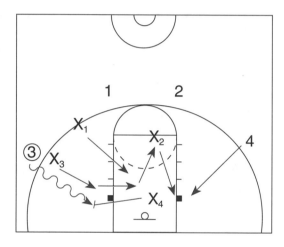

player, but seeing a good rotation the wing will pick up the open player who will be the ball-side guard.

When defensive players rotate they must all play as a team and communicate well, using such key words or phrases as *switch! I've got the ball! I've got the post! I'm back!* and *I'm up!*

Use the same scoring system as you did for the previous two drills.

Success Goal = Win more games than your opponents, with 5 points winning each game

Your Score =

   a. (#) _____ games your team won

   b. (#) _____ games opponents won

Team Defense Checks

You win with defense. Wanting to play great defense is the most important emotional factor. Have a trained observer—your coach, teacher, or a skilled player—use the checklist in Figure 10.1 to evaluate your strong-side and weak-side defensive positioning. Also, ask your coach to evaluate your defense in drills and competition, paying particular attention to your desire, knowledge, physical condition, and quickness.

Rating Your Total Progress

Each drill you completed in this book had a success goal, which helped to develop your fundamental skills and team play. The following rating chart allows you to rate your overall progress. Rate your success in basketball by writing a number in the space provided to the right of each basketball skill listed. Read each item carefully and respond objectively. Then, review your strengths and weaknesses, and set new goals.

Rating points   5 = Outstanding, 4 = Very good, 3 = Fair, 2 = Needs extra work, 1 = Weakness

FUNDAMENTAL SKILLS

The first general success goal in basketball is to develop the fundamental skills needed to play the game. How would you rate yourself on the fundamental skills?

Offensive footwork
Change of pace _____
Change of direction _____
One-two stop _____
Jump stop _____
Front turn _____
Reverse turn _____
Two-foot jump _____
One-foot jump _____
Defensive footwork
Side step, or slide _____
Attack step _____
Retreat step _____
Reverse step _____
Shooting—mental
Positive self-talk _____
Analyzing your shot's reaction on rim _____
Shooting mechanics
Sight _____
Balance _____
Hand position _____
Elbow-in alignment _____
Shooting rhythm _____
Follow through _____
Shooting skills
Free throw _____
Jump shot _____
Three-point shot _____
Hook shot
  Strong hand _____
  Weak hand _____
Layup
  Strong hand _____
  Weak hand _____

Runner
  Strong hand _____
  Weak hand _____
Passing
Chest pass _____
Bounce pass _____
Overhead pass _____
Sidearm pass _____
Baseball pass _____
Behind-the-back pass _____
Catching
Meeting the pass when overplayed _____
Catching in position to shoot
  From in front _____
  From strong-hand side _____
  From weak-hand side _____
Dribbling
Control dribble
  Strong hand _____
  Weak hand _____
Speed dribble
  Strong hand _____
  Weak hand _____
One-two stop after speed dribble _____
Footfire dribble
  Strong hand _____
  Weak hand _____
Change-of-pace dribble
  Strong hand _____
  Weak hand _____
Retreat dribble
  Strong hand _____
  Weak hand _____

Crossover dribble
  Strong hand _____
  Weak hand _____
Inside-out dribble
  Strong hand _____
  Weak hand _____
Reverse dribble
  Strong hand _____
  Weak hand _____
Behind-the-back dribble
  Strong hand _____
  Weak hand _____
Shooting off the dribble
  Dribbling to strong-hand side _____
  Dribbling to weak-hand side _____
Rebounding—emotional
Desire _____
Courage _____
Rebounding—mental
Anticipation of missed shots _____
Knowledge of opponent _____
Rebounding—physical
Quickness _____
Jumping _____
Muscular endurance _____
Strength _____
Rebounding skills
Vision _____
Balance _____
Position _____
Hands up _____
Timing _____
Jump often _____

Two-hand catch   _____

Spread-eagle   _____

Land in balance   _____

Defensive rebounding (block out)

Front turn   _____

Reverse turn   _____

Offensive rebounding

Straight cut   _____

Fake-and-go   _____

Spin   _____

Step-back   _____

Offensive moves

Getting open in low post

  When denied   _____

  When fronted   _____

Low post moves

  Drop-step baseline power move   _____

  Drop-step middle hook   _____

  Front-turn baseline bank jump shot   _____

  Front-turn baseline crossover and hook   _____

Getting open on the perimeter

  V-cut   _____

  Backdoor cut   _____

One-on-one moves

  Drive-step jump shot   _____

  Straight drive   _____

  Crossover drive   _____

  Straight drive jump shot   _____

  Crossover drive jump shot   _____

  Step-back jump shot   _____

TEAM PLAY

The second general success goal in basketball is to develop your ability to play together and communicate with your teammates, complementing each other's talents in two and three person plays, fast breaking, team offense, and team defense. How would you rate your physical and mental abilities in the following aspects of team play?

	Physical	Mental		Physical	Mental
Two person plays			**Team defense**		
Give-and-go	_____	_____	Emotional qualities		
Pick-and-roll	_____	_____	Desire		_____
Three person plays			Discipline		_____
Flash backdoor	_____	_____	Aggressiveness		_____
Screen away	_____	_____	Mental toughness		_____
Dribble screen and weave	_____	_____	Mental qualities		
Fast break			Knowledge of your opponent		_____
Starting the fast break	_____	_____	Anticipation		_____
Filling the fast-break positions	_____	_____	Concentration		_____
Fast-break scoring options			Alertness		_____
2-on-1	_____	_____	Judgment		_____
3-on-2	_____	_____	Physical qualities		
4-on-3	_____	_____	Physical condition	_____	
Fast-break swing	_____	_____	Quickness and balance	_____	
Team offense			Defense on the ball		
Passing game			Pressuring the dribbler	_____	_____
Starting the passing game	_____	_____	Defense off the ball		
Backdoor cut	_____	_____	Strong-side wing denial	_____	_____
Give-and-go	_____	_____	Weak-side help, defending guard	_____	_____
Dribble screen and weave	_____	_____	Weak-side help, defending wing	_____	_____
Downscreen	_____	_____	Defending the low post	_____	_____
Back pick (upscreen)	_____	_____	Defending the cutter	_____	_____
Elbow curl	_____	_____	Defending the flash cut	_____	_____
Cross-screen	_____	_____	Executing defensive rotations	_____	_____
Pick-and-roll	_____	_____			
Draw-and-kick	_____	_____			
Zone offense	_____	_____	Zone defense	_____	_____

About the Author

Hal Wissel is director of player personnel for the New Jersey Nets of the NBA. Before taking this position, he was a scout and special assignment coach for the Milwaukee Bucks of the NBA. Until 1990, he was a head basketball coach on the collegiate level for 24 years, including 12 years at NCAA Division I schools. His greatest coaching success came while he was at Florida Southern College, where he guided his team to three consecutive trips to the NCAA Division II Final Four and to one NCAA Division II National Championship title in 1981.

Wissel has also worked as an assistant coach and head scout for the NBA's Atlanta Hawks and served as head coach, general manager, and vice president of operations for the Westchester Golden Apples of the United States Basketball League. In addition to coaching, Wissel is the founder and president of Basketball World, Inc., a venture that organizes and runs basketball camps and clinics and produces instructional basketball books and videos. Recognized as one of the world's best basketball clinicians, Wissel conducts his popular Shoot It Better Mini Camps worldwide for players at all levels.

Wissel received his doctorate in physical education from Springfield [Massachusetts] College in 1970. His honors include being named *Coach & Athlete* magazine's Eastern Coach of the Year in 1972, sunshine State Conference Coach of the Year in 1979, 1980, 1981, and 1982, and Division II National Coach of the Year by the National Association of Basketball Coaches in 1980.

Drills and learning progressions for every area of the game

Becoming a Basketball Player

Five Videos in One

(102-minute videotape)

1990 • 1/2" VHS • Item MATH0364
ISBN 0-87322-563-5 • $49.95 ($74.95 Cdn)

Ball Handling
(21-minute videotape)
1990 • 1/2" VHS • Item MATH0371
ISBN 0-87322-558-9
$19.95 ($29.95 Cdn)

Shooting
(21-minute videotape)
1990 • 1/2" VHS • Item MATH0382
ISBN 0-87322-562-7
$19.95 ($29.95 Cdn)

Offensive Moves
(21-minute videotape)
1990 • 1/2" VHS • Item MATH0393
ISBN 0-87322-560-0
$19.95 ($29.95 Cdn)

Offensive Moves Off Dribble
(21-minute videotape)
1990 • 1/2" VHS • Item MATH0400
ISBN 0-87322-561-9
$19.95 ($29.95 Cdn)

Defense and Rebounding
(20-minute videotape)
1990 • 1/2" VHS • Item MATH0410
ISBN 0-87322-559-7
$19.95 ($29.95 Cdn)

The *Becoming a Basketball Player* video series provides a complete program of innovative drills and learning progressions that will help players develop every area of their game. Developed by Hal Wissel, the series is excellent for beginning coaches who want to learn how to teach specific basketball skills, more experienced coaches who want drill ideas for their practices, and players who want to work on basketball skills on their own.

Available on five individual tapes or as a comprehensive five-in-one video, the series covers these skills:

Ball Handling (Tape 1)—Emphasizing development of the weak hand, this video will help players develop confidence in dribbling, passing, and catching the basketball.

Shooting (Tape 2)—From lay-ups to three-pointers, this video teaches correct technique for the full range of basketball shots.

Offensive Moves (Tape 3)—This video teaches players a variety of offensive moves—like the crossover dribble, drop step, and ball fake—that will keep opponents off balance.

Offensive Moves Off Dribble (Tape 4)—This video provides additional offensive moves, including power moves, changes of pace, reverse moves, and speed and footfire dribbles.

Defense and Rebounding (Tape 5)—This video will help players develop the lateral quickness necessary for playing defense and the jumping ability important in rebounding.

Coaching Basketball Successfully

Morgan Wootten

Foreword by John Wooten

1992 • Paper • 240 pp • Item PWOO0446
ISBN 0-88011-446-0 • $18.95 ($27.95 Cdn)

Morgan Wootten covers every facet of building a successful basketball team. He presents practical skills, strategies, and drills that coaches can apply in their own program. Coaches also will learn the importance of developing a coaching philosophy. Through more than 40 personal anecdotes, Wootten explains how success should be measured in terms of effort and execution rather than outcome.

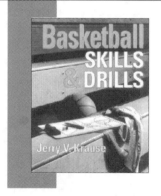

Basketball Skills and Drills

Jerry Krause

Foreword by Dean Smith

1991 • Paper • 136 pp • Item PKRA0422
ISBN 0-88011-422-3 • $16.95 ($23.95 Cdn)

This book shows coaches how to teach fundamentals that start beginners off right and reinforce basic skills in more advanced players. Part I focuses on individual basketball skills. A chapter is devoted to each skill, with drills for each to help coaches add variety and fun to practice sessions. Part II covers general team offensive and defensive principles.

Rookie Coaches Basketball Guide

American Coaching Effectiveness Program

1991 • Paper • 80 pp • Item ACEP0401
ISBN 0-88011-412-6 • $9.95 ($13.95 Cdn)

The *Rookie Coaches Basketball Guide* provides beginning coaches with detailed information on the responsibilities of a coach. It also explains the essential skills for coaching basketball, including how to teach basketball techniques and strategies to beginners.

Prices are subject to change.

To request more information or to place your order, U.S. customers call **TOLL-FREE 1-800-747-4457**.
Customers outside the U.S. use appropriate telephone number/ address shown in the front of this book.

Human Kinetics
The Information Leader in Physical Activity